Minority Religions under Irish Law

Muslim Minorities

VOLUME 31

The titles published in this series are listed at *brill.com/mumi*

Minority Religions under Irish Law

Islam in National and International Context

Edited by

Kathryn O'Sullivan

BRILL

LEIDEN | BOSTON

Cover illustration: Skellig Michael or Great Skellig, home to the ruined remains of a Christian monastery, Country Kerry, Ireland. Photo: iStock.com/MNStudio.

Library of Congress Cataloging-in-Publication Data

Names: O'Sullivan, Kathryn (Law teacher), editor.
Title: Minority religions under Irish law : Islam in national and international context / edited by Kathryn O'Sullivan.
Description: Leiden ; Boston : Brill, 2019. | Series: Muslim minorities ; volume 31 | Includes bibliographical references and index.
Identifiers: LCCN 2019011693 (print) | LCCN 2019012032 (ebook) | ISBN 9789004398252 (ebook) | ISBN 9789004398238 (hardback : alk. paper)
Subjects: LCSH: Muslim minorities--Legal status, laws, etc.--Ireland. | Religious minorities--Legal status, laws, etc.--Ireland. | Domestic relations (Islamic law)--Ireland. | Conflict of laws--Domestic relations--Ireland. | Islamic law.
Classification: LCC KDK1260.M86 (ebook) | LCC KDK1260.M86 M56 2019 (print) | DDC 342.41708/5297--dc23
LC record available at https://lccn.loc.gov/2019011693

Typeface for the Latin, Greek, and Cyrillic scripts: "Brill". See and download: brill.com/brill-typeface.

ISSN 1570-7571
ISBN 978-90-04-39823-8 (hardback)
ISBN 978-90-04-39825-2 (e-book)

This book is printed on acid-free paper and produced in a sustainable manner

Contents

Notes on Contributors

Amin Al-Astewani

is a Lecturer in Law at Lancaster University Law School. His research focuses on the role played by religious tribunals in Western legal systems. Over the past few years, he has led cutting-edge research on a novel type of religious tribunal in the UK, namely Islamic Shariah tribunals. After conducting fieldwork research at four of the most prominent of these tribunals, Dr Al-Astewani submitted written evidence to Parliament on the legal status of their decisions and practices, as part of the government's first public review of Shariah councils in the UK. His evidence was subsequently cited by over twenty media outlets, including internationally. As part of his engagement with communal organisations and bodies, Dr Al-Astewani has also advised the UK Board of Shariah Councils on the legal status of Islamic Tribunals. He continues to offer his expertise and advice to both policy-makers and Shariah councils on the legal status and role of Islamic tribunals in the modern English legal system.

M. Christian Green

is a scholar, teacher, researcher, and writer working in the fields of law, religion, ethics, human rights, and world affairs. She holds degrees from Georgetown University in history and government, Emory University in law and theology, and the University of Chicago in religion and ethics. She is currently a Senior Fellow and Research Director on Law, Religion, and Human Rights at the Center for the Study of Law and Religion at Emory University, an editor of the *Journal of Law and Religion*, and publications manager for the African Consortium for Law and Religion Studies (ACLARS). From 2016–2018, she was an academic consultant to the Commonwealth Initiative for Freedom of Religion or Belief (CIFoRB), based at the University of Birmingham in the UK.

Claire Hogan

is a barrister with a mixed civil and public law practice. She has a degree in Law and French from Trinity College Dublin, where she was elected a Scholar. She went on to obtain a Masters in Law (LL.M.) from the University of Cambridge. Claire qualified as a barrister and John Brooke Scholar in the Honorable Society of King's Inns. She returned to Trinity College Dublin to complete a Ph.D. on the theme of constitutional freedom of religion. This work was funded by the Irish Research Council for the Humanities and Social Sciences, and supervised by Prof. Gerry Whyte. Claire lectures part-time in the Honorable Society of King's Inns, and in the Law Society of Ireland.

Edana Richardson
is a Lecturer in Law at the University of Maynooth, Ireland, having previously worked as a solicitor in the London and Abu Dhabi offices of an international law firm. She is a graduate of Trinity College Dublin (where she completed her undergraduate law degree (2006) and PhD (2011)) and the University of Cambridge (where she undertook taught postgraduate study). Dr Richardson's research interests include Islamic finance and capital markets law and she has published both nationally and internationally in journals and edited collections.

Eoin Daly
is a lecturer at the National University of Ireland, Galway. He specialises in constitutional law, political theory and Church-State issues, focusing on Ireland and France. He is author, in particular, of *Religion, Law and the Irish State* (2012) and *Rousseau's Constitutionalism* (2017).

James Carr
lectures in the Department of Sociology in the University of Limerick. Building on previous scholarly and policy oriented publications, in 2016, James published his book *Experiences of Islamophobia: Living with Racism in the Neoliberal Era* (London and New York: Routledge) which focused on anti-Muslim racism in Ireland set to the international context. James has published research with the Immigrant Council of Ireland, supported by the Open Society Foundations, entitled 'Islamophobia in Dublin: Experiences and how to respond,' the recommendations of which he continue to work on with national and international partners. James is the author of the European Islamophobia Report submissions on Ireland for 2015, 2016, and 2017; and he is the contributor to the *Yearbook of Muslims in Europe* (Leiden: Brill) for Ireland for the same period.

Kathryn O'Sullivan
is a lecturer at the School of Law, University of Limerick. Her primary research interests are in Family Law, Property Law and Religion and the Law and has been published in leading national and international journals including in *Legal Studies*, the *Journal of Family Studies* and the *International Journal of Law, Policy and the Family*.

Máire Ní Shúilleabháin
is an Assistant Professor in Law at University College Dublin. Her teaching and research is primarily in the area of private international law, with a particular

focus on family law aspects. She is the author of *Cross-Border Divorce Law Brussels II bis* published by Oxford University Press in 2010, and co-author (along with Professors James Fawcett and Sangeeta Shah) of *Human Rights and Private International Law* published by Oxford University Press in 2016. She has co-edited (with Professor Jonathan Hill) the fifth edition of *Clarkson & Hill's Conflict of Laws* published by Oxford University Press in 2016.

Samia Bano

is a Senior Lecturer at SOAS, University of London, School of Law. Prior to this appointment, Samia taught at the University of Reading (2006–2013) in Family Law, Gender and Law (LLB) and Research Methods in Law (LLM) where she was also appointed deputy director of research. Samia's research interests include the practice of Muslim family law in the UK and Europe, multiculturalism, citizenship, Islamic jurisprudence and human rights and issues concerning the rights of Muslim women and gender equality. She has published widely in this field and is author of *Muslim women and Shariah Councils: Transcending the boundaries of Community and Law* (Palgrave MacMillan December 2012); *An exploratory study of Shariah Councils in England with respect to family law* (MOJ 2013) and two edited collections a special issue *Personal Narratives, Social Justice and the Law. Feminist Legal Studies*, Special Issue. (21) 3 and *Gender and Justice in Family Law Disputes: Women, Mediation and Religious Arbitration* (Brandeis Press 2017). Samia has also worked as a researcher on a number of social and policy projects and acted as an advisor for a number of working groups. She is an editorial board member for a number of journals in and is currently completing her book monograph entitled, Muslim Religious Arbitration and Civil Law in Britain. Her new research project is investigating the rise of Muslim legal services and the practice of Muslim Marriage in the UK.

Susan Leahy

is a lecturer in law at the University of Limerick. Susan's primary research interests lie in the area of criminal justice (with particular emphasis on sexual violence and victims of crime) and family law (with particular emphasis on domestic abuse and marriage). She has published her research on sexual offences in both national and international journals including *the Common Law World Review, the International Journal of Evidence and Proof, the Journal of Criminal Law, and the Irish Journal of Family Law*. She has co-authored, with Dr Margaret Fitzgerald-O'Reilly, a book entitled *Sexual Offending in Ireland: Laws, Procedures and Punishment*, which was published by Clarus Press in 2018.

CHAPTER 1

Introduction

Kathryn O'Sullivan

The legal protections that are afforded – or, in many cases, are not afforded – to religious minorities right across the world are attracting increased attention. Although concern for the plight of religious minorities is certainly not confined to Western democracies, nor is it invariably related to the rapidly growing Muslim communities in such countries, migration patterns across, in particular, the twentieth century, from Muslim majority countries to Western, usually Christian majority, countries has in no small way contributed to placing the spotlight on these protections.

Human migration is by no means a new phenomenon. It is one with which Ireland has long been intimately associated. However, while Irish history tells the often sad tale of the millions of our emigrants who left our shores in search of a better life abroad, it is only in the past quarter of a century that we have seen relatively large scale inward migration. This migration of peoples into Ireland has brought our approach to the protection of minority religions into much clearer focus.

Ireland has long been a bastion of Roman Catholicism. Since the early-fifth century (and certainly since the arrival of St Patrick in 432 AD), Catholicism has been the primary religion of the majority of the people. Although adherence to the Roman Catholic faith has dwindled in recent times, 78.3% of the population continue to identify as Roman Catholic according to Census 2016.[1] In this context, and as will be explored in this volume, Irish law and society was, until very recent times, strongly influenced by Christian (specifically Catholic) ideals and mores. How new minority, especially non-Christian, religions fit into this social and legal context is a question well worthy of study and reflection. In particular, how the fast growing Muslim community in Ireland are accommodated under Irish law is of specific importance. Islam now represents the third largest religion in the country. According to the Central Statistics Office, the community has grown by almost 30% since 2011 alone, with approximately

1 Central Statistics Office, *Census 2016 Summary Results – Part 1* (April 2017) 72. This was down from 84.2% in 2011.

 | DOI:10.1163/9789004398252_002

63,400 respondents identifying as Muslim in 2016.[2] This figure is up from just 3,873 in 1991 census, and 19,147 in 2002.[3]

With this in mind, this author sought and secured funding to hold a one-day international symposium at the School of Law, University of Limerick, Ireland. Supported by the School of Law and the University's International Activity Challenge Fund, the research event brought together, for the first time, key Irish legal researchers conducting research on issues of special relevance to minority religions and, in particular, to the Muslim community in Ireland. Influential international scholars were also invited to present and provided valuable insights. This volume represents the contributions of a number of the speakers at the symposium and is an important addition to the literature in the field.[4]

The volume is divided into three main parts. Part 1 is entitled 'Accommodating Minority Religions: The International and Irish Context' and comprises two chapters both of which serve to provide the broader framework for the protection of minority religions in Ireland. The first chapter in this section is contributed by Professor M. Christian Green of Emory University, USA. Professor Green provides a global and international overview of what she suggests is an 'emerging consensus' on the importance of minorities, especially religious minorities. Having considered the emergence and development of rights to freedom of religion or belief (FoRB) and the rights of other minority groups as group rights, she goes on to highlight political, legal and governmental initiatives in a number of countries which have been directly or indirectly aimed at managing minority religions. Building on this platform, she considers what she describes as 'overarching and transnational' themes in law and religion which may be influencing these developments. The second chapter in this Part is delivered by Dr Eoin Daly, Lecturer of Law at the National University of Ireland, Galway. It focuses the discussion in on the protections afforded to religion generally – and religious minorities in particular – under the Irish constitution, *Bunreacht na hÉireann*. In his contribution, Dr Daly argues that the Irish constitutional framework concerning religion is characterised, in large part, by

2 Central Statistics Office (n 1) 72.

3 Central Statistics Office, *Census 2011 Profile 7: Religion Ethnicity and Irish Travellers* (Dublin: Stationary Office, 2012) 16. For a discussion of Irish converts to Islam, in particular, women converts, see Yafa Shanneik, 'Muslim Women in Ireland' in Oliver Scharbrodt et al (eds) *Muslims in Ireland: Past and Present* (Edinburgh University Press, 2015) 193–215.

4 For earlier compilations of research in this area, see, in particular, Oliver Scharbrodt et al (eds) *Muslims in Ireland: Past and Present* (Edinburgh University Press, 2015) and the 2011 special edition 31(4) of the *Journal of Muslim Minority Affairs* focusing on Islam and Muslims in the Republic of Ireland.

indeterminacy rather than coherence. He highlights how the Irish Constitution can be seen to simultaneously appeal to opposing principles or worldviews concerning the relation of State and religion with case law effectively oscillating between those two views resulting in somewhat unpredictable results for religious minorities.

Part 2 turns to issues of specific concern to the largest non-Christian minority religion in Ireland – the Muslim community. Entitled 'Islam and Irish Law: Implications for the Muslim Community in Ireland', this Part of the volume opens with a contribution from Dr James Carr of the Department of Sociology at the University of Limerick, Ireland. Providing the social context for the discussion which follows, Dr Carr provides some background on the development of the diverse Muslim communities residing in Ireland today before drawing on the 2016 Census to provide insights on the make-up of these communities in 21st-century Ireland. He wraps up this contribution with a brief consideration of contemporary issues and debates relating to Islam and Muslim communities in Ireland.

Next, Dr Claire Hogan BL, interrogates the accommodation of Islam under Irish employment, education and healthcare law. She concludes that although litigation is not as extensive as it is in other jurisdictions, issues are beginning to crystallise. The following two chapters address issues of Islamic family law. First, Dr Susan Leahy and Dr Kathryn O'Sulivan, both of the School of Law, University of Limerick, Ireland investigate the recognition of Muslim marriage ceremonies under Irish law. Highlighting the intense discussion on the topic of Muslim marriage recognition in various jurisdictions, the chapter finds that issues regarding the status of Muslim marriages conducted within Ireland have attracted minimal attention. Taking readers through the key legislation, namely the Civil Registration Act 2004 (as amended), the chapter highlights concerns for the relatively small number of Muslim marriages registered over the past five years in Ireland and, having regard to the implications of non-recognition, asks where to next. Continuing the theme of marriage recognition, Dr Máire Ní Shúilleabháin, Assistant Professor at the Sutherland School of Law, University College Dublin, Ireland examines the treatment of Islamic marriage and divorce under Irish private international law – a key issue given, as she explain, that it 'seems probable that there are many Muslims now living in Ireland who have previously married or divorced in a legal system based on Islamic law'. She highlights, in particular, the failure at both a domestic and European level to develop an appropriate regime for recognition of Islamic divorces. Leaving behind issues of family law, this Part closes with a comparative review of the accommodation of Islamic Finance in Irish law delivered by Dr Edana Richardson of the Department of Law, Maynooth University, Ireland. Highlighting the fact that 'Islamic finance is one of the only aspects of Islam within Irish life that the Irish government has actively sought to address though guidelines and legislative amendments', Dr Richardson compares the Irish approach to that adopted in the United Kingdom.

The final part of this collection, Part 3, turns the focus towards Sharia Councils. Although there are no reports of such councils existing in Ireland at present, it would seem probable that as the Muslim community expands the likelihood of their emergence will increase. Entitled 'International Perspectives on Sharia Councils: Regulation and Governance', this Part comprises of two chapters contributed by UK-based academics. First, Dr Amin Al Astewani of the Law School, Lancaster University, England considers the broad approach on both sides of the Irish Sea towards the accommodation of religious tribunals generally before zoning in specifically on the regulatory model currently applied in England for governing Sharia Councils and questions whether such a model could be adopted by the Irish legal system. Dr Samia Bano, Senior Lecturer at SOAS, University of London, England, concludes the collection with her prospective analysis of the potential for institutional reform of Sharia Councils, and, in particular, the possible value and/or potential limitations of the 'parity governance' model.

What emerges quite forcefully from this collection is the sheer scale of the task which will be before the Irish courts, the Irish legislature and the Irish State in the years to come as it seeks to strike a balance in the recognition and/or accommodation of minority religions in the jurisdiction. While pressure has already come to bear on discrete aspects of Irish law which have a particular importance for minority religions such as the Muslim community,[5] this pressure is only likely to increase as Irish society becomes ever more diverse from a religious, cultural and ethnic standpoint. Deciding how we react to these changes will require hard questions to be asked and it is important that in answering, we reflect carefully and, where appropriate, learn from the experience of other jurisdictions. It is hoped that this collection will better inform these discussions in the years ahead.

5 For a broad overview of Irish law of particular relevance to the Muslim community in Ireland, see Kathryn O'Sullivan, *Annotated Legal Documents on Islam in Europe: Ireland* (Brill, 2018).

PART 1

Accommodating Minority Religions: The International and Irish Context

CHAPTER 2

Law, Religion and Religious Minorities

Reflections on International Human Rights Law and Global Trends

M. Christian Green

1 Introduction: Religious Minorities – An American Preface

'We will all have to be Islam scholars now.' This was my first thought as a law and religion scholar in the United States after the terrorist attacks in New York and Washington, D.C. on September 11, 2001. My own limited engagement with the Islamic religion had begun a few years earlier, in some research on alliances between Muslim and Christian groups at the United Nations in the aftermath of the International Conference on Population and Development in Cairo in 1994 and the Fourth World Conference on the Status of Women in Beijing in 1995. At the time, it was unusual to see Islam linking up with other religions on the international stage, though Muslim nations themselves were organized under the auspices of the Organization of the Islamic Conference, now the Organization of Islamic Cooperation (OIC). At the time of the 9/11 terrorist attacks on the United States, while working at a faith and health research organization in downtown Chicago, I was also finishing up a second project on interfaith religious congregational responses to community violence in a city adjacent to Chicago. As the project was concluding, my Chicago-based research colleagues and I began to get calls from people in the neighboring city about how to reach out to Muslims in their community. It was as if they did not know their own neighbors. In fact, Muslim communities were reporting so many well-meaning efforts at outreach that they were deluged and challenged in responding. A final anecdote will set the stage. Several years after 9/11, around 2008, I accompanied some colleagues in Atlanta to lunch with a visiting Islamic studies scholar from the U.K. At one point, our guest asked us, 'Didn't Americans know anything about Islam before 9/11?' Our answer, nearly in unison, was 'No.'

According to the latest Pew Research Center survey in 2015, Muslims still make up just barely 1% of the U.S. religious landscape.[1] Prior to 9/11, Muslim

1 The percentage of the U.S. population who are Muslim is 0.9% to be precise. See Pew Religion & Public Life Project, *America's Changing Religious Landscape* (Washington, DC, Pew

 | DOI:10.1163/9789004398252_003

minorities, mostly Arab and Asian Muslims, had the status of 'model minorities,' generally attaining levels of education and economic prosperity equal to or higher than the general population.[2] But there has also been a dramatic uptick in the number of Muslim immigrants to the U.S. in recent decades – 30% since 2010, another 26% between 2000 and 2009, and another 25% in the 1990s.[3] Slightly more than 80% of Muslims in the U.S. have arrived in the last three decades, a factor which might add to their novelty and unfamiliarity. The more recent influx of Muslims has also included migrants from impoverished, and revolution and conflict-torn regions of the world, such as Somalia, Iran, Iraq, and Central Asia. This has diversified the immigrant Muslim population in the U.S., which now includes groups who are having a tougher time integrating into the fabled 'American Dream,' due to persistent forces of poverty, racism, and suspicions of terrorism.[4] Some of these groups have even become recruiting points for the Islamic State and other jihadist movements.[5] Waves of post-9/11 discrimination continue to make it difficult to be an American Muslim, even as many communities in the U.S. do strive to welcome immigrants and refugees through projects of hospitality and sanctuary.[6] Today, in the post-9/11 era and particularly under the Trump Regime, Muslims in the U.S. appear to be experiencing some of the same pernicious forms of discrimination experienced by Irish and other immigrants groups in centuries past. This is a regrettable and distressing development in the eyes of many Americans – and,

Research Center 2015) <http://www.pewforum.org/religious-landscape-study> accessed 9 November 2018.

2 Muslim achievements in these areas, overall, continue to largely resemble the general public in the U.S. See Pew Research Center, 'U.S. Muslims Concerned About Their Place in Society, but Continue to Believe in the American Dream' (Washington, DC, Pew Research Center, 2017), <http://www.pewforum.org/2017/07/26/demographic-portrait-of-muslim-americans> accessed 9 November 2018.

3 Pew Research Center, 'U.S. Muslims Concerned.'

4 See Khaled A. Beydoun, 'America, Islam, and Constitutionalism: Muslim American Poverty and the Mounting Police State,' [2016] JLR See also Khaled A. Beydoun, *American Islamophobia: Understanding the Roots and Rise of Fear* (University of California Press 2018).

5 Some of the best information on these American would-be ISIS jihadis has been collected by the Program on Extremism at George Washington University in Washington, D.C. See, especially, their list of court and federal law enforcement documents on 'ISIS in America' cases at: https://extremism.gwu.edu.

6 For recent discussions of Muslims and Islam in America, see Abdullahi Ahmed An-Na'im, *What Is an American Muslim?: Embracing Faith and Citizenship* (OUP 2014); Denise Spellberg, *Thomas Jefferson's Qur'an: Islam and the Founders* (Vintage 2013); Juliane Hammer and Omid Safi, eds., *The Cambridge Companion to American Islam* (CUP 2013); Kambiz Ghanea Bassiri, *A History of Islam in America: From the New World to the New World Order* (CUP 2010); Edward E. Curtis, IV, *Muslims in America: A Short History* (OUP 2009).

hopefully, something that we will be able to reverse juridically, legislatively, and electorally.

But one cannot speak of Muslims as immigrants or imports to American shores without also acknowledging the long history of Islam in America – a presence that predates the very establishment of the nation. Many Muslims came to America in the bonds of slavery.[7] A few years back, the *New York Times* posted an essay by a scholar discussing slavery in colonial Georgia, including the presence on one plantation of a Muslim leader who presided over that administration of sharia law among the plantation's enslaved inhabitants.[8] The Black Muslim community in the U.S. has produced such political and cultural figures as the human rights activist Malcolm X, the civil rights educator Betty Shabazz, the international championship boxer Muhammad Ali, and U.S. Congressmen Keith Ellison of Minnesota (elected 2006) and Andre Carson of Indiana (elected 2008), who were the sole Muslim members of the U.S. Congress until the elections of 2016, in which Rashida Tlaib of Michigan and Ilhan Omar of Minnesota were elected to the House of Representatives. Tlaib and Omar are the first Muslim women elected to Congress, and Omar takes the seat of Ellison, who was elected to be Minnesota's Attorney General. The wider American Muslim community, including many immigrants of every race, ethnicity, and national origin has contributed greatly to American life, culture, science, education, politics, and other areas of endeavor.

All of the above is an American preface to the present analysis, the purpose of which is to provide a global and international overview of what I will propose is an 'emerging consensus' on the importance of minorities, especially religious minorities, that may inform discussions of Muslim religious minorities in the Irish context. First, I discuss the emergence and development of rights to freedom of religion or belief (FoRB) and other rights of other minority groups in a way that reflects a significant reframing of national and international human rights away from individual rights and toward group rights in recent decades. Freedom of religion is a right that is obviously salient to Muslim groups as Muslims, but FoRB rights also involve and invoke a host of other freedoms of speech, association, citizenship, and political participation that are essential for all minority groups, whether religious or not. Second, building on research that I have been doing as an academic consultant

7 For an important discussion of this history, see Sylviane A. Diouf, *Servants of Allah: African Muslims Enslaved in the Americas* (15th anniv edn, NYU Press 2013).

8 Peter Manseau, 'The Muslims of Early America,' *The New York Times*, (New York, 9 February 2015). For a history of religious diversity in the United States, see also Manseau's, *One Nation, Under Gods: A New American History* (Little, Brown, & Company 2015).

to the Commonwealth Initiative for Freedom of Religion or Belief (CIFoRB),[9] I assemble some data on the growing attention to religious minorities, even in some notoriously religiously torn places around the world,[10] as a way to address issues of religious freedom (or FoRB) that may offer a way around doctrinal, ethnic, political, and other divisions over religious belief, religious freedom, and the proper relationship between religion and politics, that exist in some parts of the world. Third, I lift up from this global data some core themes of recognition, identity, nondiscrimination, and equality in the treatment of religious minorities, particularly the way in which new demands for recognition of individual and group identities are also driving new calls for equal treatment and nondiscrimination in international law. Finally, I close with some reflections on religious minorities and the challenges and opportunities that the emerging consensus on religious minorities is posing for domestic and international legal systems.

2 Religious Rights and Religious Minorities in International Law

Within the system of human rights law, the religious freedom (FoRB) guarantees of Article 18 of the Universal Declaration of Human Rights (UDHR) are well known. Specifically, Article 18 provides: 'Everyone has the right to freedom of thought, conscience and religion; this right includes freedom to change his religion or belief, and freedom, either alone or in community with others and in public or private, to manifest his religion or belief in teaching, practice, worship and observance.'[11] Other provisions of the UDHR guarantee religious rights in the areas of marriage and family (Art. 16) and education (Art. 26). Article 2 of the UDHR also contains a general principle of nondiscrimination on the basis of factors including 'race, colour, sex, language, religion, political

9 The CIFoRB project was led by Baroness Elizabeth Berridge of the UK House of Lords from 2015–2018 and was based at the Edward Cadbury Centre for Public Understanding of Religion at the University of Birmingham. For more information on CIFoRB, see <www.birmingham.ac.uk/ciforb> accessed 12 November 2019. For further information on the CIFoRB project's research, see the article symposium on 'Freedom of Religion or Belief Across the Commonwealth,' *The Review of Faith of Faith & International Affairs*, Volume 16, Number 4 (Winter 2018).

10 The data are largely gleaned from our CIFoRB Twitter feed, @ciforb_uob, which has served as a powerful resource for aggregating and understanding religious, legal, and political trends throughout the Commonwealth.

11 Universal Declaration of Human Rights, G.A. res. 217A (III), U.N. Doc A/810 at 71 (1948), art. 18.

or other opinion, national or social origin, property, birth or other status.'[12] It is worth noting that Article 26 on education further provides that education, within a human rights framework, 'shall promote understanding, tolerance and friendship among all nations, racial or religious groups, and shall further the activities of the United Nations for the maintenance of peace,' thus containing one of only three specific references to 'groups,' including religious groups in the UDHR.[13]

The International Covenant on Civil and Political Rights (ICCPR) replicates many of the guarantees of the UDHR, including the general principle of nondiscrimination in ICCPR Article 2(1) and the guarantee of religious freedom in ICCPR Article 18.[14] Significant in the context of the counterterrorism framework that has been deployed and critiqued in recent years, particularly for its treatment of Muslim minorities, ICCPR Article 4 outlines circumstances in which there can be derogation from general grants of human rights. Specifically, Article 4 provides that 'In time of public emergency which threatens the life of the nation and the existence of which is officially proclaimed, the States Parties to the present Covenant may take measures derogating from their obligations under the present Covenant to the extent strictly required by the exigencies of the situation, provided that such measures are not inconsistent with their other obligations under international law and do not involve discrimination solely on the ground of race, colour, sex, language, religion or social origin.' This would appear to be a strong condemnation of discrimination or 'profiling' of groups along these important identity lines.

Equally significant in the ICCPR's iteration of the rights themselves are robust protections of equality and nondiscrimination for minority groups. Specifically, ICCPR Article 26 provides: 'All persons are equal before the law and are entitled without any discrimination to the equal protection of the law. In this respect, the law shall prohibit any discrimination and guarantee to all persons equal and effective protection against discrimination on any ground such as race, colour, sex, language, religion, political or other opinion, national or social origin, property, birth or other status.' ICCCR Article 26, thus, combines

12 Marriage, family, and childrearing are, of course, key areas of 'personal law' in which many religious groups were granted latitude or freedom by colonial powers, and they are also important dimensions of sharia law systems that many Muslim minority groups see to set up in countries to which they migrate.

13 The other two mentions are in the Article 16 description of the family as the most basic group within society and the UDHR's final nonderogation clause in Article 30.

14 International Covenant on Civil and Political Rights, G.A. res. 2200A (XXI), 21 U.N. GAOR Supp. (No. 16) at 52, U.N. Doc. A/6316 (1966), 999 U.N.T.S. 171, *entered into force* Mar. 23, 1976, art. 2(1) and 18.

the negatively framed freedom from discrimination with a positively framed principle of equality. Thus, states are not only to take measures to prevent discrimination, but also to promote equality before the law of all individuals, irrespective of the specified markers of group identity. Even so, the focus of Article 26 is, thus, still squarely on the guarantee of equality to individuals, rather than groups *per se*, as the bearers of rights.

But from the group rights perspective, things get more interesting with the immediately ensuing provision in Article 27. On the question of national, ethnic, religious, and linguistic minorities, whose claims have been increasing in number and force in recent decades, ICCPR Article 27 provides: 'In those States in which ethnic, religious or linguistic minorities exist, persons belonging to such minorities shall not be denied the right, in community with the other members of their group, to enjoy their own culture, to profess and practise their own religion, or to use their own language.' Coming nearly two decades after the 1948 UDHR, the 1966 ICCPR reflected a world being reshaped anew with the disintegration of colonialism and new movements for independence around the world. The enhanced focus on group rights, alongside the standard human rights concerns for the fundamental freedoms of individuals in the face of state power, reflected these new global realities. The new focus on group rights would make itself felt in international human rights documents in subsequent decades.

The 1981 Declaration on the Elimination of All Forms of Intolerance and Discrimination on the Basis of Religion or Belief [hereinafter, Religion Declaration],[15] which is the United Nations' highest-level revelation on religious freedom, repeats many of the provisions in the earlier human rights documents, but it also combines non-discrimination and equality principles in a robust way. Articles 1 and 2 of the Religion Declaration reiterate earlier religious rights provisions. Notably, whereas the UDHR Article 2 provision on non-discrimination was framed in exclusively negative terms as a guarantee of freedom from discrimination, Article 2 of the Religion Declaration picks up the ICCPR Article 27 combination of the negative freedom from discrimination with the positive freedom guarantee of equality of treatment. Article 2 defines the very phrase 'intolerance and discrimination based on religion or belief' to mean any distinction, exclusion, restriction or preference based on religion or belief and having as its purpose or as its effect nullification or impairment of the recognition, enjoyment or exercise of human rights and fundamental

15 Declaration on the Elimination of All Forms of Intolerance and of Discrimination Based on Religion or Belief, G.A. res. 36/55, 36 U.N. GAOR Supp. (No. 51) at 171, U.N. Doc. A/36/684 (1981).

freedoms on an equal basis.' Article 3 describes discrimination on the basis of religion or belief as an 'affront to human dignity,' a 'disavowal of the principles of the Charter of the United Nations,' a 'violation of the human rights and fundamental freedoms proclaimed in the Universal Declaration of Human Rights and enunciated in detail in the International Covenants on Human Rights,' and an 'obstacle to friendly and peaceful relations between nations.' On the matter of religious discrimination, Article 4 of the Religion Declaration further provides:

> 1. All States shall take effective measures to prevent and eliminate discrimination on the grounds of religion or belief in the recognition, exercise and enjoyment of human rights and fundamental freedoms in all fields of civil, economic, political, social and cultural life.
> 2. All States shall make all efforts to enact or rescind legislation where necessary to prohibit any such discrimination, and to take all appropriate measures to combat intolerance on the grounds of religion or other beliefs in this matter.

This nondiscrimination directive to states is supplemented by a further gesture toward equality in the next-to-last provision of the Religion Declaration Article 7, which provides that: 'The rights and freedoms set forth in the present Declaration shall be accorded in national legislation in such a manner that everyone shall be able to avail himself of such rights and freedoms in practice.' That the rights are to be available to everyone can be taken as an implicit endorsement of an equality approach.

With the 1993 Declaration on the Rights of National, Ethnic, Religious, and Linguistic Minorities [hereinafter, Minorities Declaration],[16] the United Nations moved even more explicitly toward the protection of minority rights, including the rights of religious minorities, in positive and affirmative sense. Article 1 of the Minorities Declaration calls upon states to 'protect the existence and the national or ethnic, cultural, religious and linguistic identity of minorities within their respective territories and shall encourage conditions for the promotion of that identity' and to 'adopt appropriate legislative and other measures to achieve those ends.' Thus, the concern, specifically for group identity, is a focus from the outset. Article 2 provides that minority groups are to have the rights: (1) 'to enjoy their own culture, to profess and practise their

16 Declaration on the Rights of Persons Belonging to National or Ethnic, Religious or Linguistic Minorities, G.A. res. 47/135, annex, 47 U.N. GAOR Supp. (No. 49) at 210, U.N. Doc. A/47/49 (1993).

own religion, and to use their own language, in private and in public, freely and without interference or any form of discrimination,' (2) 'to participate effectively in cultural, religious, social, economic and public life,' (3) 'to participate effectively in decisions on the national and, where appropriate, regional level concerning the minority to which they belong or the regions in which they live, in a manner not incompatible with national legislation,' (4) 'to establish and maintain their own associations,' and (5) 'to establish and maintain, without any discrimination, free and peaceful contacts with other members of their group and with persons belonging to other minorities, as well as contacts across frontiers with citizens of other States to whom they are related by national or ethnic, religious or linguistic ties.' The Minorities Declaration specifies further rights that derive from the core rights articulated in Article 2, but these basic rights of nondiscrimination, participation, and association are central. These are rights protections that may be especially relevant for Muslims in Ireland, as well as key rights for immigrant and diaspora groups and the communities that they establish around the world.

Besides these international treaties and declarations specifically on religion, there are others in the international human rights law panoply that reinforce similar themes of equality, nondiscrimination, recognition of identity and religious freedom. The 2007 Declaration on the Rights of Indigenous Peoples, for example, contains an important statement in its preamble that 'doctrines, policies and practices based on or advocating superiority of peoples or individuals on the basis of national origin or racial, religious, ethnic or cultural differences are racist, scientifically false, legally invalid, morally condemnable and socially unjust.'[17] Articles 11 and 12 contain important protections of rights to 'cultural traditions and customs,' including 'spiritual and religious traditions,' 'religious and spiritual property,' and 'religious and cultural sites.' Concern for the protection of these sorts of heritage rights as human rights has also become a feature of a growing academic movement in heritage studies, with the protection of minority groups as a key concern. The flip side of these rights based on indigeneity and heritage, as suggested earlier, has been examined increasingly in the study and protection of the rights of migrants, refugees, stateless and displaced people, and other groups whose citizenship comes under question. Overall, the early conceptions of religious rights and other fundamental freedoms are increasingly coming to be seen as not just as individual rights, but as group rights – sometimes as ones that pit majority and minority groups against another in problematic ways. A recent United Nations report noted

17 Declaration on the Rights of Indigenous Peoples, G.A. Res. 61/295, U.N. Doc. A/RES/47/1 (2007).

that minorities of various sorts, including religious minorities, constitute more than three quarters of the world's stateless people.[18] Amid such statistics, the good news may be that there seems to an emerging consensus – at least at the rhetorical level and potentially the practical legal and political level – building on the need to protect minority rights in general that may also benefit religious minorities in particular. Whether and to what extent this is the case is the subject of the next section.

3 The Plight of Minorities: An Emerging Global Consensus?

The status of religious minorities has emerged as one of several key themes of research pursued by the Commonwealth Initiative on Freedom of Religion or Belief (CIFoRB).[19] News reports, policy papers, and legislative interventions to do with FoRB across the vast global reach of the Commonwealth of Nations, have increasingly expressed concern with the plight of religious minorities – even in hotspot nations, such as Pakistan and India, which have routinely populated the lists of the violators of religious freedom,[20] as well as other "South and Southeast Asian Commonwealth" nations, such as Bangladesh, Sri Lanka, Malaysia, and Singapore, where interreligious tensions appear to be rising.[21]

18 'Minorities Make Up Most of the World's Stateless Population,' *Ethics Daily* (Nashville, TN, 16 November 2017). See underlying report at United Nations High Commission for Refugees, '"This Is Our Home": Stateless Minorities and Their Search for Citizenship,' (Geneva: UNHCR, November 17) <http://www.unhcr.org/ibelong/wp-content/uploads/UNHCR_EN2_2017IBELONG_Report_ePub.pdf> accessed 9 November 2018.

19 CIFoRB (n 9).

20 See 'U.S. Places Pakistan on "Special Watch List" for Severe Violations of Religious Freedom,' *VOA News* (Washington, DC, 8 January 8 2018 <https://www.voanews.com/a/us-redesignates-10-nations-for-violations-of-religious-freedom/4192098.html> accessed 9 November 2018; United States Commission on Freedom of Religion or Belief, 'Constitutional and Legal Challeness Faced by Religious Minorities in India' (Washington, DC: USCIRF, 8 February 8 2017). <https://www.uscirf.gov/sites/default/files/Constitutional%20and%20Legal%20Challenges%20Faced%20by%20Religious%20Minorities%20in%20India.pdf> accessed 9 November 2018. For an excellent account of the overall situation of religious minorities in Pakistan, see Farahnaz Ispahani, *Purifying the Land of the Pure: Pakistan's Religious Minorities* (CUP 2016). For an apt discussion of the situation of religious minorities in India, especially amid the growing Hindu nationalist influence, see Amrita Basu, *Violent Conjunctures in Contemporary India* (CUP 2015).

21 For accounts of the recent situation in these countries, see Ali Riaz, *Islamist Militancy in Bangladesh: A Complex Web* (Routledge 2010); Ali Riaz and Christine Fair, eds. *Political Islam and Governance in Bangladesh* (Routledge 2010); David Little, *Sri Lanka: The Invention of Enmity* (United States Institute of Peace 1993); Dian A.H. Shah, *Constitutions, Religion and Politics in Asia: Indonesia, Sri Lanka, and Asia* (CUP 2017); Andrew Harding and Dian

There is an irony for those us studying these issues from the vantage point of the United States, in that, perhaps largely because of our constitutional protection of religious freedom and our long and sad post-slavery legacy of race being a primary marker of identity, discrimination against religious minorities has often been subordinate to racial discrimination as a social and political concern. And while the U.S. has more and more celebrated its religious pluralism in recent decades, it remains a Christian majority nation.[22] While the U.S. is, at least in popular mythology, a 'melting pot' of immigrants, the assimilative norm that underlies that metaphor may work to conceal other religious, ethnic, linguistic, class, and national origin or immigrant status divisions that are so often the basis of conflict and strife elsewhere. This does not mean that such divisions do not exist, but rather that they have been subordinated in such a way as to push them below the surface of the sociopolitical imaginary. However, in other parts of the world, these other categories and groupings remain constitutive and divisive.[23] They are also 'intersectional,' in what has become the popular academic description, such that religious, ethnic, and other minority status merge and interact in different ways.[24]

In his recent study of the situation of religious minorities around the world, political scientist Jonathan Fox defines religious discrimination as 'limitations placed by a government on the practice of religion or the religious institutions

---

A.H. Shah, eds., *Law and Society in Malaysia: Pluralism, Religion and Ethnicity* (Routledge 2017).

22 See, e.g. Diana Eck, *A New Religious America: How a 'Christian Country' Has Become the World's Most Religiously Diverse Nation* (Harper One 2001). Cf. Pew Religion & Public Life Project, American Religious Landscape Survey, 2015. See also Alan Cooperman and Michael Lipka, 'U.S. Doesn't Rank High in Religious Diversity,' *Pew Research Center Fact Tank* (Washington, DC, Pew Research Center, 4 April 2014) <http://www.pewresearch.org/fact-tank/2014/04/04/u-s-doesnt-rank-high-in-religious-diversity> accessed 9 November 2018.

23 In particular, one cannot come away from reading about the founding of Pakistan in the Partition from India and not see how central religious groups identities were in the founding of relationship between those two nations and how many of troubles at the inception continue to the present day. For an excellent account of this history and its legacy for religious minorities in Pakistan and across the border in India, see Ispahani (n 20).

24 The term intersectionality was coined in a key article by law professor and critical race theorist Kimberlé Crenshaw, whose writings on the subject will be collected in the forthcoming volume, *On Intersectionality: Essential Writings of Kimberlé Crenshaw* (New Press forthcoming 2019). See also Patricia Hill Collins and Silma Bilge, Intersectionality (Polity 2016); Ange-Marie Hancock, *Intersectionality: An Intellectual History* (OUP 2016); Patrick R. Grzanka, *Intersectionality: A Foundations and Frontiers Reader* (Westview Press 2014). For a more critical analysis of the concept, see Anna Carastathis, *Intersectionality: Origins, Contestations, Horizons* (University of Nebraska Press, 2016).

within the state that are not placed on the majority religion.'[25] As Fox acknowledges and others have chronicled more extensively, this definition does not take into account political, economic and other forms of discrimination, nor does it include the sorts of social hostilities which can, along with government restrictions, exert a discriminatory force on minority religious groups, a force often explicitly or implicitly sanctioned by the government.[26] Two of the key takeaway points from Fox's study are that: (1) religious discrimination is increasing around the world and (2) that it is often distributed and experienced unequally among religious groups in a given country.[27] It is also worth noting from Fox's study that it cannot be assumed that Western nations are absolved of responsibility for FoRB violations within their own borders. Indeed, as Fox observes of his study and its categorization of FoRB violations in various parts of the world, 'Perhaps the most striking finding is that religious discrimination is present and increasing in nearly all of these subdivisions of states, including Western democracies which are supposed to be among the most tolerant in the world.'[28] Fox attributes a large part of this Western intolerance, particularly directed at Muslim minorities, to the ascendancy of 'securitization theory' in connection with perceived security threats from terrorist incidents.[29]

While to some extent focused on the government restrictions dimension of FoRB violations, Fox does not, however, ignore the social dimension of religious freedom, including the important group identity and intersectional dimensions. As he puts it:

> The concepts of religious repression and persecution have another potential meaning – discrimination on the basis of religion. This focuses not on restrictions of the right of free exercise, but rather, on any restriction placed on a religious group because they are a religious group as such. These types of restrictions do not need to have anything to do with the practice of religion or religious institutions. Rather, they can include

25 Jonathan Fox, *The Unfree Exercise of Religion: A World Survey of Discrimination Against Religious Minorities* (CUP 2016), 1.

26 Fox (n 2, 12, 14–15). The government restrictions versus social hostilities distinction has been a particular hallmark of the research of the Pew Research Center on rising religious restrictions around the world. See the various reports archived at: http://www.pewresearch.org/topics/restrictions-on-religion, esp the foundational reports on the topic, 'Global Restrictions on Religion' (Washington, DC: Pew Research Center, 17 December 17 2009) and 'Rising Religious Restrictions' (Washington, DC: Pew Research Center, 9 August 2011).

27 Fox (n 25, 2).

28 Fox (n 25, 8).

29 Fox (n 25, 42–46).

> any political, social, cultural, or economic restriction placed on an identity group defined by religion.[30]

Fox further observes that while these kinds of discrimination may be 'essentially indistinguishable from the types of persecution against minorities that are not based on religious identities' and that 'discrimination on the basis of religion does not necessarily violate the right of free exercise and is perhaps best dealt with in the context of the ethnic conflict literature,' such forms of discrimination may end up becoming FoRB violations, insofar as 'sufficient levels of discrimination or persecution on the basis of religion can in effect limit the free exercise of religion.'[31]

In a number of nations in South and Southeast Asia that constitute a populous and religiously diverse swath of the Commonwealth and are also feeder nations to the diasporic Irish Muslim community, there have been increasing calls from government and civil society to address the situation of minorities, especially religious minorities.[32] In Pakistan and India, two notorious hotspots for violation of religious minority rights, the governments have increasingly taken action to address problems of citizenship, status, and rights of various minorities. Whether these policies and pronouncements will be effective remains to be seen – for there is certainly the possibility that they are mere rhetoric or window-dressing concealing human rights violations take place under the surface. A snapshot of the issues that have emerged in these countries, just in the last few years, while not a comprehensive or fully historical portrait, can give some indication of the nature and the scope of the problem.

Pakistan, for example, has received international criticism for its treatment of minorities amid a sense of rising tensions around religion, ethnicity, and identity within its borders.[33] The European Parliament has joined the U.S. in criticism of the human rights and FoRB rights situation in Pakistan.[34] Two dozen members states of the United Nations recently criticized Pakistan's human

30 Fox (n 27, 15).

31 Fox (n 27, 16).

32 Aftab Alam, 'Taking Minority Rights Seriously,' *Countercurrents.org* (Kerala, 27 December 2016) <https://countercurrents.org/2016/12/27/taking-minority-rights-seriously> accessed 12 November 2018.

33 Anam Zakaria, 'Perceiving the 'Other' in Pakistan, Within and Across Borders,' *The Wire* (New Delhi, 19 December 2016 <https://thewire.in/external-affairs/pakistan-perceptions-religious-minority> accessed 9 November 2018. For an account of the overall situation of religious minorities in Pakistan, see Ispahani (n 20).

34 'EP Conference Raises Questions about Ethnic & Religious Rights in Pakistan and the Role of the EU,' *UNPOorg*, (Brussels, 11 May 2017) <https://unpo.org/article/20083> accessed 9 November 2018.

rights record at a universal periodic review by the U.N. Human Rights Council, citing particularly Pakistan's record on the status of women, minority rights, and FoRB.[35] Recently, however, the Pakistani government has responding to calls from activists at the national and provincial levels for greater recognition and protection of the rights of religious minorities. At least at the level of rhetoric, this is something markedly different than might be expected of a nation that is routinely cited as one of the world's worst FoRB violators.[36]

Pakistani officials have often indicated support for FoRB minority rights abroad, but they have also recently been pursuing measures to improve protections for religious minorities at home, albeit to varying receptions and degrees of success. Even with these measures, religious minorities in Pakistan continue to experience high levels of discrimination and outright persecution, and concerns about rising nationalism and sectarianism have been increasing for several decades.[37] Christian, Hindu, and Sikh minorities have all complained to the Pakistani National Security Adviser of ongoing FoRB violations, particularly misuse of the blasphemy laws and forced conversion, the latter often accomplished through kidnapping and forced marriage of teenage girls. On matters of FoRB and freedom of expression, two human rights concerns that often coincide in Pakistan's blasphemy laws, a 2016 report by the Asian Forum for Human Rights and Development, titled 'Desecrating Expression – An Account of Freedom of Expression and Religion in Asia,' reported that social media were increasingly being used to target Pakistani religious minorities.[38] As in other parts of South Asia, bloggers on political and religious matters have come under government scrutiny and have been vocal in challenging blasphemy and other laws intended to infringe upon their freedom of expression.[39]

---

35 Ehsan Rehan, 'U.N. member states criticize Pakistan's Human Rights record,' *Rabwah Times* (Chenab Nagar, 14 November 2017) <https://www.rabwah.net/u-n-member-states-criticize-pakistans-human-rights-record> accessed 9 November 2018.

36 Shamim Shahid, 'HR activists demand equal constitutional rights for minorities, *Pakistan Today* (Islamabad, 5 February 2017 <https://www.pakistantoday.com.pk/2017/02/25/hr-activists-demand-equal-constitutional-rights-for-minorities> accessed 9 November 2018.

37 Zakaria (n33).

38 Rana Tanveer, 'Social media being used as a tools against minorities,' *The Express Tribune* (Karachi, 26 December 2016) <https://tribune.com.pk/story/1272167/unregulated-hate-social-media-used-tool-minorities> 9 November 2018. See also Asia Forum for Human Rights and Development, 'Desecrating Expression – An Account of Freedom of Expression and Religion in Asia' (Forum-Asia, 2016) <https://www.forum-asia.org/?p=21941> accessed 9 November 2018.

39 'Bloggers unite to bring minorities' issues into the limelight,' *The Express Tribune* (Karachi, 28 January 2017) <https://tribune.com.pk/story/1308963/power-pen-bloggers-unite-bring-minorities-issues-limelight> accessed 9 November 2018.

The efforts of the Pakistani government to address the situation of religious minorities have sometimes been seen to involve moving 'one step forward, two steps back,' as exemplified by two recent bills on Hindu marriage and religious conversion in Sindh Province.[40] In February 2016, in what was hailed internationally as a very beneficial move for religious minorities, Sindh province passed a law recognizing Hindu marriages at the same time that the national government was considering passage of a similar law.[41] This bill supporting Hindu marriage early in 2016, was followed by passage of the Sindh Criminal Law (Protection of Minorities) Bill of 2015 in November 2016. This law prohibits conversion to Islam before the age of 18 and makes it a requirement that anyone wishing to convert to Islam take prescribed classes on other religions before so doing. The Sindh law was intended to combat a perceived growing problem of the kidnapping and forced Islamic conversion of Hindu girls.[42] The law was criticized by Muslim majority groups as overly broad for banning religious conversion outright before age 18.[43] Even so, an appeal by the Muslim majority to repeal the law just a month after its passage drew international criticism.[44] Freedoms of marriage and non-coercion in conversion have been

40 Olivia Enos, 'Religious Freedom in Pakistan Take 1 Step Forward, 2 Steps Back,' *The Daily Signal* (Washington, DC, 29 December 2016 <https://www.dailysignal.com/2016/12/29/religious-freedom-in-pakistan-takes-one-step-forward-two-steps-back> accessed 9 November 2018; Umair Jamal, 'The Politics of Religious Exclusion in Pakistan,' *The Diplomat* (Washington, DC, 18 October 2017 <https://thediplomat.com/2017/10/the-politics-of-religious-exclusion-in-pakistan> accessed 9 November 2018.

41 Ansar Abbasi, 'U.S. Commission seeks repeal of blasphemy and anti-Qadiani laws,' *The News International* (Islamabad, 23 December 2016) <https://www.thenews.com.pk/print/173924-US-commission-seeks-repeal-of-blasphemy-and-anti-Qadiani-laws> accessed 9 November 2018. See also Reuben Ackermann, 'Forced Conversions & Force Marriages in Sindh, Pakistan,' (Birmingham, UK, CIFoRB, 2018) <https://www.birmingham.ac.uk/Documents/college-artslaw/ptr/ciforb/Forced-Conversions-and-Forced-Marriages-in-Sindh.pdf> accessed 12 November 2019.

42 'Hindus in Pakistan declining due to 'forced' conversions: Pak media,' *The Deccan Chronicle* (Hyderabad, 21 June 2017) <https://www.deccanchronicle.com/world/neighbours/210617/hindu-minority-in-pakistan-reduced-to-margins-due-to-forced-conversions-pak-media.html> accessed 9 November 2018.

43 Abbasi (n 42); 'Rights activists urge government to pass minorities' bill protection,' *Dawn* (Karachi, 29 December 2016) <https://www.dawn.com/news/1305047> accessed 9 November 2018.

44 Abbasi (n 42); 'Pakistan may face isolation if Minorities Bill repealed,' *Janta Ka Reporter* (Islamabad, 26 December 2016 <http://www.jantakareporter.com/india/minorities-bill/87713> accessed 9 November 2018; Mobarik A. Virk, 'Minorities want Sindh not to repeal a bill in their favour,' *The News International*, (Islamabad, 26 December 2016) <https://www.thenews.com.pk/print/174426-Minorities-want-Sindh-not-to-repeal-bill-in-their-favour> accessed 9 November 2018.

important ones for religious minorities in South Asia and many other parts of the world, and in that context the Pakistani government's protection of its Hindu minority was seen as a welcome development.

Given its large size and large and influential diaspora communities in Europe, North America, and elsewhere, Pakistan remains a key country to watch on FoRB matters. This also makes its recent gestures toward protection of religious minorities notable, as well. In light of its status as a key training ground and source of the Taliban, Islamist religious extremists, and global terrorist organizations, Pakistan will bear monitoring for the foreseeable future. Its recent attempts at protecting religious minorities do seem, at least, to indicate a growing understanding of the problem that could have positive domestic and international implications if addressed robustly and effectively. It also remains a country that is testament to the age-old human rights problem of needing to keep malefactor nations within the circle of discussion in order to exert leverage and to persuade them to act upon their pro-human rights rhetoric.

In India, there has also been new attention paid to the situation of religious minorities.[45] The Indian system seeks to balance equal treatment of religions with the granting of special privileges in order to bring groups that have experienced discrimination and disadvantage to a level of equality with other religious groups. In some cases, Indian political parties have conducted specific outreach campaigns to bring religious minorities into their parties and the political process.[46] The government, at both federal and state levels, has also set quotas for the numbers of religious minority groups in government.[47] In some cases, India has had to balance its constitutionally mandated secularism with attempts to address injustice and equality within religious groups. For example, a leading religious minority issue in India recently has been the 'triple talaq' divorce, according to which Muslim men may divorce their wives by uttering the words 'I divorce you' three times.[48] This form of Islamic divorce is one that

45 Editorial, 'State Minority Commission,' *Daily Excelsior* (Janipura, 13 December 2016) <http://www.dailyexcelsior.com/state-minority-commission> accessed 9 November 2018.

46 'Laskar Committee for greater representation of Christians,' *Eastern Mirror* (Dimapur, 27 April 2017) <http://www.easternmirrornagaland.com/laskar-committee-for-greater-representation-of-christians> accessed 9 November 2018.

47 Koride Maheshi, 'TRS government threatens to move apex court for Muslim quota,' *Times of India* (Gurugram, 20 November 2017 <https://timesofindia.indiatimes.com/city/hyderabad/trs-government-threatens-to-move-apex-court-for-muslim-quota/articleshow/61586404.cms> accessed 9 November 2018.

48 J Venkatesan, 'Triple talaq hearing begins, 5 judges of 5 religions on SC's bench,' *The Deccan Chronicle*, (Hyderabad, 11 May 2017) <https://www.deccanchronicle.com/nation/

has been opposed heavily by Muslim feminists, among other groups.[49] In August 2017, the Indian Supreme Court ruled the so-called 'instant divorce' to be un-Islamic in a verdict that was seen by Muslim feminists in India as a victory for women's empowerment.[50] But it also, notably, required an officially secular court to render a judgment on the validity and permissibility of religious practices. Secularism in India thus rests in tension with the need to promote values of equality and gender justice in way that ends up involving the state in the management of religion.[51]

Even with these various protections, religious minorities continue to experience persecution in India, and FoRB violations are said to have increased significantly with the ascension to power of the Bharatiya Janata Party (BJP) with its 'Hindutva' Hindu nationalist philosophy under Prime Minister Narendra Modi. In January 2017, the international NGO Human Rights Watch reported attacks on religious minorities led by vigilante groups, blocks on foreign funding for NGOs, and pressure on media and civil society organizations that were critical of government policies.[52] Muslims have experienced human rights and a range of FoRB violations, up to and including religiously motivated lynchings.[53] Christian groups in parts of the country where the Hindu nationalist BJP party has enjoyed electoral success have been strategizing about ways to

current-affairs/110517/crucial-triple-talaq-hearing-begins-today-5-judges-of-5-religions-on-scs-bench.html> accessed 9 November 2018; Ambika Panditl, 'Triple talaq a social ill, not a religious issue: Muktahr Abbas Naqvi, *Times of India*, 11 May 2017.

49 I am indebted for this observation to Samia Bano, a fellow participant in the conference that produced the present volume. See also 'Conservative Muslims slam, feminists hail triple talaq ban,' *Deutsche Welle* (Bonn/Berlin) 22 August, 2017) <https://www.dw.com/en/conservative-muslims-slam-feminists-hail-indias-triple-talaq-ban/a-40190155> accessed 9 November 2018.

50 'Triple talaq: India's court bans Islamic instant divorce,' *BBC News* (London, 22 August 2017 <https://www.bbc.com/news/world-asia-india-41008802> accessed 9 November 2018.

51 In the U.S. the theoretical and practical difficulties associated with such state management of religion, especially minority religions, have been amply explored by law and religion scholar Winnifred Fallers Sullivan in *The Impossibility of Religious Freedom* (Princeton University Press, 2005). See also the work of Sullivan and colleagues on the politics of religious minorities around the world in Winnifred Fallers Sullivan and Elizabeth Shakman Hurd, *Politics of Religious Freedom* (University of Chicago Press, 2015). See also Saba Mahmood, *Religious Difference in a Secular Age: A Minority Report* (Princeton University Press 2015).

52 'Human Rights Watch voices concern over attacks on minorities in India,' *Financial Express*, (Mumbai, 14 January 2017) <https://www.financialexpress.com/india-news/human-rights-watch-voices-concern-over-attacks-on-minorities-in-india/507431> accessed 12 November 2018.

53 Rana Ayyub, 'Mobs are killing Muslims in India: Why is no one stopping the?' *The Guardian* (Surry Hills, NSW, 28 July 2017) <https://www.theguardian.com/commentisfree/2018/jul/20/mobs-killing-muslims-india-narendra-modi-bjp> accessed 12 November 2018.

strengthen the political standing of religious minorities and to prevent them from moving out of these regions.[54]

Prime Minister Narendra Modi's visions for a 'new India,' said to involve measures to 'purify the country,' have increasingly elicited concern not only within India, but around the world.[55] His appointment of Yogi Aditnayath, described as a 'firebrand Hindu cleric' in international media, to be the chief minister of Uttar Pradesh has drawn global scrutiny.[56] The European Union has demanded respect for human rights in trade talks with India.[57] Indian-American diaspora groups in the U.S. have also criticized India's human rights record.[58] India is, thus, like Pakistan, an enormously populous country with a substantial global diaspora population in a way that makes it a key nation in the region. The present path toward Hindu nationalism, coupled with ongoing communal violence and even resort to blasphemy charges, though on a lesser scale than Pakistan, means that it, too, will be a nation to watch in coming years.

Pakistan and India are two of the highest profile South Asian nations in terms of issues of treatment of religious minorities, and there are, of course, Pakistani and Indian expatriates who are part of Ireland's diverse Muslim community. But other South and Southeast Asian nations that send expats to Ireland have also had troubles over religious minorities in recent decades. For example, the nation of Sri Lanka has long experienced division and strife between its Sinhalese Buddhist majority and its ethnic Tamil population. Muslims, Christians, and

54 'Uncertain future for Indian Christians after BJP's election victories,' *World Watch Monitor*, 22 March 2017) <https://www.worldwatchmonitor.org/2017/03/uncertain-future-indian-christians-bjps-election-victories> accessed 12 November 2018.

55 Editorial Board, 'Mr. Modi's Perilous Embrace of Hindu Extremists,' *New York Times* (New York, 23 March 2017) <https://www.nytimes.com/2017/03/23/opinion/mr-modis-perilous-embrace-of-hindu-extremists.html> accessed 9 November 2018. Others have expressed greater faith in Modi's FoRB commitment to religious minorities. See, e.g., 'Minority rights more secure more safe after Modi,' *The Asian Age* (New Delhi, 12 November 2017) <http://www.asianage.com/metros/delhi/121117/minority-rights-more-secure-safe-under-pm-modi.html> accessed 9 November 2018.

56 'Mr. Modi's Embrace of Hindu Extremists,'; 'PM Modi making Yogi Adityanath UP CM is 'shocking rebuke' to religious minorities: New York Times,' *DNA* (Mumbai, 23 March 2017) <https://www.dnaindia.com/india/report-pm-modi-making-yogi-adityanath-up-cm-is-shocking-rebuke-to-religious-minorities-new-york-times-2365669> accessed 9 November 2018.

57 Lars Adaktusson, 'EU must demand respect for human rights in trade talks with India,' *Euractiv* (Brussels, 4 October 2017) <https://www.euractiv.com/section/freedom-of-thought/opinion/eu-must-demand-respect-for-human-rights-in-trade-talks-with-india> accessed 9 November 2018.

58 'Human rights abuses against minorities on rise again in India: Indian-American group,' *Hindustan Times*, (New Delhi, 24 May 2017) <https://www.hindustantimes.com/india-news/human-rights-abuses-against-minorities-on-rise-in-india-indian-american-group/story-pYVmC22dDJfQ4Ro1ousclK.html> accessed 9 November 2018.

other groups have also reported FoRB violations. Sri Lanka's constitution gives a privileged place to Buddhism, which was declared the state religion in 1978.[59] Preferential treatment of the Buddhist majority has been controversial and was linked to the development of a separatist Tamil Tiger movement, which was largely ethnically based, but also drew significantly from the Hindu religious community. The clash between these groups produced a thirty-year civil war that ended in 2009. As in Myanmar/Burma, another country in the region with religious minority issues, the Sri Lankan state's commitment to the protection of Buddhism has given to Buddhist nationalist sentiments. Sri Lankan and Burmese Buddhist nationalism, with growing Hindu nationalism, has thus marked the larger phenomenon of religious nationalism as a problem for religious minorities in South and Southeast Asia.

Sri Lanka's response to this problem of rising religious nationalism has been to embark on a range of efforts aimed at creating 'peace,' 'unity,' 'tolerance,' and 'harmony' among religious groups that have not been without controversy.[60] Local newspapers editorials cite the need for religion to 'build bridges, not walls,'[61] and broadcast messages from religious leaders on Independence Day.[62] Prime Minister Ranil Wickremesinghe recently declared the government's full support for reconciliation among religious groups in service of a unitary country.[63] A government-sponsored National Unity and Reconciliation movement has sought to bring religious leaders together for dialogue about the country's new constitution, which was proposed in 2018.[64] However, some aspects of the emerging religious scene in Sri Lanka remain unclear. Notably,

---

59 Constitution of the Democratic Socialist Republic of Sri Lanka, 1978, amended 2015, Ch. II, art 9. Protection of 'religion or belief' is later referenced at Ch. III, art 10 and 14(e).

60 'Racial and religious harmony' as a rationale for restricting rights is also referenced several times in Ch. III, art 15 of the Constitution. Religion and other factors bearing on national 'unity' are referenced in Ch. VI, art 27(e)(5–6). Art 27(11) of this same chapter on directive principles of the state promises further: 'The State shall create the necessary economic and social environment to enable people of all religious faiths to make a reality of their religious principles.'

61 'Religions meant to build bridges, not walls,' (editorial) *Daily Mirror.lk* (Colombo, 18 January 2017) <http://www.dailymirror.lk/article/Religions-meant-to-build-bridges-not-walls-122315.html> accessed 9 November 2018.

62 'Independence Day messages from Religious leaders,' *Daily News.lk* (Colombo, 4 February 2017) <http://www.dailynews.lk/2017/02/04/local/106682/independence-day-messages> accessed 9 November 2018.

63 'Sri Lankan Prime Minister declares government's full support for religious reconciliation,' *ColomboPage* (Colombo, 29 March 2017) <http://www.colombopage.com/archive_17A/Mar29_1490808608CH.php> accessed 9 November 2018.

64 'Sri Lankan monks, bishops propose religious councils,' *Herald Malaysia* (Kuala Lampur, 14 March 2017) <http://www.heraldmalaysia.com/news/sri-lankan-monks-bishops-propose-religious-councils/35243/2> accessed 9 November 2018.

the reconciliation movement encountered difficulties bringing the island nation's Buddhist, Hindu, Muslim, Christian, and other groups together.[65]

Sri Lanka's quest for tolerance, peace, harmony, unity, and reconciliation among religions, at least at the normative and rhetorical level and in the context of constitutional reform, is a promising development. However, it also exemplifies a growing problem that can be seen in especially strong form in South and Southeast Asia and increasingly around the world – namely, the problem of religious majorities acting like religious minorities. This happens when majority religions claim protection from the state, in a victim-like way, vis-à-vis minority religions. In the religiously diverse nations of Southeast Asia, such as Myanmar/Burma, Malaysia, Indonesia, and Vietnam, this has given rise to numerous laws protecting majority religions, under the guise of promoting 'respect,' 'tolerance,' 'peace,' 'unity,' and 'harmony.' Under these laws, majority religions are said to demand respect as the price for extending tolerance to religious minorities. Sometimes these laws include rights-limiting language referencing the need to protect public morality, virtue, and safety in parceling out respect to majorities and tolerance to minorities. Blasphemy or quasi-blasphemy restrictions are the frequent result of the implementation of these laws in practice. They end up operating against freedoms of speech, religion, and other civil and political rights, creating a patina and veneer of civility that stifles resistance and critique. While these South and Southeast Asian struggles may seem exotic in the Irish context, they are reflective of tendencies occurring in many parts of the world over issues of majority-minority religious relations, and they are perhaps even consonant and resonant with the blasphemy and defamation of religion issue, specifically blasphemy against Christianity, as recently aired in Ireland.[66]

4 Recognition and Identity, Non-Discrimination and Equality: The Normative Challenges Regarding Religious Minorities

Consonant with the shift in focus from individual rights to a group rights in international law and the challenges around religious minorities set forth in

65 S. Ratnajeevan H. Hoole, 'Navalar Myths Aborting Reconciliation,' *Colombo Telegraph* (Colombo, 14 December 2016) <https://www.colombotelegraph.com/index.php/navalar-myths-aborting-reconciliation> accessed 9 November 2018.

66 See Steve Pinkerton, 'Blasphemy law is repealed in Ireland but remains a problem for Christians and Muslims,' Religion News Service (Columbia, MO, 8 November 2018) <https://religionnews.com/2018/11/08/blasphemy-law-is-repealed-in-ireland-but-remains-a-problem-for-christian-and-muslims/?fbclid=IwAR05Fr3SDabp489D3gs3IODZkfVIU8eGuGHDeZM3nKStDWOi18zT1zG355> accessed 12 November 2018.

the countries discussed above are some overarching and transnational themes in law and religion that may be the real determinants. The term 'recognition' is one that is widely used in discussions of human rights. We speak of the 'recognition of rights' and the 'recognition of status' of various groups. But more and more, the term 'recognition' is taking on new meaning in connection with another oft-heard term of late – namely, 'identity.'[67] Philosophers such as Kwame Anthony Appiah have written of the 'ethics of identity.'[68] The Nobel Prize-winning philosopher-economist Amartya Sen has written powerfully on the connection between identity and violence.[69] French political theorist Dominique Moïsi has proclaimed our era to be the 'age of identity.'[70] This has occurred even as the new emphasis on 'intersectionality' across many scholarly fields has complicated the notion of identity itself.

Who decides an individual or group's identity? Who prioritizes among the various racial, ethnic, gender, linguistic, national, socioeconomic, and other dimensions of identity – particularly with regard to the increasingly fraught subject of religious identity under discussion here? Is identity fixed or can it change, as through religious proselytization and conversion, to invoke two controversial practices in the area of FoRB? If an individual changes religion or becomes marginalized by changes (e.g. radicalization, extremism) occurring within a religious group, does such change imply apostasy or blasphemy, to invoke two more challenging terms?[71] Who has the responsibility – individuals, groups, religions, states – for determining, articulating, and recognizing identity? And why does religious identity seem to operate on a different plane from other categories of identity, prompting scholars of religion and conflict to

67 Much of the discussion in the fields of philosophy and political theory comes from a debate between theorists Nancy Fraser and Axel Honneth over whether recognition of identity or redistribution of socioeconomic and political goods is the central question in modern societies. The debate is captured in the volume *Redistribution or Recognition?: A Political-Philosophical Exchange* (Verso 2003).

68 See Kwame Anthony Appiah, *The Ethics of Identity* (Princeton University Press 2007) and *The Lies that Bind: Rethinking Identity* (Liveright/W.W. Norton 2018).

69 See Amartya Sen, *Identity and Violence: The Illusion of Destiny* (W.W. Norton, 2006).

70 See Dominique Moïsi, *The Geopolitics of Emotion: How Cultures of Fear, Humiliation, and Hope are Changing the World* (Doubleday 2009).

71 For a review of recent literature on apostasy, including apostasy among young Muslims drawn to jihadism and in Islamic jurisprudence, see M. Christian Green, 'Apostasy through Doubt and Dissent,' [2016] JLR. For a review of recent literature and debates on blasphemy, also with a focus on Islam, see M. Christian Green, 'Between Blasphemy and Critique: Freedom of Religion and Freedom of Speech,' [2014] JLR.

observe that when a conflict is 'religionized,' it typically becomes more violent and intractable?[72]

The new emphasis on recognition and identity goes hand-in-hand with another pair of terms that have become the subject of much recent commentary in the interdisciplinary field of law and religion, especially in law. For alongside the shift from individual rights to group rights, on matters to do specifically with FoRB and the treatment of religious minorities, we may also be seeing a shift from an earlier norm of nondiscrimination to a new norm of equality. Increasingly, it has seemed that mere nondiscrimination is not enough, or perhaps more correctly, it may be enough to address problems of government restrictions on religion, but it is not enough to tackle problems of social hostility and social discrimination, including the "majorities acting like minorities" phenomenon, which may have a greater impact on religious minority groups.

In the U.S., for example, we remain in the midst of an ongoing debate over same-sex marriage and religious freedom in the aftermath of the decision of the Supreme Court of the United States in the case of *Obergefell v. Hodges*, which legalized same-sex marriage in the summer of 2015.[73] Now, conservative groups are raising challenges on behalf of wedding vendors – purveyors of cakes, flowers, photography, and other wedding-related goods and services – that their FoRB rights need to be protected, especially insofar as their status as Christian marriage traditionalists makes them a religious minority within the wider U.S. culture. This has been framed in terms of their experiencing 'stigmatization' of or 'animus' toward their religious beliefs in a way that makes them a religious minority in need of protection. A baker in the case of the *Masterpiece Cakeshop v. Colorado Civil Rights Commission*, ended up winning his case based on the 'animus' toward his religion said to have been demonstrated in remarks by the Colorado Commissioners.[74]

The issue of same-sex marriage and religion is currently also a live one in Australia, where 61% of the population recently voted in a national plebiscite in support of same-sex marriage, leading to its legalization by action of the National Assembly. But the government also quickly convened an inquiry into the status of religious freedom in Australia, resulting in a document, the Ruddock report, that was kept secret for months after its completion in May

72 Brian J. Grim and Roger Finke, The Price of Freedom Denied: Religious Persecution and Conflict in the 21st Century (CUP 2011).

73 *Obergefell v. Hodges*, 576 U.S. ___, 135 S.Ct. 2071 (2015).

74 *Masterpiece Cakeshop v. Colorado Civil Rights Commission*, 584 U.S. ___, 38 S. Ct. 1719 (2018).

2018 – a development that drew condemnation from many, including former Australian High Court Justice Michael Kirby.[75] Though the contents and conclusions of the Ruddock report remain unknown at the time of this writing, central to the discussion informing it was the question of whether religious individuals and organizations should be exempt from laws guaranteeing non-discrimination against and equal treatment of religious and other minorities.

Same-sex marriage debates in the U.S. may seem quite different from debates over the status of Muslims in Ireland and other parts of Europe, but there are many areas of practical and normative overlap. Protection of traditional Christian definitions of marriage opens the door for protection of other forms of forms of marriage and marriage and family laws, including sharia-based systems. Indeed, this fact has not been lost on some Australians, who are now worried that protection of same-sex marriage might also pave the way for Muslim marriage and sharia more generally.[76] These concerns are also reflective of the new focus in some areas of law and religion scholarship on questions of 'legal pluralism,' or the coexistence of secular and religious legal models around the world. The fact that much of this legal pluralism comes from global migration and diaspora makes the issue of minority religious groups particularly salient for pluralistic and multicultural societies, who may be called upon to question

75 For discussion of the Australian religious freedom report, see "Read the full 20 recommendations from the religious freedom review, *Sydney Morning Herald* (Sydney, 12 October 2018) https://www.smh.com.au/politics/federal/read-the-full-20-recommendations-from-the-religious-freedom-review-20181011-p50918.html> accessed 9 November 2018. See also, "Former judge takes aim at religious freedom report delay," *SBS News* (Sydney/Melbourne, 4 October 2018) <https://www.sbs.com.au/news/former-judge-takes-aim-at-religious-freedom-report-delay> accessed 9 November 2018; Paul Karp, "Michael Kirby attacks Coalition for refusal to release Ruddock report," *The Guardian* (Surry Hills, NSW, 4 October 2018) <https://www.theguardian.com/australia-news/2018/oct/04/michael-kirby-attacks-coalition-for-failure-to-release-ruddock-religious-freedom-report> accessed 9 November 2018; Paul Karp, "Ruddock religious freedom review: what is it and what do we know so far?" *The Guardian* (Surry Hills, NSW, 11 October 2018) <https://www.theguardian.com/australia-news/2018/oct/11/ruddock-religious-freedom-review-what-is-it-and-what-do-we-know-so-far> accessed 9 November 2018; Jonathan Pearlman, "Australian plan to protect religious freedom stirs debate," *Straits Times* (Singapore, 27 October 2018) <https://www.straitstimes.com/asia/australianz/australian-plan-to-protect-religious-freedom-stirs-debate> accessed 9 November 2018.

76 David Crowe, 'Warning over sharia law in push for religious freedom,' *The Australian* (Surry Hills, NSW, 27 November 2017) <http://www.theaustralian.com.au/national-affairs/warning-over-sharia-law-in-push-for-religious-freedom/news-story/7e5d52ec5aa6ff24148715d7eb397af2> accessed 9 November 2018.

and revise earlier norms of assimilation and to propose new social and legal norms to manage diversity.[77]

In this context, recognition of identity also becomes significant as a new transnational norm. Domestic laws, with international laws, have also typically been framed in terms of individuals rather than groups, especially in areas such as FoRB and other civil and political rights. But it is significant that international laws reference marriage, family, and education of children in lists of fundamental rights and as FoRB rights. Marriage and family laws, of course, not only affect individuals, but are constitutive of families and wider forms of community. They are where the proverbial 'rubber hits the road' when it comes to FoRB and group rights. Thus, it is no accident that social and legal definitions of Christian marriage, Hindu marriage, Muslim marriage, and marriage and family laws of other groups continue to be the subject of domestic debates and national legislation.

The opportunity that may come from these legal debates is the possibility of allowing self-determination of minority religions in societies in ways that respect rights and meet the individual and collective needs of people and communities in these minority groups. It may even be the case that facilitating self-determination of minority religions on some of these issues can bypass some of the doctrinal and 'culture wars' types of divisions that might otherwise contribute to social discord and greater discrimination against minority groups. A focus on protection of religious minorities may also offer ways around doctrinal aspects concerning religious beliefs themselves and definitions of religious freedom. Such a focus is also exemplary of what seems to be a new international consensus on the need to protect religion and other minorities.

A final issue to continue to watch in this area has to do with the relationship between norms of nondiscrimination and equality, for it increasingly seems that nondiscrimination will not be sufficient when it comes to minority religious groups. More and more, one hears calls not just for nondiscrimination against religious minorities, but for equal treatment of religious groups and even equal treatment of religious and nonreligious views. These calls for equality raise a number of further issues. First, as noted above, research has shown that mere norms of nondiscrimination can become a cover for government inaction and failure to more robustly protect minority rights. This is the

77 The relationship between religion and diaspora has gained particular attention over the last decade. See, e.g. Waltraud Kokot, Khachig Tölölyan, and Carolin Alfonso, eds., *Diaspora, Identity, and Religion: New Directions in Theory and Research* (Routledge, 2016). The diaspora experience and problems of belonging and assimilation have also been discussed increasingly in connection with global Muslim groups. See, e.g., Raymond William Baker, *One Islam, Many Muslim Worlds: Spirituality, Identity, and Resistance* (OUP 2015).

difference between governments that merely refrain from government restrictions on FoRB rights and those which play a more robust role of intervention in social hostilities that can lead to FoRB violations. Second, these normative projects of equality will demand more from governments in the form of positive and affirmative protection of rights, particularly of groups. Third, as one noted scholar of Muslim minority groups and I brainstormed together in discussion at a conference a few years back, liberty is often in tension with equality in some of these projects.[78] That is to say, programs aimed at promoting religious equality or equality among religions, particularly in service of the rights of minority religions, may require that members of the majority be prepared to compromise or revise some of their normative preferences – e.g. secularism versus accommodation, desires for uniformity and universality of law, integrative migration practices, and others – in order to support minority rights. Resolution of these issues will be an important part of any emerging consensus on religious minorities.

5 Conclusion: Muslim Minorities in Ireland and America

For a group that comprises such a small percentage of the American religious landscape, Muslims play have played an outsize role in the American political imaginary in recent decades, particularly since 9/11. The 9/11 terrorist attacks were for many in the United States a wake-up call to recognize the identity of the Muslims in our midst. It has not always gone well. On the one hand, scholars of Islam were rapidly hired to religious studies departments. New groups of young, Muslim legal scholars formed and began to hold conferences on emerging voices in Islamic jurisprudence. One the other hand, these leaps forward in knowledge and understanding of Muslims at home and abroad were not always known to the wider U.S. public, who were all too susceptible commentators and organizations who rose up to denounce mosque construction in our cities, to raise the specter of sharia overtaking the U.S. Constitution as the law of the land, and to continue to perpetuate links between Islam and terror, even though most of the terrorism in the U.S. comes from mass shootings and domestic terrorists born or radicalized within our own borders.

Perhaps because of its history of slavery, minority status in the U.S. remains peculiarly linked to notions of race. The U.K. and European nations that were once colonial powers divided colonized peoples into religious and

78 The scholar was the late Saba Mahmood, who wrote on these issues in *Religious Difference in a Secular Age*. Sadly, her untimely death prevents further conversation.

ethnic groups as a matter of colonial policy and governance. It is hard to read of British colonialism in India and the creation of separate nations of Pakistan and India, for example, and not see the persistence of patterns of group self-conception as religious minorities. In those contexts, religion appears as fundamental as race. And as we have seen in the development of international law on religion, the trajectory appears to be moving away from universal rights and toward recognition of particular identities and rights of groups in many cases. There is potential peril in such developments, as there can be with any forces that push individuals and groups too narrowly into particular categories of what are often more complex identities. But there are also important new emphases on legal pluralism – the coexistence of secular and religious laws – alongside religious pluralism that suggest ways to honor both the universal and particular.

The various chapters included in this conference volume on religious demographics, accommodation, education, employment, healthcare, marriage, finance, and religious courts all attest to important developments afoot in Ireland to provide normative and practical solutions to the needs of Ireland's Muslim community. It is an important discussion to be having and an important place to be having it. Even as Ireland continues to modernize and, to a great extent, to secularize, there is a strong normative core of justice at the heart of the Irish experience. If there is an emerging consensus on religious minorities and their just and equal treatment, particularly of immigrant groups, Ireland will, almost certainly, be a strong contributor to that dialogue and consensus.

Bibliography

Abdullahi, A.A., *What Is an American Muslim?: Embracing Faith and Citizenship* (OUP, 2014).

Appiah, K.A., *The Ethics of Identity* (Princeton University Press, 2007).

Asia Forum for Human Rights and Development, 'Desecrating Expression – An Account of Freedom of Expression and Religion in Asia' (Forum-Asia, 2016). The entire report is accessible at: https://www.forum-asia.org/?p=21941.

Basu, A., *Violent Conjunctures in Contemporary India* (CUP, 2015).

Beydoun, K.A., *American Islamophobia: Understanding the Roots and Rise of Fear* (University of California Press, 2018).

Cooperman, A. and Lipka, M., 'U.S. Doesn't Rank High in Religious Diversity,' *Pew Research Center Fact Tank*, 4 April 2014.

Crenshaw, K., *On Intersectionality: Essential Writings of Kimberlé Crenshaw* (New Press, forthcoming 2019).

Diouf, S.A., *Servants of Allah: African Muslims Enslaved in the Americas* (15th anniv edn, NYU Press, 2013).

Eck, D., *A New Religious America: How a 'Christian Country' Has Become the World's Most Religiously Diverse Nation* (Harper One, 2001).

Fox, J., *The Unfree Exercise of Religion: A World Survey of Discrimination Against Religious Minorities*(CUP, 2016),

Fraser, N. and Honneth, A., *Redistribution or Recognition?: A Political-Philosophical Exchange* (Verso, 2003).

Green, M.C., 'Apostasy through Doubt and Dissent,' *Journal of Law and Religion* 31(2) (July 2016): 261–273.

Green, M.C., 'Between Blasphemy and Critique: Freedom of Religion and Freedom of Speech,' *Journal of Law and Religion* 29(2) (February 2014): 176–196.

Grim, B.J. and Finke, R., The Price of Freedom Denied: Religious Persecution and Conflict in the 21st Century (CUP, 2011).

Harding, A. and Shah D.A.H., eds., *Law and Society in Malaysia: Pluralism, Religion and Ethnicity* (Routledge, 2017).

Ispahani, F., *Purifying the Land of the Pure: Pakistan's Religious Minorities*(CUP, 2016).

Kokot, W., KTölölyon, K., and Alfonso, C., eds., *Diaspora, Identity, and Religion: New Directions in Theory and Research* (Routledge, 2016).

Little, D., *Sri Lanka: The Invention of Enmity* (United States Institute of Peace, 1993).

Mahmood, S., *Religious Difference in a Secular Age: A Minority Report*(Princeton University Press, 2015).

Manseau, P. 'The Muslims of Early America,' *The New York Times*, (New York, 9 February 2015).

Manseau, P., *One Nation, Under Gods: A New American History* (Little, Brown, & Company, 2015).

Masterpiece Cakeshop v. Colorado Civil Rights Commission, 584 U.S. ___, 38 S. Ct. 1719 (2018).

'Minorities Make Up Most of the World's Stateless Population,' *EthicsDaily* (Nashville, TN, 16 November 2017) <https://www.ethicsdaily.com/minorities-make-up-most-of-worlds-stateless-population-cms-24476/> accessed 9 Nov 2018.

Moïsi, D., *The Geopolitics of Emotion: How Cultures of Fear, Humiliation, and Hope are Changing the World* (Doubleday, 2009).

Obergefell v. Hodges, 576 U.S. ___, 135 S.Ct. 2071 (2015).

Pew Religion & Public Life Project, *America's Changing Religious Landscape* (Washington, D.C.: Pew Research Center, 2015).

Pew Research Center, 'U.S. Muslims Concerned About Their Place in Society, but Continue to Believe in the American Dream' (Washington, DC: Pew Research Center, 2017).

Riaz, A., *Islamist Militancy in Bangladesh: A Complex Web* (Routledge, 2010).

Riaz, A. and Fair, C., eds. *Political Islam and Governance in Bangladesh* (Routledge, 2010)
Sen, A., *Identity and Violence: The Illusion of Destiny* (W.W. Norton, 2006).
Shah, D.A.H., *Constitutions, Religion and Politics in Asia: Indonesia, Sri Lanka, and Asia* (CUP, 2017).
Sullivan, W.F., *The Impossibility of Religious Freedom* (Princeton University Press, 2005).
Sullivan, W.F. and Hurd, E.S., *Politics of Religious Freedom*(University of Chicago Press, 2015).
United Nations General Assembly. Universal Declaration of Human Rights, G.A. res. 217A (III), U.N. Doc /810 at 71 (1948), art. 18.
United Nations General Assembly. International Covenant on Civil and Political Rights, G.A. res. 2200A (XXI), 21 U.N. GAOR Supp. (No. 16) at 52, U.N. Doc. A/6316 (1966), 999 U.N.T.S. 171, *entered into force* Mar. 23, 1976, art. 2(1) and 18.
United Nations General Assembly. Declaration on the Elimination of All Forms of Intolerance and of Discrimination Based on Religion or Belief, G.A. res. 36/55, 36 U.N. GAOR Supp. (No. 51) at 171, U.N. Doc. A/36/684 (1981).
United Nations General Assembly. Declaration on the Rights of Persons Belonging to National or Ethnic, Religious or Linguistic Minorities, G.A. res. 47/135, annex, 47 U.N. GAOR Supp. (No. 49) at 210, U.N. Doc. A/47/49 (1993).
United Nations General Assembly. Declaration on the Rights of Indigenous Peoples, G.A. Res. 61/295, U.N. Doc. A/RES/47/1 (2007).
United Nations High Commissioner for Refugees, '"This Is Our Home": Stateless Minorities and Their Search for Citizenship,' (Geneva: UNHCR, November 17) <http://www.unhcr.org/ibelong/wp-content/uploads/UNHCR_EN2_2017IBELONG_Report_ePub.pdf> accessed 9 November 2018.

CHAPTER 3

Accommodating Religious Minorities in Ireland

The Constitutional Framework

Eoin Daly

1 Introduction

While religious minorities in Ireland have been accommodated in a rather ad hoc way in practice – without reference to any overarching, authoritative principles, whether of secularism, multiculturalism and so forth – the potential role of the Constitution in this respect remains underexplored. While it would be easy to overstate the specificity of the constitutional provisions in terms of the principles, philosophies and ideologies that they represent or embrace, they still offer a constraint, at least, upon the policy choices that might be adopted in relation to religious minorities. The rather distinctive prohibition on the endowment of religions, for example, clearly precludes certain policy choices in relation to religious minorities. In this contribution, I will argue that the constitutional framework concerning religion is characterised, in large part, by *indeterminacy* rather than *coherence* – that is to say, it lacks a specific guiding principle or philosophy. In general, the Constitution can be read as appealing simultaneously to two opposing principles or worldviews concerning the relation of State and religion, and the case law essentially oscillates between these two views. To summarise, the first of these approaches recognises religion as a public good, and supports active state intervention aimed at recognising and sustaining religion – albeit in a pluralistic sense – as a part of the social fabric. For the sake of convenience, I will label this the 'recognition approach'. According to an alternative view, religion is understood as a protected sphere of private activity, in which the State may not generally intrude, whether for benign reasons or otherwise. This I will call the 'neutrality approach'. This contrast is particularly salient in the area of education, but it is potentially of great relevance in relation to policies concerning accommodation of religious minorities more generally. A crucial difference between each approach – and a likely point of contention in the future – is the question of whether or not the State must constitutionally adopt a hands-off approach with regard to the substance of religious doctrine or religious law. This will likely influence or constrain the manner in which religious minorities are accommodated in legislation.

 | DOI:10.1163/9789004398252_004

2 The Constitutional Text

The oscillation between 'liberal' and 'conservative' understandings of religion – and therefore, between corresponding ideas of 'neutrality' and 'recognition' – is evident in the relatively detailed provisions of Article 44 of the Constitution, dealing with religion. On the one hand, there are certain bellicose, even triumphalist provisions that place religion in general, and even Christian religion specifically, at the centre of public identity. Article 44.1 states: 'The State acknowledges that the homage of public worship is due to Almighty God. It shall hold His Name in reverence, and shall respect and honour religion'. Article 6 states: 'all powers of Government ... derive, under God, from the people'. The preamble acknowledges 'the Most Holy Trinity' as the authority 'to whom and from whom as our final end, all actions both of men and States must be referred'. Moreover, the people are depicted as 'humbly acknowledging all our obligations to our Divine Lord, Jesus Christ'.

In this light, McCrea, in particular, argues that the Constitution 'defines its ultimate notion of the good in explicitly religious terms'.[1] Similarly, writing prior to his appointment as a judge, Mr. Justice Donal Barrington described the Constitution as 'mak[ing] an open profession of Christianity'.[2]

However, these professions of Christianity and religiosity are mitigated by a number of provisions – less vivid, but of greater practical importance – which more closely correspond to a 'liberal' worldview concerning religion – and which, in particular, prescribe denominational neutrality on the part of the State notwithstanding the Constitution's largely symbolic recognition of Trinitarian Christianity or at least, of monotheism. In particular, Article 44.2, while guaranteeing the 'free practice and profession of religion', also prohibits the State from imposing any 'disability' or 'discrimination' on grounds of religious profession, belief or status. Equality in the State funding of religious schools is also specifically enshrined, as is the right to opt out of religious instruction in State-funded denominational schools.[3] Most strikingly, perhaps – at least in comparative terms – Article 44.2.2 also restricts any potential State financing of religions in providing that the State 'guarantees not to endow any religion' – a strikingly separationist principle in a European context where many jurisdictions retain established churches.

1 R. McCrea, *Religion and the Public Order of the European Union* (Oxford: Oxford University Press, 2010), p. 56.

2 D. Barrington, 'The Irish Constitution x. Article Forty-Four. 11. Church and State' (1953) 81 *The Irish Monthly* 1, p. 3.

3 Article 44.2.4.

Indeed, Irish law in general has historically followed a model of formal neutrality towards religion. While legislation, until recent decades, was often attuned substantively speaking to Catholic social teachings, it rarely, if ever, explicitly incorporated religious concepts, criteria or classifications. In other words, the close Church-State relationship had little formal legal basis, compared with other European countries.[4] Notwithstanding a close Church-State relationship over much of the twentieth century, religions have remained 'private' on the legal, if not the social and political levels, since the disestablishment of the Church of Ireland in the nineteenth century.[5] It was held in early cases such as *State (Colquhoun)* v *D'Arcy*[6] that the legal status of religions in Ireland is that of private voluntary associations, whose legal framework is founded primarily on contract.[7] Their governing authorities were referred to as 'domestic tribunals', similar, in a sense, to private sporting authorities, underscoring the essentially private status of religious law.[8] The 1937 Constitution did not change this.

Moreover, there has been little political appetite to legally regulate religions or bring their administration within the public remit. There is little understanding of the State as having a legitimate role in the organization and administration of religions.[9] There has been no equivalent in Ireland of the proposals encountered in European states such as France (and even the UK),[10] calling for state intervention in minority religions, for the purpose of curbing extremism – or even creating a 'French Islam'.[11] Even in secular France, the State played an instrumental role in establishing a public representative body for Muslims, the *Conseil Français du Culte Musulman*, and there was some discussion of the possibility of amending the law so as to allow the State to subsidise 'moderate' mosques.[12] In this comparative perspective, the Church-State relationship in Ireland is underpinned by a somewhat liberal

4 See further E. Daly, *Religion, Law and the Irish State* (Clarus, 2012), Chapter 7.

5 See Chapter 6.

6 See 'New Board of Imams to Tackle Extremists', *The Times*, 3 July 2008.

7 *State (Colquohan) v Darcy* [1936] IR 641.

8 See *O'Callaghan v Sullivan* [1925] 1 IR 90.

9 See generally J. Whyte, *Church and State in Modern Ireland* (Dublin: Gill and Macmillan, 1980).

10 M. Zeghal, 'La constitution du Conseil Français du Culte Musulman: reconnaissance politique d'un Islam Français ?' (2005) 129 *Archives de sciences sociales des religions* 1.

11 See generally G. Robbers (ed.), *Church and State in the European Union* (Baden-Baden: Nomos, 2005).

12 Zeghal (n 10).

ethos.[13] In the past decade, the Government has undertaken quasi-formalised dialogue procedures with the main denominational groups, including humanists, but this remains non-statutory and purely consultative in nature.[14]

3 The Historical Context

The relative incoherence of the constitutional provisions – or at least their relative indeterminacy from a principled or philosophical standpoint – is unsurprising given the historical context in which they were drafted, and particularly the fact that the relevant text emerged as a political compromise between rival strands of nationalist and republican thought. Certain of the religiously inflected references in the text – especially the invocation of 'Almighty God' in Article 44 and to the 'Holy Trinity' in the preamble – reflected the Gaelic and Catholic-oriented nationalism that was in the ascendancy at the time the Constitution was drafted, and which was also evident in much of the social legislation enacted during the 1930s. On the other hand, the text was also influenced, at least indirectly, by a different, less sectarian and more inclusive strand of thought, appealing to republican ideals.[15] An earlier draft of Article 44 proclaimed: 'The State acknowledges that the true religion is that established by Our Divine Lord Jesus Christ Himself, which He committed to His Church to protect and propagate, as the guardian and interpreter of true morality. It acknowledges, moreover, that the Church of Christ is the Catholic Church'.[16] However, De Valera and other members of the Executive Council resisted pressures for stronger recognition of the Roman Catholic Church, and as Hogan, especially, has noted, the final version of the Constitution was in

13 As Whyte points out, the Irish government has never played any role, even consultative or formal, in the appointment of Irish bishops. Whyte (n 9), p. 15.

14 Article 16C of the Treaty of Lisbon commits EU member states to 'open, regular and transparent' dialogue with religious associations and non-confessional bodies, while committing the Union to respecting the status under national law of churches and religious associations. See generally Foret and Schlesinger, 'Religion and the European Public Sphere', in Fossum and Schlesinger, *The European Union and the Public Sphere: a Communicative Space in the Making?* (London: Routledge, 2007). On the implementation of the dialogue structures, see the speech of former Taoiseach Bertie Ahern on this theme, on 4 February 2008: http://www.taoiseach.gov.ie/eng/Government_Press_Office/Taoiseach's_Speeches_2008/Speech_by_the_Taoiseach,_Mr_Bertie_Ahern,_T_D_,_at_a_Reception_in_honour_of_Sean_Cardinal_Brady_in_Dublin_Castle,_on_Monday_4_February,_2008_at_7_00_p_m_.html.

15 D. Keogh and A. McCarthy, *The Making of the 1937 Constitution* (Cork: Mercier, 2007) p. 153.

16 *ibid.*

fact relatively liberal, especially by contemporary standards. This, he says, is overshadowed by the largely symbolic provisions on religion, which generated 'so much fuss'.[17] Bearing in mind the peculiar political context of the 1930s, it is arguable that, contrary to received wisdom, the religious provisions were in fact a 'skilful endorsement of religious pluralism'.[18] And the recognition of religion that was settled on in Article 44 – affirming the 'special position' of the Roman Catholic Church – had little more than symbolic effect in practice.[19] While the Church was recognised as 'the guardian of the Faith professed by the great majority of the citizens', also recognised were the Protestant churches, the Jewish congregation, and other religions existing in Ireland at the time. (The 'special position' clause was, in any event, abolished by the Fifth Amendment of the Constitution in 1972.)

In this spirit, the historian Joe Lee captured this philosophical and ideological indeterminacy in the Constitution in arguing that 'De Valera's text constituted an ingenious squaring of the formal circle, circumventing Catholic clericalist demands for more triumphalist recognition, and residual republican resistance to any recognition at all'.[20] None of this is to deny the conservative and sometimes clericalist character of politics and society during this period. The point, rather, is that this found little expression, ultimately, in the Constitution. Indeed one Cardinal complained that 'the Constitution makes us no better than the Quakers'.[21]

4 Case Law: Neutrality versus Recognition of Religion

Based on the above analysis, it seems there is no single, overarching doctrine or principle concerning State and religion in the Constitution; in reality, it synthesises conflicting ideological views based, roughly speaking, on state neutrality versus state recognition of religion. In one view, religion is a private

17 G. Hogan, preface to Keogh and McCarthy, *ibid* p. 17.

18 G. Hogan and G. Whyte, *JM Kelly: The Irish Constitution* (Dublin: Butterworths, 2003), para 7.6.248.

19 Article 44.1.2° recognised 'the special position of the Holy Catholic Apostolic and Roman Church as the guardian of the Faith professed by the great majority of the citizens'. However, also recognised were the Protestant churches, the Jewish congregation, and other religions existing in Ireland at the time. The 'special position' clause was abolished by the Fifth Amendment of the Constitution in 1972.

20 J.J. Lee, *Ireland 1912–1985: Politics and Society* (Cambridge: Cambridge University Press, 1989), p. 202.

21 Cardinal Joseph MacRory, Letter to the Papal Nuncio, 9 April 1937. Cited in Keogh and McCarthy, (n 15), p. 17.

affair protected against State interference whether benign or otherwise; in the other, the State is authorized to undertake benevolent intervention of the kind that affirms religion as a public good and as a component of national identity.

This ambiguity is reflected in the case law as well as the constitutional text. The earlier constitutional case law – or such little as existed – certainly did not treat religion merely as a purely private affair, or embrace a doctrine of State 'neutrality' in any significant sense. Overall, however, there has been a marked shift over time in favour of the more 'liberal' view – a shift which echoes the overall trajectory of social change in Ireland in the same period.

In particular, the earlier case law is more inclined to affirm the rights or status of religion *as such*. In 1951, for example, the Supreme Court, in *Re Tilson*, referred to the 'right' of the Catholic Church to 'guard the faith' of its adherents, in a case concerning guardianship of children. It affirmed that 'religion holds in the Constitution the place of honour which the community has always accorded to it'.[22] And of course, this is supported by the various, aforementioned provisions that affirm the symbolic value of religion, or indeed perhaps of Christianity, in public life. And as late as the 1980s, a Supreme Court affirmed in *Norris v Attorney General*[23] that the people, enacting the Constitution, had 'an intention to adopt a Constitution consistent with that conviction and faith and with Christian beliefs'[24] – a premise invoked to uphold the constitutionality of laws criminalizing male homosexual activities. In effect, the majority of the Court found that Christian religious doctrines could legitimately be used to delimit the scope of constitutional rights and of the criminal law. In a similar spirit, a Supreme Court judge observed in 1972 that 'Our Constitution reflects a firm conviction that we are religious people'.[25] While *McGee v. Attorney General*, which struck down the ban on contraception within marriage, might be perceived as a liberal judgment highlighting secular constitutional themes, in fact it strongly emphasised the importance of Christianity and of God in the Constitution. It rejected any denominationally specific form of religious recognition – embracing only State neutrality *between* denominations – while plainly precluding any notion of neutrality *towards religion as such*, with religion as such being embraced both as a cornerstone of constitutional identity and as an inspiration for constitutional rights.[26] As Walsh J put it, 'The Constitution

22 *Re Tilson* [1951] IR 1 14.

23 [1984] IR 36.

24 [1984] IR 36, 64–65.

25 [1972] IR 1, 11.

26 [1972] IR 1, 11. The courts could not 'be asked to choose … between the different views of religious denominations' [1974] IR 284, pp. 317–318.

acknowledges God as the ultimate source of all authority',[27] albeit while rejecting the view that the Court could choose between the competing views of different denominations.

It would be difficult to pinpoint the start of a shift away from this view, although the shift towards a more secular reading of the Constitution has certainly tracked the wider process of secularization in society at large. Over the lifespan of the Constitution, the predominant political rhetoric concerning religion, and its place in public life, was transformed beyond recognition. In 1951 Taoiseach John A. Costello told the Dáil: 'I, as a Catholic, obey my Church authorities' – to whom he offered 'complete allegiance'.[28] By contrast, the scale of the change that occurred over subsequent decades was underlined when Taoiseach Enda Kenny, in 2013, responded to an implicit threat of excommunication in saying: 'My book is the Constitution ... That's the people's book and we live in a republic ...'[29] – and contrasting a 'Republic of Laws' with the 'elitism' and 'narcissism' of the Vatican.[30]

In some senses, the constitutional jurisprudence on religion has echoed these wider political and social changes. In recent decades, the Supreme Court has tended to offer a more liberal interpretation of the constitutional framework – concerning religious education in particular – despite the lack of major substantive amendments.[31] In particular, and in its *obiter dicta* at least, the Court moved away from the previous idea that religions were entitled to constitutional recognition or constitutional status *as such*, or that religion formed an intrinsic part of the common good. In *Campaign to Separate Church and State v Minister for Education*,[32] the Court considered the constitutionality of State financing for secondary school chaplaincies, but also elaborated on the

27 *McGee v Attorney General* [1974] IR 284, 317.

28 *Dáil Éireann Debates*, Vol 125, Col 784, 12 April 1951. The Taoiseach continued: 'Members of my Government have all the one faith ... That is our attitude and I have no hesitation in saying that we, as Government, representing a people, the overwhelming majority of whom are of the one faith, who have a special position in the Constitution, when we are given advice or warnings by the authoritative people in the Catholic Church, on matters strictly confined to faith and morals, so long as I am here – and I am sure I speak for my colleagues – will give to their directions, given within that scope – and I have no doubt that they do not desire in the slightest to go one fraction of an inch outside the sphere of faith and morals – our complete obedience and allegiance'.

29 V. Browne, 'In Kenny's book the Constitution is king, not the Church', *Irish Times*, 15 May 2013, emphasis added.

30 P. Cullen, 'Vatican Relationship at New Low', *The Irish Times*, 21 July 2011. He also said: 'The law of the land should not be stopped by a collar or a crozier'.

31 With the exception of the Fifth Amendment, which abolished the 'special position' clause.

32 [1998] 3 IR 321.

constitutional justification for public funding of religious schools in general. It reasoned that State financing of religious education was justified as a form of support for parental choice – making no reference to any 'rights', or other status of religions, as educators, per se. Thus, implicitly, religion and religious education were valued and protected not in their own right, as components of public and constitutional identity, but rather, only to the extent that they represented authentic expressions of private choice. Implicitly, in turn, a choice of religious education is valued no more than that of a non-religious education. Similarly, in the realm of childcare and education, Hardiman J asserted in the *Baby Anne* case that 'the Constitution prefers parents to third parties ... [whether] priest or social worker ... as the enablers and guardians of children's rights'.[33]

It is worth noting that this ideological shift in constitutional discourse has been rather uneven in temporal terms. This was evident in *McNally v Ireland*,[34] a case concerning the constitutionality of a law regulating Catholic Mass cards. In response to concerns surrounding the sale of fraudulent or inauthentic Mass cards, the Charities Act 2009 created an offence of selling a Mass card 'other than pursuant to an arrangement with a recognised person'. 'Recognised persons' were defined as a bishop, or the provincial of an order of priests, recognised by the 'Holy Catholic Apostolic and Roman Church'.[35] This attempt to regulate the sale of religious products raised interesting constitutional questions concerning the permissibility of State intervention in internal religious function. MacMenamin J held that the United States authorities, premised on a principle of Church-State separation, were of limited value in interpreting Article 44 of the Constitution – given that the Irish Constitution acknowledges, he said, 'a monotheistic Christian ethos'.[36] He observed that whereas 'in United States jurisprudence there is a wall of separation ... under the Constitution of Ireland there is a constitutional 'domain' of religious recognition'.[37]

Nonetheless, on the whole there has been a marked shift towards a more liberal view in which the State is understood as being neutral not only between religions, but towards religion as such. According to the older conception, State support of religious education reflects an understanding of religion itself as an aspect of the common good, whereas in this more recent case law it is merely an expression of private choice, with the State remaining neutral towards the value or indeed, the truth, of religion *as such.*

33 *N v Health Service Executive* [2006] 4 IR 374, 504.
34 [2009] IEHC 573.
35 Charities Act 2009, s 99 (3).
36 [2009] IEHC 573, para 133.
37 [2009] IEHC 573, para 135.

With neutrality emphasised over recognition, any role for religion in public life then becomes rather contingent and conditional. In the education sector, facilitation of religious needs accordingly becomes bound up with the vagaries of private 'choice'. Whereas previously, the 'patronage' model in Irish education might have been understood as affirming the importance of religion as such, it is now re-interpreted as a mechanism for affirming or facilitating parental choice, where 'choice" is defined in religiously neutral terms. There has been a shift, indeed, both in constitutional and political discourse, in which the emphasis is placed on the rights of *parents*, almost as educational consumers, rather than of the religious denominations per se. Indeed Barrington J suggested, in the *Campaign* case, that 'parents have the ... right to have religious education provided in the schools which their children attend. They are not obliged to settle merely for religious "instruction"'.[38] This rationalises State support for religious education purely with reference to *individual* choice, phrased in ostensibly liberal and pluralist terms. Indeed this is somewhat contradictory, as there are very minimal provisions for taking account of parental choice in practice – with little reason to understand the religious education that is publicly financed as being a direct expression of parental 'choice'. O'Sullivan suggests that, in broader terms, the ascendant ideology of mercantilism in education generally is 'totally consistent with the assertion of difference in the realm of religious sentiments'.[39] Indeed Kitching argues that 'choice' operates as a political rationality which holds parents – understood largely as consumers – responsible for making 'authentic' choices – with diversity 'mobilised as a positional good' in a framework where the dynamics of school choice are grafted to the metaphor of the competitive marketplace. Thus, we can understand the increasing emphasis on choice, in relation to religious education, both as a reflection of neoliberal ideology as well as the product of a secularized, liberalized understanding of the constitutional framework. Indeed, one of the hallmarks of neoliberalism in general has been the State's active encouragement of competitive and entrepreneurial dispositions, as well as dynamics of market choice, outside narrowly economic domains.[40]

Certainly, these subtle transformations in constitutional discourse reflect wider social shifts, O'Sullivan, for example, argues that there has been a shift from a 'theocentric' to a 'mercantilist' paradigm in education policy in general since the 1950s, with the State aiming less to cultivate virtuous dispositions

38 [1998] 3 IR 321, 358 (emphasis added).

39 D. O'Sullivan, *Cultural Politics and Irish Education since the 1950s: Policy, Paradigms and Power* (Dublin: Institute of Public Administration), p. 201.

40 O'Sullivan.

linked to Christianity, and more the entrepreneurial virtues of market citizenship.[41] He describes this paradigm shift in terms of 'a transition from an institution that had God at its centre to one in which 'trade/exchange' is at its core'. He notes that 'in contrast to this [older] dogmatic prescriptiveness about the purpose of education, the mercantile paradigm assumes a populist approach holding that what education is for is a matter for consumers of the system'.[42] More generally we might speculate that the shift in constitutional discourse has been influenced, indirectly, by the ascendancy of a discourse of consumership and competition in relation to education in general.

However, from a constitutional-rights perspective, this discourse of 'choice' entails a number of anomalies and contradictions, because religious rights, including the right to freedom of religion, are, in short, subject to the vagaries of parental choice and thus, to the crude contingencies of religious demographics. Accommodation is, crudely speaking, subject to the vagaries of local demand, along with other contingencies.[43] More generally, the idea of protecting religious education as an expression of private choice, where the State professes to remain neutral between religious and non-religious choices, sits uneasily in a constitutional framework which recognizes the central importance of religion in national life. Little distinction is made between the satisfaction of preference *as such* and the recognition of religion as a constituent identity, in a sense that is irreducible to utilitarian preference. The now-dominant understanding of religious freedom in terms of 'choice' arguably reflects a broader neoliberal ideology in which the public good is simply an aggregation of private utility, and where citizenship is understood, metaphorically or otherwise, in largely consumer terms.[44] Yet if religion is protected merely as an expression of private choice – a choice in relation to which the State remains neutral – how can this be reconciled with the *privileged* recognition extended to religion *as such* in Article 44?

On the one hand, this predominant emphasis on choice and religious neutrality simply reflects a greater acceptance of equality as between religious and non-religious views. Yet equally, it is impossible to fully reconcile this premise with the competing idea of religious recognition in the Constitution; the State cannot recognize, and thereby privilege religion, while fully respecting the equality of non-religious viewpoints. There is some textual basis in the

41 D. O'Sullivan, *Cultural Politics and Irish Education since the 1950s: Policy, Paradigms and Power* (Dublin: Institute of Public Administration).

42 *ibid*, p. 113.

43 See *O'Sheil v Minister for Education* 1999] 2 IR 321.

44 See generally O'Sullivan (n 41).

Constitution for both these conflicting principles, but the trends of recent decades can be understood as placing a greater emphasis on the value of neutrality, at the expense of religious recognition.

5 Accommodating Religious Minorities within the Neutrality-recognition Dichotomy

Insofar as the constitutional framework for religions has been defined within a conceptual dichotomy between incommensurable principles of recognition and neutrality – corresponding, more or less, with competing 'liberal' and 'communitarian' ideologies – it is worth considering how each of these principles, or rather *sensibilities*, impacts on practical questions of religious accommodation, and minority accommodation in particular.

Of course, it may be argued that the liberal, neutrality-based approach protects minorities insofar as it prevents the State from privileging any dominant religion and therefore, from marginalizing or denigrating minority religions in public life. However, any such argument operates at a necessarily very abstract level, since any recognition of Catholicism tended to have merely symbolic effects, at most. Certainly, the constitutional recognition of religion was always *relatively* pluralistic, at least – eschewing outright privilege for the Catholic Church, notwithstanding its considerable influence in politics and social policy.

Equally, the liberal-neutrality reading of the Constitution may pose its own hazards from the minority perspective. Crucially, neutrality, as a principle, will tend not only to mean neutrality in a majority-minority perspective, or even neutrality as between religions. Rather, it may require a hands-off approach in general, and in particular, a prohibition on any recognition or accommodation of specific denominational imperatives. The liberal rationale, familiar in U.S. constitutional law, suggests that any efforts at accommodating religion cannot entail state recognition of the substance of religious belief or indeed of religious law, simply because such matters may involve theological controversies into which the State may have no right to intrude or inquire.[45] Thus to an extent, neutrality may come *at the cost* of religious accommodation. This may, for example, limit the possibility of accommodation in the form of exemptions, for religious communities, from laws that negatively impinge on their practices.

---

45 *Employment Division v. Smith* 494 US 872, 879 (1990).

These tensions were illustrated in the landmark case *Quinn's Supermarket v Attorney General*,[46] the first ruling to elucidate the constitutional principles concerning religion. Quinn's Supermarket constitutionally challenged its prosecution under ministerial regulations on trading hours,[47] because these exempted Jewish kosher shops, in order to facilitate Sabbath observance. The law prohibited the sale of meat in the evenings, but observance of the Jewish Sabbath required two Jewish shops in Dublin to close between sundown on Friday and sundown on Saturday. The law would otherwise would have caused commercial disadvantage to the shops, as well as preventing observant Jews from purchasing meat at certain times.

The plaintiff claimed that this kind of law – one aimed at accommodating a religious minority through differential treatment – amounted to unconstitutional discrimination on the grounds of religious 'belief, profession or status' under Article 44.2.3°. What is significant, in particular, is that the Supreme Court ruled that Article 44.2.3° prohibits not only negative invidious discrimination, but, at least *prima facie*, all forms of differential treatment based on religion, including 'positive' discrimination: discrimination was not solely defined as 'discrimination against'; thus giving this provision a much stricter ambit than the general equality clause of Article 40.1, which allows broad scope for 'positive' discrimination of various kinds based on legislative judgement.

In principle, this would prevent minorities from any invidious discrimination, but it would also limit the scope of any legislative accommodation aimed at recognizing specific religious imperatives, or exempting minority religions from generally applicable laws. However, the doctrine is of limited significance in practice, because the Supreme Court ultimately ruled that this otherwise strict principle of non-discrimination (or effectively, non-differentiation) must nonetheless be qualified where necessary to protect religious freedom. What this means, in effect, is that the Oireachtas is constitutionally permitted to exempt minority religions from generally applicable laws – only where this is necessary to permit the free practice and profession of religion as provided for under Article 44.2.1°.

Walsh J stated:

> Any law which by virtue of the generality of its application would by its effect restrict or prevent the free profession and practice of religion ... would be invalid having regard to the provisions of the Constitution,

46 [1972] IR 1.

47 Victuallers' Shops (Hours of Trading on Weekdays) (Dublin, Dun Laoghaire and Bray) Order, 1948 (SI no 175 of 1948), pursuant to s 25 of the Shops (Hours of Trading) Act 1938.

> unless it ... saved from such restriction or prevention the practice of religion of the person or persons who would otherwise be so restricted or prevented.[48]

What this signaled, furthermore, is that religious accommodation of this kind is not only constitutionally permitted, but constitutionally required where it is necessary to protect religious freedom. And this sets the Irish constitutional position clearly apart from the more liberal model, focused on neutrality, that has prevailed in the United States. In *Employment Division v Smith*, the Supreme Court controversially held that legislatures were not constitutionally required to exempt religious practitioners from laws that were 'neutral' and 'generally applicable' towards religion. However, legislatures were not constitutionally prohibited from providing such exemptions.

What *Quinn's Supermarket* suggests in theory at least – although it has been of little impact in practice – is that the Oireachtas has virtually no *discretion* whether or not to grant legislative exemptions to religious minorities.[49] The Supreme Court's approach suggests that all religious exemptions in statute are unconstitutional *unless* constitutionally required by religious freedom – which thereby removes religious accommodation from political choice. This potentially overlooks exemptions that are aimed at accommodating particular religious needs, but which cannot be classified as necessary to religious 'freedom' as such. Perhaps not all legitimate interests in religious accommodation can be described as a matter of religious freedom, yet on a strict reading of *Quinn's Supermarket*, such forms of legislation are not permitted. A court facing this problem might attempt to artificially bring the religious 'interest' at stake within the ambit of 'religious freedom'. Indeed it is unlikely that in practice, the *Quinn's Supermarket* doctrine would prevent the Oireachtas from enacting religious accommodations of this pragmatic kind. Religious freedom is likely to be given a very broad definition, which encompasses the broad interests of religious groups in being facilitated in religious practice, in particular by being exempted from regulatory burdens. This is apparent from the ruling in *Quinn's Supermarket* itself. Although the exemption for Jewish butcher shops went beyond what was 'necessary' and was accordingly unconstitutional, this arose only because the regulations exempted Jewish butcher shops from closing hours on *all* weekdays other than Saturday, going beyond what was necessary to compensate the Jewish shopkeepers for the loss of trade on the Sabbath. Yet the Court appeared to regard a more limited exemption, for the purpose of

48 [1972] IR 1, 23.

49 See generally *Estate* of Thornton v *Calder*, 472 US 703 (1985).

compensating Jewish shops from loss of trade, as somehow 'necessary' to religious freedom within the doctrinal framework it established. Walsh J described the exemption from Saturday trading hours as avoiding '*pressures* upon the practice of the Jewish religion'.[50] The hypothetical, more limited exemption on Saturday evening, which Walsh J regarded as constitutionally permissible, would have merely enabled observant Jews to purchase meat on Saturday evenings, following Sabbath observance, rather than on Saturday mornings, during Sabbath observance (all butcher shops were permitted to open on Sunday). A failure to exempt kosher shops on Saturdays, which Walsh J saw as constitutionally required, would not have prevented Jewish persons from observing the Sabbath, nor was the purchase of meat on Saturday evenings itself a requirement of the Jewish religion (furthermore, as the Court acknowledged, the advent of modern refrigeration techniques lessened the strict necessity even of the Saturday exemption by the date of hearing of this case).[51] Had the exemption not been granted, even on the limited Saturday evening period that the Court saw as constitutionally required, the only result would have been that observant Jews would have been unable to purchase meat on Saturdays, while kosher butchers would have enjoyed fewer trading hours due to Sabbath observance.

A further point, worth emphasizing, is that the Court gave no consideration to the *limits* on the constitutional right of minority religions to be accommodated in this potentially difficult way. Although the Court did not explicitly mention it, the imperative of exempting religious communities is subject to the qualification of 'public order and morality' referred to in Article 44.2.1°. It seems self-evident that the constitutional imperative of exemption is subject to a range of exceptions, which would involve weighing up the burden on religious practice that a law entailed, against the public interest in its uniform application. Thus, *Quinn's Supermarket* does little to clarify how, for example, the Constitution might protect the claim to use sacramental drugs in Ireland as part of a bona fide religious ritual. Nor, unfortunately, did the judgment indicate whether religious practitioners' right to exemption applied only to discrete religious communities on the basis of their recognised doctrines or extended, also, to individual objectors with unorthodox or obscure beliefs.

A final, but crucial point concerning the impact of the *Quinn's* judgment is that the Supreme Court implicitly accepted that in granting religious accommodations, the State – whether at the legislative or judicial levels – would have to make inquiries as to the content and the imperatives of religious law. In

50 [1972] IR 1, 26, emphasis added.

51 *ibid.*

the *Smith* judgment, by contrast, the United States Supreme Court was heavily influenced by the idea that granting religious accommodations in legislation would require legislatures, and potentially courts, to inquire into the substance of religious belief, in order to ascertain the necessity and the extent of any exemptions – thus violating the separation of Church and State (in the guise of the First Amendment 'establishment clause'). This conceptual problem, which has been much better recognised in the United States than in Ireland, is described by Eisgruber and Sager dilemma as follows:

> The problem goes roughly like this: in order to protect religious liberty we have to define what religion is, and once we are in the business of saying that some beliefs, commitments, and projects are entitled to special treatment as 'religious' while others are not, we are creating a sphere of orthodoxy of exactly the sort that any plausible understanding of religious liberty should deplore.[52]

Thus, we can say that on balance, the imperatives of religious recognition, in Ireland, outweighed the principle of strict neutrality. A question arises as to how the Courts, or indeed the Oireachtas, identifies and interprets those religious beliefs and doctrines that are, conditionally at least, entitled to exemption from generally applicable statutes. The Supreme Court, in *Quinn's*, simply took evidence from the Chief Rabbi of Ireland concerning the doctrinal Sabbath requirements of the Jewish religion, in order to determine the extent of the necessary exemption.[53] However, this seemingly pragmatic approach makes potentially problematic assumptions concerning the capacity of secular institutions to ascertain the content of religious doctrines and practices – particularly in contexts of internal religious heterogeneity. It may wrongly assume a certain unity and uniformity in religious practices and beliefs. Having surveyed Jewish dietary rules in order to ascertain the religious obligation which the law in question had sought to accommodate, the Court stated:

> If, however, at some future date there is a change in these dietary laws to the extent that they are *no longer binding* upon members of the Jewish religion ... then the position alters and such an exemption might no longer be justifiable ... the validity of the exempting provision would depend

52 C. Eisgruber and L. Sager, 'Does it Matter what Religion Is?' (2009) *Notre Dame Law Review* 807, p. 808.

53 [1972] IR 1, 3.

> upon *the existing state of fact, which in this case would be that these dietary laws are a binding part of the Jewish religion.*[54]

This approach was confirmed in the aforementioned *McNally* ruling, where the Supreme Court appeared to accept that the Oireachtas was entitled to cognize the content of religious law, for the purposes of giving legislative effect to religious imperatives and prescriptions. MacMenamin J held that in light of what he termed a constitutional 'domain of recognition' for religion, Article 44 of the Constitution allows the legislature to give effect to the 'disabilities and discriminations' internal to particular religions, and correspondingly, to lend the weight of legislative sanction to these. This might involve 'discriminating' in favour of a particular religious viewpoint over a rival one, a situation U.S. doctrine has been eager to avoid. Indeed, as an aside, it seems the Oireachtas is free to enact legislation giving sanction to the internal doctrine requirements of particular faiths, but nothing prevents it from doing so in a rather ad hoc way, assisting certain denominations but not others.[55] Thus, the recognition-oriented approach, in this instance at least, risks a certain inconsistency or inequality as between the accommodations extended to various different denominations.

Furthermore, what is depicted, in *Quinn's Supermarket,* simply as 'the existing state of fact' regarding religious law or doctrine, may often, as already argued, be a matter of deep doctrinal controversy, and not amenable to being adjudicated by any public authority. Indeed, the Supreme Court, in a later case concerning blasphemy, declared: 'the State is not placed in the position of an arbiter of religious truth'.[56] However, the full practical implications of this principle have not yet surfaced.

A possible, troubling implication of this aspect of the *Quinn's Supermarket* approach is that it potentially excludes dissident or unorthodox religious freedom claims, at the fringe of established religious doctrines. Unorthodox individual claimants may be unable to point to any 'existing state of fact' underlying their claim. Alternatively, it is entirely plausible that in the event of such an obscure religious claim, a court might simply appraise and accept the sincerity of that belief. That the *Quinn's Supermarket* ruling referred to doctrinal, clerical authority may not necessarily mean that individual claimants must always be able to provide any similar form of 'proof' as to the validity of their conviction. Nonetheless, Walsh J referred to Jewish 'laws' as the basis

54 [1972] IR 1, 25.

55 See Daly (n 4), Chapter 7.

56 *Corway v Independent Newspapers* [1999] 4 IR 484.

for exemption, suggesting a unitary, majority-based assessment. The language used implies that the necessity and indeed the validity of any legislative exemptions depends on the central doctrinal authority within a religion. Moreover, practical considerations probably prevent exemptions from being given on a case-by-case basis in courts.

Due in part to the rarity of litigation involving religion, Irish constitutional jurisprudence has yet to develop a coherent, distinctive stance on the challenges posed by the exemption doctrine. Yet certainly the embryonic doctrines already available suggest a much greater receptiveness to a jurisprudence of *recognition* – in certain contexts at least – manifested specifically as a willingness to inquire into and ascertain the content of religious belief. In general, the approach taken has been pragmatic and ad hoc, rather than adherence to overarching principle. While this distinguishes the rather piecemeal Irish jurisprudence from its American equivalent, it introduces a range of anomalies and conceptual problems in relation to practical questions of religious accommodation.

There remains a further point of caution in relation to a 'liberal', neutrality-oriented model of religious accommodation. The tendency under the liberal-neutrality model has been to treat all religions equally, but to treat religion in general as merely a private preference. And, in the education setting at least, this tends to institutionalize and reinforce various social inequalities, simply because the recognition and exercise of religious choice depends, in reality, on the social, political and economic capital that different communities can marshal in negotiating the school-recognition process. In the wider perspective, then, we can surmise that a strict neutrality approach, at least, risks a kind of indifference towards religion in general and minority religions in particular.

5.1 *Minority Religious Accommodation in Practice*

Curiously, while the *Quinn's Supermarket* judgment might suggest a potentially fruitful constitutional framework for the protection of religious freedom, there has been practically no litigation surrounding religious practices of the kind that have been the subject of legal dispute and political controversy in neighbouring states. For example, in 2007, the Garda Síochána commissioner ruled against permitting the Sikh turban for members of the force. While this prompted some controversy, it provoked no constitutional challenge, and little serious public discussion of what level of accommodation of such practices, if any, the Constitution requires.[57] It was stated that 'the prohibition was necessary to safeguard the impartiality of the police force in a context where

57 Garda Siochána Press Office, *Garda Uniform*, statement of 23 August 2007. Accessible at *http://www.garda.ie/Controller.aspx?Page=3155&Lang=1* (last accessed 1 September 2011).

religion has often threatened the peaceful coexistence of religious communities'.[58] It was argued that 'the [Garda] standing in front of you should be representative of the police force – not a Sikh police officer, not a Catholic police officer, not a Jewish police officer'.[59] The Commissioner also stated he would re-examine the toleration of ashes being displayed on members' foreheads on Ash Wednesday.[60]

Controversy also erupted surrounding the refusal of a school principal in Gorey, Co. Wexford, to permit a pupil to wear the *hijab*.[61] There are no legislative or regulatory provisions specifically governing religious attire in schools, with this being left to individual school management, and no litigation arose from the affair.

This lack of a unified approach is evident in the divergent approaches taken to accommodating religious practices in different statutes. Some use denominationally specific criteria for exempting religious practice, whereas other provisions accommodate a broader, denominationally neutral category of religious practices, exempting religious practice or belief as a general category, rather than enumerating particular denominations. Indeed, this more general formula – accommodating religion as a broad category rather than as specific denominational needs – may have the advantage of reconciling religious freedom with the countervailing constitutional requirement of non-discrimination as between the different denominations that may require accommodation.[62] Thus, for example, 'ministers of religion', presumably a broad category, are exempted from jury service under the Juries Act 1976.[63] Similarly, tax legislation has typically referred to 'clergy or ministers of religion'.[64] Secondary legislation on nursing-home regulations require that 'any dietary restriction on ... religious grounds shall be respected'[65] – thus avoiding any attempt to exhaustively enumerate different religious dietary regimes. In similarly general terms, the Prison Rules 2007 provide that 'each prisoner shall, in so far as is practicable

58 S. Mullally and D. O'Donovan, 'Religion and Ireland's "Public Squares": Education, the Family and Expanding Equality Claims' (2011) *Public Law* 284, p. 289.

59 F. O'Toole, 'The Choice is Simple: All or Nothing' *The Irish Times*, 28 August 2007.

60 K. Holland, 'Turban Ban Forces Garda into Rethink of Catholic Symbols', *The Irish Times*, 27 August 2007.

61 See general T. Hickey, 'Freedom as non-Domination and the Islamic *Hijab* in Irish Schools' (2009) 31 *Dublin University Law Journal* 128.

62 See Article 44.2.3°, discussed separately in Chapter 3. Given that the Fifth Amendment of the Constitution in 1972 deleted all references to any specific denominations, it seems likely that the Constitution accords protection to 'religion' as a broad category, rather than to any exhaustive list of recognised denominations, as further discussed below.

63 First Schedule, Part 2.

64 Taxes Consolidation Act 1997, s 837.

65 Nursing Homes (Care and Welfare) Regulations, 1993, SI no 226/1993, s 6(2).

and subject to the maintenance of good order and safe and secure custody, be permitted to practice and comply with the rules, observances and norms of behaviour of the religious denomination of which he or she is a follower or member'.[66]

However, a number of enactments contain denominationally specific provisions, potentially raising constitutional difficulties.[67] Legislation on juries recognises the 'Old' and 'New' testaments as the texts upon which 'Christian' and 'Jewish' jurors swear oaths.[68] The Slaughter of Animals Act 1935 makes denominationally specific provision for Jewish and 'Mohammadan' slaughter methods, although these are not the only religions that have particular requirements for animal slaughter.[69] As already mentioned, such denominationally specific provisions raise the issue of equality in the accommodation extended to different religious groups. Even if such enactments treat all such existing groups evenly and fairly, a new religious group might emerge in Ireland – for example, a denomination whose practices conflicted with animal-slaughter laws – in a manner that had not been envisaged when the statute in question was enacted. Then, a question may arise as to whether it could challenge the constitutionality of its non-exemption based on a comparison with similarly situated denominations already accommodated,[70] whether on grounds of religious freedom or non-discrimination. Alternatively, it might be argued their claim ought to be left instead to the political and legislative process, although this might put constitutional religious freedom on a precarious footing. Similarly, the Charities Act 2009, which establishes a specific scheme for regulating the sale of Mass cards on the basis of approval granted to retailers by certain Catholic authorities,[71] makes specific provision for the needs of a named denomination.

In summary, religious needs and religious-freedom claims have been facilitated on a largely ad hoc basis, with little sense, if any, of how the Constitution

66 Prison Rules 2007, s 34(1).

67 See further Chapter 3, Sections I and II.

68 s 17, Juries Act 1976. However, s 18(3) provides: 'a juror who states that he has a religious belief but that he is neither of the Christian nor of the Jewish faith may, if the judge so permits, be sworn in any manner that the juror states to be binding on him'.

69 s 15(2).

70 This would almost certainly be excluded based on separation of powers considerations. In relation to the constitutional equality guarantee in Article 40.1, it has been held that the courts cannot remediate discriminatory treatment in statute by extending a discriminatory benefit to those excluded, by virtue of the separation of powers. In general terms, they may only strike out a discriminatory clause, rather than extend its application. See J. Casey, *Constitutional Law in Ireland* (Dublin: Thomson Round Hall, 2000), p. 451.

71 The retailer must demonstrate the existence of an 'arrangement' either with a Catholic bishop, or the provincial of an order of priests. Charities Act 2009, s 99.

frames or guides these various claims to accommodation in an era of greater religious diversity. In legislation, as already discussed, there is little sign of any coherent, overarching principle guiding statutory accommodations of religion. Indeed, notwithstanding the *Quinn's Supermarket* doctrine and the theoretical arguments surrounding its merits, the reality has been that exemptions are effectively extended based on administrative or political contingency rather than with reference to overarching principles. To illustrate this inconsistency, medical professionals are exempted from any requirement to dispense contraception or abortion information,[72] yet upon the enactment of a Civil Partnership scheme for same-sex couples in 2010, the claim of some Catholic civil registrars to exemption from same-sex ceremonies was roundly rejected, and even ridiculed, across the political spectrum.[73] It seems questionable whether this ad hoc, piecemeal approach is desirable or sustainable in the long run. Recent controversies seem to support Mullally and O'Donovan's argument that 'as the implicit contract between Church and State unravels, the cleavages between faith communities, and between religious citizens and secularists, are likely only to increase'.[74]

6 Conclusion

I have argued that Irish constitutional doctrine, reflecting the text itself, has oscillated between principles of neutrality and recognition as regards religion. In turn, this has led to rather unpredictable and ad hoc results for religious

72 Section 11 of the Health (Family Planning) Act 1979 provides: 'nothing in this Act shall be construed as obliging any person to take part in the provision of a family planning service, the giving of prescriptions or authorisations for the purposes of this Act, or the sale, importation into the State, manufacture, advertising or display of contraceptives'. Similarly, s 13 of the Regulation of Information (Services outside the State for Termination of Pregnancies) Act 1995 provides that no person may be obliged to provide information on abortion services available outside of the State.

73 Senator Paschal Donohoe noted on his website: 'the law is the law. We cannot chose what parts of the law we want to implement based on our own views or beliefs. We've seen to our cost as a country what happens when the universal application of law to all, regardless of their status and wealth, is either subverted or not implemented'. Press release, *Freedom of Conscience and the Civil Partnership Bill*, 2 December 2009, available at http://www.paschaldonohoe.ie/?p=2752, 4 July 2011. The then Minister for Justice, Dermot Ahern, said that it would be 'against public policy to permit State officials to choose not to perform certain of their official functions on the grounds that to do so would be contrary to their religious beliefs'. See Marie O'Halloran, 'No Exemption from Bill on Grounds of Belief–Ahern', *Irish Times*, 28 January 2010.

74 S. Mullally and D. O'Donovan, 'Religion and Ireland's "Public Squares": Education, the Family and Expanding Equality Claims' (2011) *Public Law* 284, p. 289.

minorities – although the degree to which the constitutional provisions actually *determine* such policy approaches could easily be overstated. There is no single, coherent *principle* in the Constitution concerning the State's relationship with minority religions, and the alternation between competing, competing principles provides for a great deal of flexibility – and equally, of uncertainty – regarding the development of constitutional doctrine in the future. Finally, there is no reason for concluding that in general, the recognition-based or neutrality-based approach is more favourable for religious minorities, in the long run. Under each, the actual form of accommodation extended remains highly dependent on the vicissitudes of governmental indifference and administrative expediency.

Bibliography

Books

Casey, James, *Constitutional Law in Ireland* (Dublin: Thomson Round Hall, 2000).

Daly, Eoin, *Religion, Law and the Irish State* (Dublin: Clarus, 2012).

Hogan, Gerard and Gerry Whyte, *JM Kelly: The Irish Constitution* (Dublin: Butterworths, 2003).

Keogh, Dermot and Andrew McCarthy, *The Making of the 1937 Constitution* (Cork: Mercier, 2007).

Lee, J.J., *Ireland 1912–1985: Politics and Society* (Cambridge: Cambridge University Press, 1989).

McCrea, Ronan, *Religion and the Public Order of the European Union* (Oxford: Oxford University Press, 2010).

O'Sullivan, Denis, *Cultural Politics and Irish Education since the 1950s: Policy, Paradigms and Power* (Dublin: Institute of Public Administration).

Robbers, Gerhard (ed.), *Church and State in the European Union* (Baden-Baden: Nomos, 2005).

Whyte, John, *Church and State in Modern Ireland* (Dublin: Gill and Macmillan, 1980).

Articles

Barrington, Donal, 'The Irish Constitution x. Article Forty-Four. ii. Church and State' (1953) 81 *The Irish Monthly* 1.

Eisgruber, Christopher and Lawrence Sager, 'Does it Matter what Religion Is?' (2009) *Notre Dame Law Review* 807.

Hickey, Tom, 'Freedom as non-Domination and the Islamic *Hijab* in Irish Schools' (2009) 31 *Dublin University Law Journal* 128.

Mullally, Siobhán and Darren O'Donovan, 'Religion and Ireland's 'Public Squares': Education, the Family and Expanding Equality Claims' (2011) *Public Law* 284.

Zeghal, Malika, 'La constitution du Conseil Français du Culte Musulman: reconnaissance politique d'un Islam Français ?' (2005) 129 *Archives de sciences sociales des religions*.

Book chapters

Fossum, John Erik and Philip Schlesinger, 'Religion and the European Public Sphere', in Fossum and Schlesinger, *The European Union and the Public Sphere: a Communicative Space in the Making?* (London: Routledge, 2007).

Newspaper articles

Browne, Vincent, 'In Kenny's book the Constitution is king, not the Church', *Irish Times*, 15 May 2013, emphasis added.

Cullen, Paul, 'Vatican Relationship at New Low', *The Irish Times*, 21 July 2011.

Holland, Kitty, 'Turban Ban Forces Garda into Rethink of Catholic Symbols', *The Irish Times*, 27 August 2007.

O'Halloran, Marie, 'No Exemption from Bill on Grounds of Belief–Ahern', *Irish Times*, 28 January 2010.

O'Toole, Fintan, 'The Choice is Simple: All or nothing', *The Irish Times*, 28 August 2007.

PART 2

Islam and Irish Law: Implications for the Muslim Community in Ireland

CHAPTER 4

Muslims in Ireland

History, Demographics and Debates

James Carr

1 Introduction

One aspect of the vision statement of the Islamic Cultural Centre of Ireland is to preserve 'Islamic identity as well as encouraging the positive integration of Muslim's, both Irish and Non-Irish into the Inter-Cultural society we now live in.'[1] This latter reference to contemporary Irish society that Muslims are part of is fascinating in that it points up the manner in which the religious composition of Ireland has changed so much over the years, as will be discussed. Moreover, it also underscores that Muslims and Islam are now an integral part of Irish society. The purpose of this chapter is to provide some background on the development of Muslim communities residing in Ireland today. Commencing with a snapshot of the historic development of Islam in the State, the focus will move to engage with data provided from the most recent Census to provide insights on the make-up of twenty-first century Ireland's diverse Muslim communities. These new data will be set to extant published researches on Islam and Muslim communities in Ireland to put them in context. These new Census data provide insights on the socio-economic class, age, sex, and ethno-national background all of which will be elaborated upon in-turn. Moving from the historic and statistical, the remainder of what follows below will engage with contemporary issues and debates relating to Islam and Muslim communities in Ireland. Here topics such as the political climate in Ireland; experiences of exclusion and integration; as well as discourses and debates within Ireland's Muslim communities will be explored. In all, the following provides a context for the remainder of this book providing, as it does, insights into contemporary Islam in Ireland.

1 Islamic Cultural Centre of Ireland, 'About Us' <https://islamireland.ie/about/about-icci/> accessed 24 March 2018.

 | DOI:10.1163/9789004398252_005

2 Migration[2]

The relationship between Muslims, Islam and Ireland is not a new phenomenon. Although the numbers of Muslims residing in the State are considerably larger than at any other time, there is a long history of interaction. Research demonstrates that, from as early as the eighteenth century, Muslim communities started to lay a footprint, albeit faint at first, on the island. In addition to notable individuals such as Mir Aulad, (1832–98),[3] originally from India, who would become a Professor of Languages at Trinity College Dublin, early records note that Muslims in Ireland occupied a range of roles including 'visitors, students, servants of former colonial officials, or firemen lodging temporarily in Irish port cities.'[4] As Scharbrodt notes, this presence was, at this stage, predominantly 'transitory' and there was no sense of an established 'Muslim' presence in Ireland at that time.[5] This pattern continued somewhat into the early twentieth century: we see small numbers of Muslim men and their families, mainly those from the shipping industry or working in medicine, coming to make Ireland their home.[6] These instances of 'Muslim' migration to Ireland were low in number and speaking of a 'Muslim community' in Ireland at this point would be misleading.[7]

The intervening periods since these early days have witnessed Muslim communities in Ireland grow steadily from the mid-twentieth century onward. Sakaranaho places the number in Ireland in 1959 at circa three-hundred individuals but this may be an overestimation.[8] These numbers were made up primarily of South African students of Indian background who had moved to

2 For detailed histories of Muslim migration to Ireland please see Bryan Fanning, *Migration and the Making of Ireland* (University College Dublin Press 2018); Kieran Flynn, 'Understanding Islam in Ireland,' (2006) 17(2) Islam and Christian-Muslim Relations; Tuula Sakaranaho, *Religious Freedom, Multiculturalism, Islam: Cross-reading Finland and Ireland* (Brill 2006); Oliver Scharbrodt, 'Muslim immigration to the Republic of Ireland: trajectories and dynamics since World War II' (2012) 47(1) Éire-Ireland.

3 Fanning (n 2).

4 Scharbrodt (n 2) 225.

5 Scharbrodt (n 2).

6 Fanning (n 2).

7 Both Fanning (n 2) and Scharbrodt (n 2) note the problems of referring to any Muslim 'community' as a unified homogenous whole. Firstly, in doing so one reduces these otherwise diverse communities to one aspect of their identities: the religious; further, Muslims while ostensibly sharing religious identities should not be perceived as a unitary whole for a range of reasons: including levels of religiosity, ethno-national background, socio-economic etc. as will be demonstrated below.

8 Sakaranaho (n 2); for example, Flynn (n 2) places the Muslim population at three-hundred in 1969; In any case, the number is probably in the low hundreds.

Dublin to study medicine in the apartheid era. To these could be added a small number of both Malaysian and Arabic Muslims.[9] These numbers were to gradually increase over time. Some of those who initially came to study on a short term basis decided to remain on, post-graduation, for occupational reasons and also to settle down with families of their own.[10] In addition, the numbers of students coming to Ireland to study continued to grow with the numbers of Arabic and Malaysian students, in particular, increasing.

The latter decades of the twentieth century witnessed this growth continue. In addition to students, UK entrepreneurs of Pakistani background saw Ireland as an ideal business opportunity and moved here to exploit this by to opening restaurants inter alia.[11] High level initiatives such as the development of international diplomatic relations between the Irish Government with Arabic Gulf nations saw a further development of Muslim communities in Ireland with Arabic communities forming the majority ethnic group of Ireland's Muslims in the 1980s.[12]

During the 1990s in addition to continued growth in numbers of Muslim people coming to Ireland, we start to see a change in the demographic make-up of these individuals. In addition to students, we start to see increases in the numbers of asylum seekers and refugees from Muslim majority societies, including Bosnia and Middle Eastern States, coming to Ireland to flee conflict and persecution.[13] Furthermore, the then successful economic climate in Ireland, the so-called Celtic Tiger, acted as a 'pulling factor' for migration.[14] These factors resulted in not only increasing the numbers of Muslims living in Ireland but also the diversity of these communities.

As noted above, the numbers of Muslims living in Ireland in the 1950s and 60s was in the low hundreds. In 1991, the first year for which we have official national figures, the number of Muslims in Ireland stood at 3,875. Eleven years later, this figure stood at 19,147. The first decade saw a continued 'massive increase'[15] in Ireland's Muslim population. In 2006, the number of Muslims in Ireland was 32,539 before moving to 49, 204 five years later.[16] In the summer of 2017, a national newspaper ran with the headline: 'Islam is Ireland's third

9 Scharbrodt (n 2).
10 Scharbrodt (n 2).
11 Sakaranaho (n 2).
12 Scharbrodt (n 2).
13 Sakaranaho (n 2); Scharbrodt (n 2).
14 Sakaranaho (n 2) 271.
15 Scharbrodt (n 2) 230.
16 Central Statistics Office, 'Statistical Tables: Profile Educations, Ethnicity, and Irish Traveller Tables' (Census 2011) <http://www.cso.ie/en/media/csoie/census/documents/census2011

largest religion.'[17] This was based on the most recent Census figures which now placed Ireland's Muslim communities at 63,443, constituting 1.3% of the population.[18]

3 Age, Sex and Ethno-national Background

Census data reveal that the vast majority of Muslims in Ireland live in the Dublin region.[19] However, these data also reveal that while urban centres such as Limerick, Galway, Cork and Waterford predictably have larger numbers, there is a notable presence of Muslim adults and children spread right across the State.[20] These communities, at an average age of 26 years, are younger than the national comparator which stands at just over 37 years-of-age. In terms of sex and the demographic composition, there are more Muslim men than women (129 Muslim men for every 100 women) although this gap has narrowed in the 2011–16 inter-censal period.[21]

Ireland's Muslim communities are incredibly diverse.[22] Over half of all Muslims in Ireland are Irish nationals (55.6%). Outside of this, Pakistani nationals make up the next largest community at 11.4%. Other nationalities include those from across Europe, Saudi Arabia, Bangladesh, and Afghanistan inter alia (see table 4.1 for more insights).[23] When it comes to ethnic background, the data provided for through the categories utilised in the Census is of limited utility due to the conflation of national/racial/macro ethnic groupings.[24] However, research undertaken by the author with Ireland's Muslim communities

---

profile7/Profile_7_Education_Ethnicity_and_Irish_Traveller_Tables_and_appendices.pdfaccessed> accessed 23 March 2018.

17 Joyce Fegan, 'Islam is Ireland's third largest religion' *Irish Examiner* (Cork, 7 June 2017) <https://www.irishexaminer.com/ireland/islam-is-irelands-third-largest-religion-451879.html> accessed 23 March 2018.

18 Central Statistics Office, 'Census of Population 2016 – Profile 8 Irish Travellers, Ethnicity and Religion' (Census 2016) <http://www.cso.ie/en/releasesandpublications/ep/p-cp8iter/p8iter/p8rnc/> accessed 24 March 2018.

19 Central Statistics Office (n 18).

20 Central Statistics Office, 'Statistical Database' (Census 2016) <http://www.cso.ie/px/pxeirestat/Statire/SelectVarVal/Define.asp?maintable=E8055&PLanguage=0> accessed 23 March 2018.

21 Central Statistics Office (n 18).

22 Scharbrodt (n 2).

23 Central Statistics Office (n 20).

24 Central Statistics Office, 'Statistical Database' (Census 2016) <http://www.cso.ie/px/pxeirestat/Statire/SelectVarVal/Define.asp?maintable=E8009&PLanguage=0> accessed 23 March 2018.

can provide more insight in this regard. In a survey undertaken to ascertain insights on Islamophobia in Ireland completed by 323 individuals, participants were asked: 'How would you describe your cultural identity?'[25] Participants self-identified a range of cultural backgrounds which at times conflated with national identities (table 4.2).

TABLE 4.1 Census 2016 Data on 'Population Usually Resident and Present in the State 2011 to 2016 (Number) by Religion, Sex, Nationality and Census Year' (Central Statistics Office of Ireland 2018)

Muslim (Islamic)	**2016**
Both sexes	
All nationalities	62,032
Irish	33,971
French	366
German	153
Italian	71
Latvian	191
Lithuanian	126
Polish	200
Romanian	92
Spanish	73
UK	2,069
Other EU28	725
Other European	1,437
African	5,293
Indian	496
Other Asian	15,138
American(US)	113
Brazilian	9
Other American	98
Other nationalities	482
Not stated, including no nationality	929

25 James Carr, *Experiences of Islamophobia: Living with racism in the neoliberal era* (Routledge 2016).

TABLE 4.2 Self-proclaimed Cultural Identities of Muslims in Ireland (Carr 2016)

	2016
Self-identified Cultural Identities	
Irish; Irish Muslim,	Muganda
Arabic	Kashmiri
Bangladeshi	Oromo
Bengali	Pashtun
European (British; Dutch; Kosovar; etc.)	Punjabi
Iraqi	Sindhi
Kashmiri	Swahili
Malay	Yoruba

4 Muslims in Ireland: Socio-economic Class

The pattern of migration of Muslims to Ireland over the twentieth and into the twenty-first centuries raises interesting differences in terms of socio-economic background within these communities. Excluding the aforementioned relatively isolated instances of particular individuals, those who migrated to Ireland from the mid-twentieth century were primarily from a middle class background. As noted, medial students and professionals dominated Muslim immigration in those early years. Towards the end of the twentieth century, this pattern of middle-class migration changed. Instead of students and professionals, Muslim men and women migrating to Ireland included those coming to seek employment in the service industry, people seeking asylum, and refugees.[26]

It is somewhat problematic to assume that all of these newer migrants were of a lower educational standing than earlier arrivals. Nonetheless, there is arguably at least some difference in levels of educational/professional qualifications given the diversity of the communities and reasons for migration. Scharbrodt's argument that a 'socio-economic gap' developed between early and latter waves of migration presents an interesting insight into the communities with

26 Fanning (n 2); Sakaranaho (n 2); Scharbrodt (n 2).

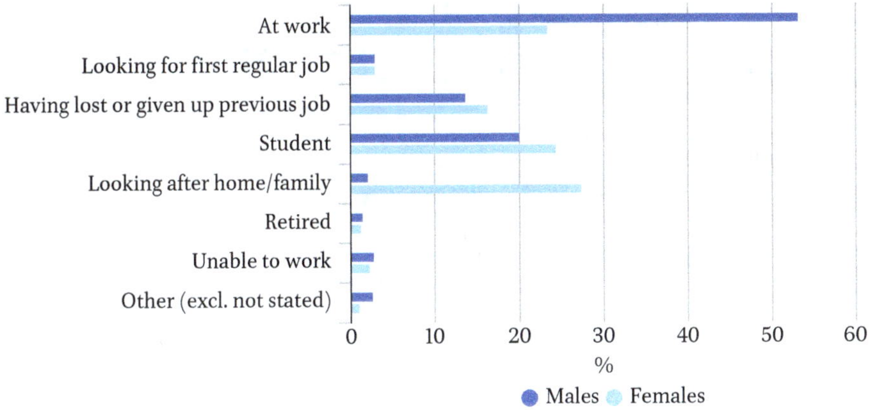

FIGURE 4.1 Principal Economic Status of Muslims in Ireland (Central Statistics Office of Ireland 2018)

newer arrivals being less privileged than earlier migrants.[27] Scharbrodt argues that this in turn impacts upon migrant integration opportunities, with those earlier arrivals, due to class, access to resources, professional and educational advantage (including linguistic skills) being better positioned to integrate than the latter category, those who may be deficient in some or all of these capitals.[28]

Data from the most recent Census provide interesting up-to-date insights on the socio-economic positions of Muslim men and women in Ireland. In particular, data on occupational status is useful in this regard as a proxy for class.[29] At a base level, figure 4.1 demonstrates the differences between Muslim men and women. As demonstrated, 53.3% of Muslim men are classed as 'at work' compared to less than 23.6% of Muslim women. Far more Muslim women (27.4%) are 'looking after the home/family' than their male co-religionists (2.3%) and the national average for all women in the State (14.9%). Interestingly, more Muslim men (2.3%) are classed as home-makers compared to the total population (1.1%).

These data indicate that the professions today, standing at 23.5%, account for the largest occupational category among Muslim communities in Ireland. Moreover, within this, the medical profession is the largest recorded occupation among Muslim communities standing at 12%, deviating immensely from the national total for the same field which is 0.7% (see figure 4.2). It is also interesting to note, while the data at first reading reflect historic occupational

27 Scharbrodt (n 2) 235.
28 Scharbrodt (n 2).
29 Central Statistics Office (n 18).

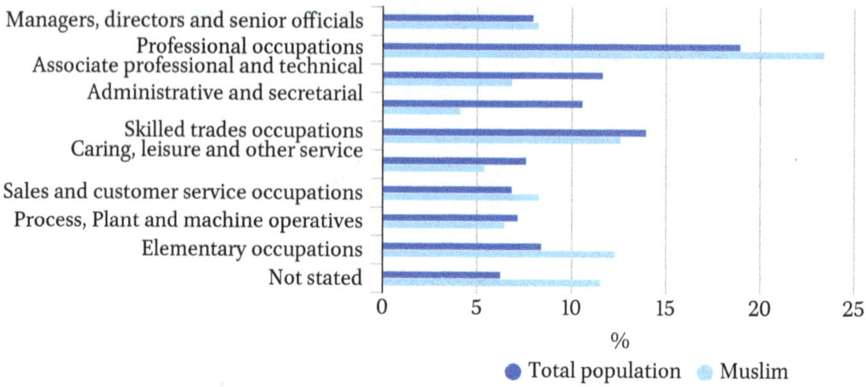

FIGURE 4.2 Major occupational groups of Muslims and of the total population in Ireland in 2016 (Central Statistics Office of Ireland 2018)

TABLE 4.3 Top ten occupations of Muslim workers, 2011–2016 (Central Statistics Office of Ireland 2018)

Occupations (SOC2010)	2011	2016
Medical practitioners	1,725	2,102
Chefs	954	1,349
Sales and retail assistants, cashiers and checkout operators	912	1,045
Kitchen and catering assistants	391	589
Security guards and related occupations	462	560
Managers and directors in retail and wholesale	373	504
Taxi and cab drivers and chauffeurs	295	464
Restaurant and catering establishments managers and proprietors	313	392
Programmers and software development professionals	140	316
Hairdressers, barbers, beauticians and related occupations	150	308
Other (including not stated)	6,813	9,914
Total	12,528	17,543

patterns, a closer look suggests somewhat of a blurring of the heretofore socio-economic gap within the communities although this is hard to confirm in the absence of detailed historical data. Nonetheless, despite the top heavy number of medical practitioners, Census data reveal the presence of Muslim communities across a range of occupational sectors (see table 4.3).

5 Muslims in Ireland: Establishing Institutions

As noted above, what were predominantly student migrations in the early-mid twentieth century formed the backbone of what was to become sustained Muslim immigration to Ireland. These early migrations heralded the first efforts vis-à-vis the establishment of Islamic institutions in Ireland.[30] The educational and professional standing of these early Muslim immigrants to Ireland meant that they had the expertise required to establish an institutional presence in the State.[31] Detailed accounts of the development of Islamic institutions are provided elsewhere.[32] Nonetheless, it is worth noting a number of key milestones.

The late 1950s witnessed the establishment of the first organised Muslim presence in Ireland known as the Dublin Islamic Society (DIS).[33] In these early years, the predominantly student Muslim population used a residential premises close to the Royal College of Surgeons of Ireland (RCSI) campus in Dublin city centre to facilitate communal prayers. Throughout the 1960s, discussions took place on the topic of establishing a dedicated mosque and communal facility in the city. These discussions were maintained across the 1960s, energised by the continued to growth of Muslim communities in Dublin and their needs. At this point, the communities were still utilising venues close to/on the RCSI campus for religious gatherings.[34]

In 1969, the DIS agreed to source charitable donations to enable the purchase of a location that would be dedicated to the needs of Dublin's communities. By the mid-1970s, as a result of international financial support, the DIS purchased premises on Harrington Street in Dublin city centre.[35] The Dublin Islamic Centre formally opened in 1977.[36] As Muslim communities continued to grow, the venue on Harrington Street quickly became unfit-for-purpose. A new location, an old Presbyterian church on South Circular Road, Dublin was procured, financed through a private donation. The then new Dublin Mosque

30 Scharbrodt (n 2).

31 Scharbrodt (n 2); Sakaranaho (n 2).

32 See various contributions in: Oliver Scharbrodt, Tuula Sakaranaho, Adil.Hussain Khan, Yafa Shanneik, and Vivian Ibrahim (eds.) *Muslims in Ireland: Past and Present* (Edinburgh University Press 2015).

33 Fanning (n 2); Adil Hussain Khan, 'Early Muslim Organisations and Mosques in Ireland' in Oliver Scharbrodt, Tuula Sakaranaho, Adil .Hussain Khan, Yafa Shanneik, and Vivian Ibrahim (eds.) *Muslims in Ireland: Past and Present* (Edinburgh University Press 2015).

34 Khan (n 33).

35 Khan (n 33).

36 Khan (n 33).

opened in 1983 and the DIS changed its name to the Islamic Foundation of Ireland. In 1990, the first Muslim national school opened on the same premises.[37]

The development of Islamic institutions in the capital has continued apace in subsequent decades. Arguably most notable in this regard was the construction of a purpose built mosque, primary school and cultural centre in the Dublin suburbs of Clonskeagh. In the early 1990s, Sheikh Hamdan Ben Rashid al-Maktoum agreed to fund the construction of this purpose built mosque and broader complex. This then new mosque and associated facilities opened in 1996 under the name of the Islamic Cultural Centre of Ireland (ICCI).[38]

Over the intervening years, the ICCI in Clonskeagh has come to be known, somewhat problematically given the diversity of Muslim communities in Ireland, as *the* representative body for Islam in the State.[39] The ICCI does fulfil a crucial role in the infrastructure of Islamic communities in Ireland, acting as a channel through which funding from the al-Maktoum Foundation is provided to other mosques around the country; this in turn 'present[s] a unified [Muslim] front to Irish society' despite the diversity of Muslim communities in the State.[40]

Despite the ICCI being perceived as the 'go-to' organisation for Islam in Ireland, a number of other organisations in the State could also lay claim to representing Muslim communities. There is a sizeable Shi'a community in Ireland, although exact numbers vis-à-vis size are unattainable, Fanning places the figure at circa five-thousand individuals.[41] Around the same time the ICCI opened in Clonskeagh (1996), the Ahlul Bayt Shi'a mosque and community centre opened in nearby Milltown.[42] More recently, a second Shi'a mosque has opened in North Dublin.[43] In the absence of dedicated Shi'a mosques, Shi'i in Ireland have used Sunni aligned facilities for prayers.[44] Anwar-e-Madina Sufi mosque, now home to the Irish Sufi Foundation, opened in Dublin's inner city in 2008.[45]

The establishment of the IFI, the construction of the ICCI, and that of the Ahlul Bayt centre, and the creation of the Irish Sufi Foundation can usefully be thought of as high visibility activities located in Dublin. To these though can

37 Fanning (n 2); Khan (n 33); Sakaranho (n 2).
38 Fanning (n 2).
39 Sakaranaho (n 2).
40 Fanning (n 2) 245.
41 Fanning (n 2) 245.
42 Sakaranaho (n 2).
43 Fanning (n 2).
44 Sakaranaho (n 2).
45 Fanning (n 2).

be added an array of smaller mosques and prayer facilities located across the city of Dublin in less visible locales such as industrial estates.[46]

However, Dublin is not the only location in Ireland to have a Muslim presence. Outside of Dublin, Islamic centres/mosques taking various forms are dotted across Ireland including all of the main cities as well as other more rural locations.[47] According to a spokesman for the ICCI, there are an estimated seventy-eight mosques around the country.[48] Indeed, the first purpose built mosque in Ireland was constructed in the 1980s in the rural town of Ballyhaunis, Co. Mayo in the West of Ireland to meet the needs of a sizeable Muslim staff working in a halal slaughtering facility.[49] There are also Shi'a mosques outside of Dublin in Cork city and an Ahmadiyya community mosque in Galway.

In terms of governance of these various Islamic institutions, different groups have laid claim to taking the lead over the past two decades. In 1996, the Irish Council of Imams was established, affiliated with the ICCI and the IFI, however, Fanning argues that this Council 'has a projected a mostly symbolic unity' with only limited consensus on issues relevant to Islam in Ireland. More recently, the Irish Muslim Peace and Integration Council, led by Sheikh Dr Umar Al-Qadri has also stepped up to act as a representative Muslim organisation in Ireland. IMPIC includes members from Muslim centres across various cities in Ireland and speaks out on a range of issues.[50] These are but two organisations of note and there is limited utility in listing all those who would lay claim to representing Islam in Ireland.[51] It is worth stressing though that, given the diversity of Muslim communities in Ireland, it is highly problematic to regard any one organisation as 'representative' of Islam in the State.

6 Muslims in Ireland: Contemporary Issues and Debates

When it comes to Islam as a faith in Ireland, Sakaranaho argues that the overriding perception among Muslim communities in the Republic is that as a

46 Fanning (n 2).

47 Fanning (n 2); Sakaranaho (n 2).

48 Patsy McGarry, 'Muslim academic apologises for 'confusion' over FGM comments' *The Irish Times* (Dublin, 19 February 2018).

49 Fanning (n 2).

50 Irish Muslim Peace and Integration Council, 'Homepage' <http://impic.ie/> accessed 23 March 2018.

51 For more see for example: Irish Sufi Foundation, 'Facebook page' <https://business.facebook.com/IrishSufi/> accessed 23 March 2018; Ahlul Bayt Islamic Centre, 'Homepage' <http://homepage.tinet.ie/~ahlulbyteassociation/> accessed 23 March 2018; Muslim Association of Ireland <http://maionline.ie/>accessed 23 March 2018.

religious country (at least perceived as such), there is greater respect for religion than in other European nations.[52] Furthermore, the fact that common ground can be found in relation to shared histories of Ireland and Muslim majority societies vis-à-vis colonialism has also underpinned good relations.[53] Maintaining this positive outlook, Fanning noted recently that 'the visible presence of Muslims in the Republic of Ireland has not become politicised to the extent that it has in several other European countries.'[54] These points are, of course, debatable as the argument to follow will demonstrate. The following subsections outline some of the key issues and debates impacting on Muslim communities in Ireland. These are arguably 'headline' issues, and it should not be taken as exhaustive. Nonetheless, the issues and debates described here are incredibly important. Moreover, the following also demonstrates the nexus between the experiences of Muslims in Ireland and the wider international context.

7 Islam in Ireland: The Political Climate

As noted above, in many ways, Muslim communities and Islam in Ireland have not been subject to the sort of politicisation that is visible in other nation states. This should not be read however as an absence of negative political activity vis-à-vis Muslims in Ireland. As has been documented elsewhere, the last number of years have witnessed elected officials from mainstream political parties in Ireland publicly make anti-Muslim/Islam statements.[55] In one incident, an elected representative raised a question in Parliament as to how many Muslims had applied for citizenship in Ireland. The following month a local councillor stated that most Muslims in Ireland do not want to work and preferred living on welfare.[56] More recently, a local councillor from the leading party in Government, Fine Gael, claimed on social media that: 'Sharia law is operating in Ireland and most of the political class either do not know or do not care. It is a subversion of our legal system.'[57]

52 Sakaranaho (n 2).

53 Sakaranaho (n 2).

54 Fanning (n 2) 253.

55 See entries for Ireland in the European Islamophobia Reports for 2015, 2016, 2017 at European Islamophobia Report, 'Homepage' <http://www.islamophobiaeurope.com/> accessed 23 March 2018.

56 James Carr, 'Ireland 2016' European Islamophobia Report (SETA 2017) <http://www.islamophobiaeurope.com/wp-content/uploads/2017/03/IRELAND.pdf> accessed 22 March 2018.

57 Cormac McQuinn, and Kathy Armstrong, 'We will take any necessary action' – Taoiseach distances himself from FG councillor's comments on Islam and refugees' *Irish Independent* (Dublin, 7 September 2017).

Overt anti-Muslim positions from members of mainstream political parties in Ireland are relatively isolated. Somewhat more worrying anti-Muslim and anti-Islam activities have been developing on the fringes of Irish politics in recent years. One such group, Identity Ireland, put forward a candidate for elected office, most recently in the 2016 general election, wherein he returned with only 0.4% of votes in the Cork North Central constituency.[58] Outside of running for office, Identity Ireland has developed links with the German based PEGIDA movement, addressing supporters in Dresden in January 2016.[59] Indeed, Identity Ireland attempted, unsuccessfully, to establish a PEGIDA affiliate in the State in early 2016, hosting the founder of the English Defence League and then key figure in PEGIDA UK Tommy Robinson in the lead up to the attempted launch.[60] In addition to Identity Ireland can be added the National Party; a group that are led by Justin Barrett who has been outspoken against Islam and the Muslim presence in Ireland. It is worth noting that Barrett has also attended meetings of groups such as Italian neo-fascist group Forza Nuova.[61] 2017 also saw the emergence in Ireland of Generation Identity UK and Éire (GI), an affiliate of the Identitarian movement present across EU Member States.[62] GI have been active since mid-summer 2017, particularly in the context of high visibility social media campaigns and on-street activities warning of the 'risk' of Islam/Muslims and immigration.[63]

8 Muslims in Ireland: Exclusion and Integration

It is important not to overstate the influence of these groups, who, as election results indicate, attract vanishingly small numbers of supporters. Nonetheless, for present purposes, the mere presence of these groups in Ireland points up the manner in which the Irish context is not dislocated from international anti-Muslim/Islam discourses. As noted above, the religious background of the Irish State and shared histories of colonialism present the Irish context in an optimistic light for Muslim communities. Indeed, speaking in a recent media

58 Raidió Teilifís Éireann, 'Election2016: Cork Norh-Central' <https://www.rte.ie/news/election-2016/constituencies/cork-north-central/> accessed 23 March 2018.

59 Carr (n 56).

60 Carr (n 56); see also: Hope Not Hate, 'A Short History of Pegida' <https://www.hopenothate.org.uk/research/investigations/pegida-uk/a-short-history/> accessed 24 March 2018.

61 Carr (n 56).

62 James Carr, 'Ireland 2017' European Islamophobia Report (SETA 2018) <http://www.islamophobiaeurope.com/wp-content/uploads/2018/04/Ireland.pdf> accessed 6 November 2018.

63 Ibid.

interview, a sample of young Irish Muslims in Dublin shared their views that Ireland is more accommodating for Muslims and Islam than other EU States. However, these same young people also shared their experiences of anti-Muslim hostility and discrimination.[64] Therefore, while at least some Muslims in Ireland perceive their situation to be better than elsewhere, it is important to recognise the negatives. These include the impact of anti-Muslim/Islam discourses and political activities; the failure to meaningfully address exclusion by the State; and the manner which these impact on the lives of Muslims in the State as the following sections demonstrate.

Various studies over the past number of years have elucidated the realities of anti-Muslim hostility and discrimination in Ireland. Research published in 2016 demonstrated the manner in which Muslim men and women in Ireland have been subjected to physical and verbal abuse; targeted on the basis of their religious (including perceived) identity. In terms of physical abuse, this has ranged from being spat at to having hijabs torn from heads; from having bottles thrown to serious assault. When it comes to verbal abuse, people have reported receiving comments that associate them with terrorism, Osama bin Laden, Al-Qaida through to the so-called Islamic State, and the recent humanitarian crisis involving migration into Europe. It is evident in these reports that Muslimness/ Islam and Irishness are deemed mutually exclusive by assailants.[65] Moreover, what is also evident from the limited available statistical insight, is that Muslim women are almost twice as likely to experience anti-Muslim hostility than their male co-religionists.[66] Calls have been made for the implementation of hate crime legislation in the Irish context to challenge anti-Muslim hostility and indeed broader forms of hate crime. However, at the time of writing, Ireland remains without the specific legislative means to address hate crime.[67]

These aforementioned studies also illuminate experiences of discrimination reported by Muslim communities on the basis of their religious identity. These have included experiences of discrimination in/looking for work, with the hijab being reported as a key factor for women in this regard. Other contexts

---

64 Patsy McGarry, 'What is it like to grow up Muslim in Ireland?' *The Irish Times* (Dublin, 28 January 2017) <https://www.irishtimes.com/news/social-affairs/religion-and-beliefs/what-is-it-like-to-grow-up-muslim-in-ireland-1.2949144> accessed 27 March 2018.

65 Carr (n 25); James Carr, 'Islamophobia in Dublin: Experiences and How to Respond (Immigrant Council of Ireland 2016); Carr (n 56); Carr (n 62).

66 Carr (n 25).

67 Sorcha Pollak and Elaine Edwards, 'Hate crime legislation needed 'as matter of urgency' *The Irish Times* (Dublin, 23 March 2017) <https://www.irishtimes.com/news/social-affairs/hate-crime-legislation-needed-as-matter-of-urgency-1.3022528> accessed 27 March 2018.

where discrimination is reported include accessing goods and services, including shops and restaurants and public transport. An area that has been reported as particularly problematic relates to young Muslim children accessing the schools of their choice. Admissions policies serve to restrict access to those of minority or no faith identities while simultaneously prioritising the religious ethos of the school in question which in Ireland is overwhelmingly Catholic.[68] Remaining within the education context, recent researches also evidence the manner in which Muslim children can and do experience discriminatory treatment from their teachers in the classroom environment.[69]

These exclusionary experiences of hostility and discrimination, in addition to international discourses of Muslim 'Otherness', are informed at a local level by a perception that to be Irish one cannot be Muslim; that to be Irish one must be Catholic.[70] Extant research evidences the manner in which Irish Muslims have to repeatedly assert their Irishness; that to be Muslim and Irish is to betray the nation. This perceived incompatibility between Irishness and Islam, frequently invoked in anti-Muslim hostility, has a profound impact on Irish Muslims, their identity and sense of belonging.[71] Sakaranaho notes the manner in which Muslims in Ireland 'must find the right balance between keeping one's identity, on the one hand, and integrating into a host society.'[72]

It is important to recognise though that the vast majority of Muslims in Ireland now are Irish citizens as noted above. Moreover, almost a third (29%) of Muslims in the State were born here.[73] Muslim participants in a study undertaken in Dublin on anti-Muslim racism in 2015 referred to experiencing a type of identity crisis. This crisis is an output of being Muslim and Irish but frequently being met with the incredulous responses of others.[74] Male and female participants in this study referred to being met with questions of 'where are you really from?'; this despite being born in Ireland and having strong Irish accents. The young Muslims who took part evidenced a sense of frustration at having to convince others of their Irishness. Speaking of his experiences, Irish born and reared Samir[75] succinctly sums up the crisis of identity lived by him

68 Carr (n 56).
69 Carr (n 65).
70 Carr (n 25).
71 Carr (n 25).
72 Sakaranaho (n 2) 285.
73 Central Statistics Office (n 20).
74 Carr (n 65).
75 Pseudonym.

and some of his peers: 'You don't know where you belong… but your identity is Irish.'

Feelings of not belonging such as these behove the State to engage in social, political and legal initiatives that promote integration. Any such integration initiatives that are undertaken in this regard must run both ways and not just focus on integrating Muslim communities into broader Irish society. As noted, very many Muslims in Ireland are Irish by birth and up-bringing, highlighting this would arguably go some way towards challenging anti-Muslim acts and sentiments. Moreover, Muslim communities are incredibly active in Irish society across a range of sectors, notably working with homeless groups on the streets of Ireland's cities, reaching out to communities through exhibitions and participating in local events, and engaging in political activites including demonstrations against the European Court of Justice ruling on the wearing of the hijab to name but a few.[76] However, no meaningful action vis integration has been taken to date by the Government. Indeed, in a very troubling development, the most recent Governmental strategy document on integration in Ireland, published in 2017, only referred to Muslims/Islam in the following manner:

> Radicalisation has been a particular issue for other European societies where ideologies that seek to undermine the state have prompted some young people, particularly second-generation Muslim immigrants, to undertake terrorist actions. The risk of radicalisation leading to terrorist activity is a risk for all societies. The challenge will be to reach out to young people at risk of radicalisation to encourage them to participate constructively in Irish society.[77]

---

76 James Carr, 'Ireland' in Oliver Scharbrodt, Samim Akgönül, Ahmet. Alibašić, Jørgen S. Nielsen, Edgūnas Račius (eds.) Yearbook of Muslims in Europe, Volume 8 (Brill 2017); James Carr, 'Ireland' in Oliver Scharbrodt, Samim Akgönül, Ahmet Alibašić, Jørgen S. Nielsen, Edgūnas Račius (eds.) Yearbook of Muslims in Europe, Volume 9 (Brill 2018). See also Kerry Islamic Outreach, 'Homepage' <http://www.kerryislamicoutreach.org/mission.html> accessed 27 March 2018; Muslim Sisters of Éire, 'Homepage' <http://msoe.ie/> accessed 27 March 2018; Sorcha Pollak, 'Protestors warn ECJ ruling to further alienate Muslim women' *The Irish Times* (Dublin, 21 March 2017) <https://www.irishtimes.com/news/social-affairs/protesters-warn-ecj-ruling-to-further-alienate-muslim-women-1.3019176> accessed 27 March 2018.

77 Department of Justice, 'The Migrant Integration Strategy: A Blueprint for the Future' (Department of Justice 2017) <http://www.justice.ie/en/JELR/Migrant_Integration_Strategy_English.pdf/Files/Migrant_Integration_Strategy_English.pdf> accessed 27 March 2018.

9 Islam in Ireland: Who Speaks for Whom?

When it comes to debates within Muslim communities in Ireland, media reports present a window into the various positions being taken by key Islamic figures in the Irish context. To be clear, there is a sense of frustration among Ireland's Muslim communities, particularly among the youth, that media outlets in the State tend to engage with the same individuals during interviews. As such, while the following presents an insight into some of the key debates among the communities at time of writing, it should not be taken as representing all of the issues being debated and voices therein.[78] Nonetheless, the following analysis of media reports in 2017 and into 2018 presents four of the most publicly debated issues vis-à-vis Muslim communities in Ireland. These include the question of radicalisation and the role of mosques in challenging this phenomenon, the regulation of religious activities and the recent response to comments made by a leading figure in Irish Islam on the topic of female genital mutilation (FGM).

9.1 *Radicalisation*

The question of radicalisation within Ireland's Muslim communities was amplified in media reports in the summer of 2017. Shortly after the terrorist attacks on London Bridge in the UK, a press conference was held in the Al Mustafa Islamic Centre in Dublin, organised by Sheikh Dr Umar Al-Qadri. During this press conference an Irish female convert to Islam 'Aalyia' claimed that there was approximately one-hundred-and-fifty 'Muslim extremists' living in Ireland. Moreover, these extremists believed Ireland to be a soft touch when it comes to counter-terror policing.[79]

Around the same time, reports in the media emerged that an Irish male convert to Islam was posting 'inflammatory messages' on social media under the name of 'Abu Yusuf Al-Irlandi.' In addition to inflammatory messages, Al-Irlandi was critical of Muslims who condemned jihad.[80] Sheikh Al-Qadri denounced the activities of this individual and encouraged other imams in Ireland to distance themselves from him. Moreover, Sheikh Al-Qadri claimed that Al-Irlandi 'actually engages a lot with the Muslim youth in the South Circular

78 Carr (n 65); McGarry (n 64).

79 Nicola Anderson, 'There are at least 150 extremists here who see Ireland as a soft touch'; Nicola Anderson talks to a young Muslim woman about how she be-came deradicalised after being a jihadi wife' *Irish Independent* (Dublin, 10 June, 2017).

80 Katie O'Neill and Ali Bracken, 'The Irish Voice of Islamist Fanatics; Hard line Muslim convert spouts hate speech online and is 'engaging' with mosque youths. London Terror Aftermath: The Irish fanatic defending jihad' *Irish Daily Mail* (Dublin, 7th June 2017).

Road mosque and the other mosques and therefore I find that the imams there must be very loud and clear that these hate messages have nothing to do with Islam.'[81] Sheikh Al-Qadri was also critical of Sheikh Hussein Halawa, imam at the *ICCI*, for being 'friends' with Al-Irlandi on Facebook; that in doing so was providing Al-Irlandi with 'legitimacy.'[82]

The response from the imam at the Dublin mosque on South Circular Road was to distance himself and his community from Al-Irandi.[83] Responding to the above claims, Sheikh Halawa dismissed the online friendship with Al-Irandi, downplaying his own use of social media and noting that he does not support his position. Sheikh Halawa was also unequivocal in his condemnation of terrorism, before stating again that he is not a member of the Muslim Brotherhood; the latter question being one that is repeatedly directed toward him.[84] On the question of radicalisation, Sheikh Halawa stated: 'the Muslim community in Ireland just doesn't accept any radicalism or terrorism – they despise it and they vocally put effort into despising it… The majority [of Muslims] would disown anyone that has those opinions.'[85]

Touching on the issue of integration, Sheikh Al Qadri called for the Irish authorities to play a greater role in facilitating the integration of Muslim communities in Ireland, that, '[W]hen people feel part of a community and valued, the risk of radicalisation disappears.'[86] Moreover, Al-Qadri has called for the Government to draft and implement a counter-radicalisation programme in Ireland, criticising the State for not already doing so.[87] It is interesting to note that ICCI affiliated groups such as the Irish Muslim Board, meeting in January 2017, have also raised the issue of promoting the integration of Ireland's Muslim communities. However, the position of the IMB vis-à-vis 'extremism' and radicalisation is at odds with that of Al-Qadri, underscoring the difference of opinion present in debates within Muslim communities in Ireland.[88]

---

81 O'Neill and Bracken (n 80).

82 O'Neill and Bracken (n 80).

83 O'Neill and Bracken (n 80).

84 Sunday Independent (2017) 'Islam does not accept any form of terrorism,' says Sheikh Halawa' *Sunday Independent* (Dublin, 11 June 2017).

85 Katie O'Neill, 'Muslims in Ireland have no tolerance for radicals;' *Irish Daily Mail* (Dublin, 8 June 2017).

86 John Meagher, 'Muslims in Ireland: a growing community that's keen for more integration' *Irish Independent* (Dublin, 22 April 2017).

87 Irish Examiner, 'Assessing jihadist levels: optimism will not stop terror attack' *Irish Examiner* (Cork, 30 August 2017).

88 Sorcha Pollak, 'Greater effort needed to ensure inclusion of Irish Muslims, group hears,' *The Irish Times* (Dublin, 19 January 2017).

9.2 *Regulating Islam in Ireland*

The preceding section demonstrates different perspectives within Ireland's Muslim communities on the topic of radicalisation and the responses from key actors therein. On a related but distinct issue, Sheikh Umar Al-Qadri has called for the introduction of a State sponsored regulatory body for Islam in Ireland.[89] For Al-Qadri, this body would be inclusive of a range of aspects of Islam and serve to, inter alia, oversee and achieve consensus on items including the delivery of educational curricula for madrassas and, for example, uniformity on messages to be delivered in sermons.[90]

This call for a State regulatory body was a reiteration of calls made previously by Al-Qadri which were rejected by the Government.[91] In terms of regulating Islam, Al-Qadri has been critical of other Islamic cultural centres and organisations in Ireland in relation to inviting international Islamic scholars to Ireland. Indeed, Sheikh Al Qadri stated in 2017 that he supports 'legislation that bans hate preachers from entering the EU and also deports their sympathisers.'[92] Furthermore, Al-Qadri has called for a State regulation of international funding for the construction of mosques in Ireland, alleging what he perceives as the influence of Wahabi Islam in the case of one such proposed development in Blanchardstown in Dublin.[93]

Sheikh Al-Qadri has called on the Irish State to support Ireland's Muslim communities by working with and providing support for those Islamic Centres whose perspectives align with that of the State. By working together with these officially approved bodies, common standards can be established across

89 Limerick Civic Trust, 'Autumn Lecture Series 2017, Sheikh Dr Umar Al-Qadri discusses Immigration and Integration' <https://www.youtube.com/watch?v=IxdvWdcv2bE&t=1945s> accessed 28 March 2018.

90 Limerick Civic Trust (n 89).

91 Brian Hutton, 'Berlin-style terror attack in Ireland 'cannot be ruled out,' Enda Kenny warns' *Irish Independent* (Dublin, 24 December 2016).

92 Ralph Riegel, 'As Muslims, it is our duty to speak up against extremists;' *Irish Independent* (25 May 2017).

93 Limerick Civic Trust (n 89); As a point of note, the proposed new mosque and community centre in Balnchardstown will be funded by Dr Taufiq Al Sattar, and Irish based neuro-surgeon, drawing from his own private resources, donations from the public in the UK city of Leicester, where Dr Al-Sattar's wife and children tragically died, as well as through fund raising initiatives with medical students in Pakistan and Saudi Arabia for more see: Jack Power, 'Plans submitted for large mosque centre in Blanchardstown' *The Irish Times* (Dublin, 2 September 2018) <https://www.irishtimes.com/news/ireland/irish-news/plans-submitted-for-large-mosque-centre-in-blanchardstown-1.3206484?mode=sample&auth-failed=1&pw-+origin=https%3A%2F%2Fwww.irishtimes.com%2Fnews%2Fireland%2Firish-news%2Fplans-submitted-for-large-mosque-centre-in-blanchardstown-1.3206484> accessed 27 March 2018.

Islamic organisations which will have to be met if they are to receive State support. In doing so, such initiatives on the part of the State would eliminate foreign influences on Islam in Ireland according to Al-Qadri.[94]

9.3 *FGM*

The early part of 2018 witnessed a range of responses from within Muslim communities come to the fore in response to the comments made by a leading figure of Islam in Ireland on the topic of FGM. Appearing on national television in February 2018, Dr Ali Selim, a theologian at the Islamic Cultural Centre of Ireland in Clonskeagh, Dublin addressed the issue of FGM. The programme was engaging with the topic of FGM following the Dublin launch of an international campaign to eradicate the practice worldwide. Speaking on the programme Dr Selim stated, inter alia:

> I'm not an advocate of female genital mutilation but I am an advocate of female circumcision. We see female circumcision in the same way we see male circumcision. It might be needed for one person and not another, and it has to be done by a doctor and practiced in a safe environment.[95]

Dr Selim continued:

> The same medical reason that would justify male circumcision would be the same for females. It is not an obligation, but it should be allowed by law if needed and a medical doctor can decide if it is needed or not.

Addressing the question of whether or not FGM was justified in Islam, Dr Selim replied: '… If a doctor advises it is needed, then it has to be done. Religion says it does not have to be practiced, our religion says ask the people of knowledge.'

Dr Selim's comments were met with a range of dissenting voices both from within and without Muslim communities in Ireland. Imam of the Ahmadiyya mosque in Galway, Ibrahim Noonan stated that 'FGM has nothing to do with Islam' urging Dr Selim to be more careful in making statements such as the above.[96] Sheikh Dr Umar Al-Qadri declared a fatwa against FGM and called 'on all Muslims to speak against this practice, stop it if they are aware of its

94 Limerick Civic Trust (n 89).

95 Kathy Armstrong, 'Female circumcision "should be allowed by law" – member of Ireland's Islamic Cultural Centre' *Irish Independent* (Dublin, 9 February 2018); Aine McMahon, 'Leading Muslim figure Ali Selim backs female circumcision' *The Irish Times* (Dublin, 8 February 2018).

96 Ibrahim Noonan, 'FGM is nothing to do with Islam,' Letters and Editorial Comment, *Irish Independent* (Dublin, 15 February 2018).

occurrence, and report any knowledge of it to the authorities.'[97] Ifrah Ahmed, the Irish-Somali Muslim woman behind the campaign to eradicate FGM, joined Sheikh Al-Qadri in calling for a review of Dr Selim's position in the ICCI and Trinity College Dublin while also calling on Islamic leaders to speak out and say: 'this has nothing to do with Islam and nothing to do with religion.'[98]

Perhaps more interesting than the response from Sheikh Dr Umar Al-Qadri was that of Muslim medical professionals in Ireland who spoke out against Dr Selim's opinion on FGM. Consultant neonatologist Prof Afif El-Khuffash responded by stating that the perspective of Dr Selim on FGM was not that of the majority of Muslims before going on to note that he would not attend the mosque in Clonskeagh while these views were supported.[99] Consultant pediatrician Prof Farhana Sharif, referred to FGM as a 'mutilating procedure' without any 'medical justification.' Similarly, consultant pediatrician Dr Rizwan Khan, stated that there is no difference between FGM and female circumcision, before going on to note that the physical and psychological impacts of FGM are profound for women.[100]

In the days following his television appearance, Dr Selim addressed his earlier comments. Stating to the media that: 'I condemn FGM and I condemn circumcision that gives the same meaning as FGM. I totally apologise for the confusion.' Dr Selim reiterated that he is not a medical professional and that his understanding of the issue is that of a 'layman in this field, and hence contributed to this confusion.'[101] Dr Selim also stated: 'Female genital mutilation (FGM) means the total or partial distortion of female genitals for non-medical reasons, I am 100 per cent against that ... I condemn it in the strongest terms.'[102]

10 Conclusion

This chapter has set the stage for the discussions to follow. An important point to take away from what is stated above is that, while discussing the faith of

97 Patsy McGarry, 'Dublin imam issues fatwa against female genital mutilation; Leading obstetrician calls on all religious leaders, including the Pope to support the ban' *The Irish Times* (Dublin, 13 February 2018).

98 McGarry (n 97).

99 Susan Mitchell, 'Mosque leaders condoning "criminal" act, says obstetricians' institute' *The Sunday Business Post* (Dublin, 10 February 2018).

100 Sorcha Pollak, 'Comments on female circumcision "distorted",' *The Irish Times* (Dublin, 13 February 2018).

101 P. McGarry, 'Muslim academic apologises for "confusion" over FGM comments,' *The Irish Times* (19 February 2018).

102 S. Pollak (n 100).

Islam, the issues elaborated upon above impact upon Muslim men, women and children. Discussions about the religion of Islam in Ireland should not be just about the Islamic religion, which of course needs to be provided for, but instead position the needs of Muslim men, women and children as people, as Irish citizens or otherwise to the fore. There are a range of backgrounds, and perspectives within the communities which make the notion of a 'homogenous' Muslim community impractical. As has been presented above, Muslim communities are a diverse, vibrant part of twenty-first century Irish society. The following chapters will engage in more detail, and from a legal perspective, on some of issues raised above, as well as others, that impact upon Ireland's Muslim communities today.

Bibliography

Ahlul Bayt Islamic Centre, 'Homepage' <http://homepage.tinet.ie/~ahlulbyteassociation/> accessed 23 March 2018.

Anderson, N., 'There are at least 150 extremists here who see Ireland as a soft touch'; Nicola Anderson talks to a young Muslim woman about how she be-came deradicalised after being a jihadi wife' *Irish Independent* (Dublin, 10 June, 2017).

Carr, J., *Experiences of Islamophobia: Living with racism in the neoliberal era* (Routledge 2016).

Carr, J., 'Islamophobia in Dublin: Experiences and How to Respond (Immigrant Council of Ireland 2016).

Carr, J., 'Ireland 2016' European Islamophobia Report (SETA 2017) <http://www.islamophobiaeurope.com/wp-content/uploads/2017/03/IRELAND.pdf> accessed 22 March 2018.

Carr, J., 'Ireland 2017' European Islamophobia Report <http://www.islamophobiaeurope.com/wp-content/uploads/2018/04/Ireland.pdf> accessed 6 November 2018.

Carr, J. 'Ireland' in Scharbrodt, O., Akgönül, S., Alibašić, A., Nielsen, J.S., Račius, E., (eds.) *Yearbook of Muslims in Europe*, Volume 8 (Brill, Leiden, 2017).

Carr, J., 'Ireland' in Scharbrodt, O., Akgönül, S., Alibašić, A., Nielsen, J.S., Račius, E., (eds.) *Yearbook of Muslims in Europe*, Volume 9 (Brill, Leiden, 2018).

Central Statistics Office, 'Statistical Tables: Profile Educations, Ethnicity, and Irish Traveller Tables' <http://www.cso.ie/en/media/csoie/census/documents/census2011profile7/Profile_7_Education_Ethnicity_and_Irish_Traveller_Tables_and_appendices.pdfaccessed> accessed 23 March 2018.

Central Statistics Office, 'Statbank' <http://www.cso.ie/px/pxeirestat/Statire/SelectVarVal/Define.asp?maintable=E8058&PLanguage=0>accessed 27 March 2018.

Department of Justice, 'The Migrant Integration Strategy: A Blueprint for the Future' (Department of Justice 2017) <http://www.justice.ie/en/JELR/Migrant_Integration_Strategy_English.pdf/Files/Migrant_Integration_Strategy_English.pdf> accessed 27 March 2018.

European Islamophobia Report, 'Homepage' <http://www.islamophobiaeurope.com/> accessed 23 March 2018.

Fanning, B., *Migration and the Making of Ireland* (University College Dublin Press 2018).

Fegan, J., 'Islam is Ireland's third largest religion' *Irish Examiner* (7 June 2017) <https://www.irishexaminer.com/ireland/islam-is-irelands-third-largest-religion-451879.html> accessed 23 March 2018.

Flynn, K., 'Understanding Islam in Ireland' (2006) 17(2) Islam and Christian-Muslim Relations (2006) 17(2).

Hope Not Hate, 'A Short History of Pegida' <https://www.hopenothate.org.uk/research/investigations/pegida-uk/a-short-history/> accessed 24 March 2018.

Hutton, B., 'Berlin-style terror attack in Ireland 'cannot be ruled out' Enda Kenny warns,' *Irish Independent,* (Dublin, 24 December 2016).

Irish, Examiner, 'Assessing jihadist levels: optimism will not stop terror attack;' *Irish Examiner* (Cork, 30 August 2017).

Irish Muslim Peace and Integration Council, 'Homepage' <http://impic.ie/> accessed 23 March 2018.

Irish Sufi Foundation, 'Facebook page' <https://business.facebook.com/IrishSufi/> accessed 23 March 2018.

Islamic Cultural Centre of Ireland, 'About Us' <https://islamireland.ie/about/about-icci/> accessed 24 March 2018.

Kerry Islamic Outreach, 'Homepage' <http://www.kerryislamicoutreach.org/mission.html> accessed 27 March 2018.

Khan, A.H., Early Muslim Organisations and Mosques in Ireland' in Scharbrodt, O., Sakaranaho, T., Khan, A.H., Shanneik, Y., and Ibrahim, V., (eds.) *Muslims in Ireland: Past and Present* (Edinburgh University Press 2015).

Limerick Civic Trust, 'Autumn Lecture Series 2017, Sheikh Dr Umar Al-Qadri discusses Immigration and Integration' <https://www.youtube.com/watch?v=IxdvWdcv2bE&t=1945s> accessed 28 March 2018.

McGarry, P., 'What is it like to grow up Muslim in Ireland?' *The Irish Times* (Dublin, 28 January 2017) <https://www.irishtimes.com/news/social-affairs/religion-and-beliefs/what-is-it-like-to-grow-up-muslim-in-ireland-1.2949144> accessed 27 March 2018.

McGarry, P., 'Muslim academic apologises for "confusion" over fgm comments' *The Irish Times* (Dublin, 19 February 2018).

McQuinn, C., and Armstrong, K., 'We will take any necessary action – Taoiseach distances himself from FG councillor's comments on Islam and refugees' *Irish Independent* (Dublin, 7 September 2017).

Meagher, J., 'Muslims in Ireland: a growing community that's keen for more integration' *Irish Independent* (Dublin, 22 April 2017).

Muslim Association of Ireland <http://maionline.ie/>accessed 23 March 2018.

Muslim Sisters of Éire, 'Homepage' <http://msoe.ie/> accessed 27 March 2018.

O'Neill, K., 'Muslims in Ireland have no tolerance for radicals' *Irish Daily Mail* (Dublin, 8 June 2017).

O'Neill, K., and Bracken, A., 'The Irish Voice of Islamist Fanatics; Hard line Muslim convert spouts hate speech online and is 'engaging' with mosque youths. London Terror Aftermath: The Irish fanatic defending jihad' *Irish Daily Mail* (Dublin, 7th June 2017).

Pollak, S., 'Greater effort needed to ensure inclusion of Irish Muslims, group hears' *The Irish Times* (Dublin, 19 January 2017).

Pollak, S., 'Protestors warn ECJ ruling to further alienate Muslim women' *The Irish Times* (Dublin, 21 March 2017) <https://www.irishtimes.com/news/social-affairs/protesters-warn-ecj-ruling-to-further-alienate-muslim-women-1.3019176> accessed 27 March 2018.

Pollak, S., and Edwards, E., 'Hate crime legislation needed 'as matter of urgency,' *The Irish Times* (Dublin, 23 March 2017) <https://www.irishtimes.com/news/social-affairs/hate-crime-legislation-needed-as-matter-of-urgency-1.3022528> accessed 27 March 2018.

Power, J., 'Plans submitted for large mosque centre in Blanchardstown' *The Irish Times* (Dublin, 2 September 2017) <https://www.irishtimes.com/news/ireland/irish-news/plans-submitted-for-large-mosque-centre-in-blanchardstown-1.3206484?mode=sample&auth-failed=1&pw-+origin=https%3A%2F%2Fwww.irishtimes.com%2Fnews%2Fireland%2Firish-news%2Fplans-submitted-for-large-mosque-centre-in-blanchardstown-1.3206484> accessed 23 March 2018.

Riegel, R., 'As Muslims, it is our duty to speak up against extremists' *Irish Independent* (Dublin, 25 May 2017).

Sakaranaho, T., *Religious Freedom, Multiculturalism, Islam: Cross-reading Finland and Ireland* (Brill 2006).

Scharbrodt, O., Sakaranaho, T., Khan, A.H., Shanneik, Y., and Ibrahim, V., (eds.) *Muslims in Ireland: Past and Present* (Edinburgh University Press 2015).

Scharbrodt, O., 'Muslim immigration to the Republic of Ireland: trajectories and dynamics since World War II' (2012) 47(1) Éire-Ireland.

Sunday Independent (2017) 'Islam does not accept any form of terrorism' says Sheikh Halawa;' *Sunday Independent* (Dublin, 11 June 2017).

CHAPTER 5

The Accommodation of Islam in the Irish Workplace, Classroom and Hospital

Claire Hogan

Introduction

The aim of this article is to examine the current level of accommodation of Islam in Irish education, employment and healthcare law.

At the outset, it should be noted that the Irish legal system is very receptive towards religion. The Constitution is replete with references to God and Christianity. For example, the Preamble contains the line, 'Humbly acknowledging all our obligations to our Divine Lord, Jesus Christ, Who sustained our fathers through centuries of trial', and Article 44.1 provides: 'The State acknowledges that the homage of public worship is due to Almighty God. It shall hold His Name in reverence, and shall respect and honour religion'.

In the landmark case of *Quinn's Supermarket v Attorney General*, it was recognised by Walsh J that 'Our Constitution reflects a firm conviction that we are religious people'.[1] In this case, a tension between two articles of the Constitution was identified. Article 44.2.1° of the Irish Constitution provides: 'Freedom of conscience and the free profession and practice of religion are, subject to public order and morality, guaranteed to every citizen'. The Constitution also forbids the State from discriminating on religious grounds (Article 44.2.3°). The Court recognised that discrimination in the sense of recognising and catering for different religious needs may be necessary in order to guarantee free practice. Therefore, Walsh J held that distinctions or discriminations made between people in order to uphold the guarantee of the free profession and practice of religion would not be unconstitutional. Furthermore, it was held that laws of general application may even require adjustment in order to cater for the needs of religious people.

The parameters of this duty on the State are unclear, and in a society with a religious landscape that is markedly different to that of the *Quinn's Supermarket* era, the legal implications of this Supreme Court authority are more relevant than ever. How will Irish courts decide a case where a language

1 [1972] IR 1 (SC), 23. Hereafter referred to as *Quinn's Supermarket*.

 | DOI:10.1163/9789004398252_006

support teacher claims the right to wear a *niqab* (veil covering the face) in the classroom?[2] How will they deal with the objections of a parent to their daughter's participation in mixed swimming lessons?[3] What of Muslim parents who claim damages from a hospital in respect of their son's disabilities, in circumstances where the father, for religious reasons of modesty, refused the presence in the delivery room of a male doctor who wished to carry out certain tests?[4]

Part 1 of this article will discuss employment law, Part 2 will analyse education and Part 3 will examine healthcare law. In Part 4, conclusions will be discussed.

1 The Accommodation of Islam in Irish Employment Law

Ireland has experienced some employment litigation centring on claims made by members of minority faiths, including Islam. The litigation has thus far not involved constitutional challenges, and instead has consisted of cases taken under employment legislation designed to protect employees.

1.1 *The Unfair Dismissals Acts 1977–2015 and the Employment Equality Acts 1998–2015*

Section 6(2)(b) of the Unfair Dismissals Act 1977 (as amended by the Unfair Dismissals (Amendment) Act 1993) provides that a dismissal is deemed unfair if it results wholly or mainly from the 'religious or political opinions of the employee'.

The Employment Equality Act 1998 was a far-reaching piece of legislation prohibiting discrimination in the workplace on nine substantive grounds, including, most relevantly for present purposes, the religious ground (see Section 6(2)).

Some changes were made to the 1998 Act by the Equality Act 2004, which was introduced to transpose, inter alia, the Employment Equality and Racial Equality Directives, a pair of far-reaching EU anti-discrimination directives.[5]

2 *Azmi v Kirklees Metropolitan Borough Council* [2007] ICR 1154.

3 *Osmanoğlu and Kocabaş v Switzerland*, [2017] ECHR 14.

4 'Muslims fined for refusing male doctor at childbirth' 11 June 2008, http://www.expatica.com/fr/news/local_news/French-Muslims-fined-for-refusing-male-doctor-at-childbirth-.html, accessed 31 January 2018.

5 Council Directive 2000/78/EC of 27 November 2000 establishing a general framework for equal treatment in employment and occupation, OJ 2000 L303/16, and Council Directive 2000/43/EC of 29 June 2000 implementing the principle of equal treatment between persons irrespective of racial or ethnic origin, OJ L 180/22.

Successive amendments to the 1998 Act mean that the legislation is now referred to as the Employment Equality Acts 1998–2015. While it is generally considered that the constitutional guarantees and injunctions relating to religious freedom and equality are applicable only to the State, this equality legislation is also applicable to parties in private law relationships, and thus revolutionised the rights and responsibilities of all in this jurisdiction.

Section 2(1) provides that 'religious belief' includes religious background or outlook. Section 6(2)(e) defines discrimination 'on the religion ground' as differential treatment based on the fact that one person 'has a different religious belief from the other, or that one has a religious belief and the other has not'. The legislation is wide in scope, prohibiting direct and indirect discrimination in a variety of areas relevant to employment in both the public and private sectors. Section 8 prohibits discrimination by employers with regard to access to employment, conditions of employment, training or experience for or in relation to employment, promotion or re-grading, or classification of posts. The Acts also apply to collective agreements, equal pay, advertising and dismissal.

Section 6(1)(a) of the Acts provides that discrimination occurs where 'a person is treated less favourably than another person is, has been or would be treated in a comparable situation' on any of the discrimination grounds, which either exists, existed but no longer exists, may exist in the future, or is imputed to the person concerned. Although not labelled as such, this discrimination corresponds to the notion of 'direct discrimination'.

There is no general objective justification for direct discrimination. Section 85A(1) places the burden of proof on the respondent (the employer etc). Therefore, if a complainant establishes facts from which it may be presumed that discrimination has occurred, then the onus is on the respondent to prove that discrimination did not occur.

Section 31 provides that indirect discrimination will be held to occur where an apparently neutral provision puts persons at a 'particular disadvantage' compared to other persons (of a differing religious belief or none). In terms of justification for indirect discrimination, a provision must be 'objectively justified by a legitimate aim and the means of achieving that aim are appropriate and necessary'.

The Acts prohibit harassment, defined in Section 14(A)(7) as 'any form of unwanted conduct related to any of the discriminatory grounds'. Victimisation is also prohibited, and Section 74(2) defines this as dismissal or other adverse treatment of an employee by his or her employer occurring as a reaction to taking action around the enforcement of equality rights set out in the legislation.

It is important to note the following exemptions from discrimination in the Acts. Section 37(2) provides an exemption where a religious characteristic constitutes a genuine and determining occupational requirement:

> (2)For the purposes of this Part a difference of treatment which is based on a characteristic related to any of the discriminatory grounds (except the gender ground) shall not constitute discrimination where, by reason of the particular occupational activities concerned or of the context in which they are carried out–
>
> (a)the characteristic constitutes a genuine and determining occupational requirement, and
>
> (b)the objective is legitimate and the requirement proportionate.`

1.2 *Decisions under the Employment Legislation*

Employment legislation provides extensive protection from discrimination in employment for those from minority faiths, such as Islam. Cases are litigated in the Workplace Relations Commission (WRC).[6] From an analysis of decisions based on the equality legislation, it appears that many of the cases concerning the religion ground have been founded on direct discrimination, harassment and victimisation. Furthermore, the religion ground is usually combined with the race ground.

For example, in *Tsourova v Icon Clinical Research*,[7] Ms Tsourova claimed that her employer directly discriminated against her on the grounds of religion and race in relation to her conditions of employment. She also claimed that she was victimised. Among the allegations relating to religion, the employee claimed that when invited to socialise with her colleagues, she declined and said that as a Muslim, she could not drink or smoke. After this, she stated felt a change in attitude from her colleagues. She alleged that she received a negative reaction from fellow employees when she put a Muslim planner at her work space, and also when she fasted during *Ramadan*. Finally, she submitted that she had difficulties in getting a half-day for the *Eid* festival. Ultimately, the Equality Officer who heard the case found that there were many inconsistencies and insufficiencies in the complainant's evidence. Accordingly, she failed to establish a prima facie case of direct discrimination, and of victimisation.[8]

6 The discussion names other fora which prior to 1 October 2015 had jurisdiction to hear employment disputes, as well as appeal courts.

7 DEC-E2005/027.

8 The decision was affirmed by the Labour Court in the subsequent appeal; EDA071, 18 January 2007.

As another example, the case of *Ahmed v ICTS*[9] involved a black African Muslim who applied for a job as a security officer at Dublin Airport and alleged that the interviewer asked him several discriminatory questions; including asking almost immediately whether he was a Muslim, and whether he remembered the Lockerbie tragedy. The employer denied this version of events. The Equality Officer held that a prima facie case of discrimination in selection for employment had not been established on the facts, but made a number of non-binding recommendations to the employer to ensure fair and transparent selection procedures.

On the issue of time off for religious observance, in February 2016 the Employment Appeals Tribunal (EAT) decided a case concerning a Muslim man who brought an action against his Co Mayo employer when he was dismissed after taking a three week holiday to go to Mecca for the Hajj pilgrimage.[10] A Rights Commissioner upheld Mr Zulfaqar Ali's claim for unfair dismissal. However, the EAT overturned the Rights Commissioner's ruling, and found that Mr Ali left his work in October 2012 without permission to go to the Hajj, and that this was tantamount to gross misconduct. In its determination, the EAT accepted that while Mr Ali 'felt a religious duty to attend the Hajj, he had booked this trip without consulting his employer', and he had been been fully advised of the consequences of taking unauthorised leave. This boiled down to a simple case of unauthorised leave taking, and did not squarely raise the issue of accommodation of religion in the employment context.

As regards religious dress, there are two instances of Muslim headscarf cases. In 2005, a Dublin amusement arcade receptionist was fired after she told her employer she intended to wear a Muslim headscarf at work and wanted a prayer room. She was awarded €6,160 compensation for unfair dismissal by the EAT.[11] The Tribunal found that the dismissal of the employee over the phone was 'wholly in breach of fair procedures and natural justice'. However, it was unanimously decided that the reason for the dismissal was not her intention to wear a *hijab* at work or her demand for a prayer room, but the manner in which this information and request was presented to her employer. Essentially, there were time-keeping and behavioural problems prior to the request. The employee was given a written final warning about her behaviour after taking time off at Christmas 2003 to go on holiday. When the employee returned after this holiday, she had a heated phone call with the employer at which point she informed her she would be wearing the *hijab* to work and that she wanted a

9 DEC-E2003-047.

10 UD463/2014, PW55/2014.

11 See Andrew Bushe, 'Tribunal awards Muslim woman €6,160' *The Irish Times*, 6 October 2005.

prayer room. The employer suggested the woman did not like the contents of the warning letter and was blackmailing her with demands about her religion. In conclusion, although the case involved aspects of expression of Islam, these were not central to the case. The finding of unfair dismissal rested on the manner in which the employee was dismissed over the phone.

In 2012, it was reported that the case of a former Dunnes Stores sales assistant, Loreta Tavoraite, who sued the company for unfair dismissal as she claimed she was not permitted to wear a *hijab* at work, was settled.[12] Thus unfortunately no determination issued. The EAT had heard that Dunnes Stores staff wore a standard uniform of a blouse, trousers or a skirt, and a type of cardigan, and that no alteration to the style of the uniform was allowed.

The intertwining of religion in Irish public law is a fact that can have an impact on cases. In August 2007, a member of the Sikh community stated that he would not take up his post in the Garda Reserve, having been informed that he could not wear his turban as part of the uniform. The Irish Sikh Council criticised the decision and stated that police forces in the UK and the US permitted the wearing of turbans. The Garda Press Office defended the move, stating that An Garda Síochána has, historically, been seen as providing an impartial police service, and that accommodating variations to the standard uniform would affect that traditional stance and image.[13]

It is arguable that An Garda Síochána has a dubious claim to religious neutrality. The force regularly organises Catholic Masses and in terms of uniform, the Garda badge itself reflects Celtic Christianity, with four decorative circles positioned at each quadrant resembling a cross.

A case was subsequently taken to Court by the person concerned. However, the case was dismissed as members of the Garda Reserve are not 'employees' within the meaning of the Employment Equality Acts 1998–2015 and therefore it was held that the legislation did not apply.[14] An opportunity for a judicial pronouncement on religion in employment was lost on this occasion.

As a recent indication of how the State, as employer, is prepared to accommodate the expression of faith in the workplace from those outside of the Catholic faith, the turban controversy sets a precedent of low-level accommodation.

12 Barry Roche, 'Dunnes Stores case over hijab is settled' *The Irish Times*, 14 November 2012.

13 Patsy McGarry, 'Garda defends its policy on wearing of religious dress' *The Irish Times*, 3 September 2007.

14 *Ravinder Singh Oberoi v The Commissioner of An Garda Síochána* [2013] IEHC 267.

1.3 *Future Employment Accommodation Scenarios*

Ireland has not had a significant amount of litigation on uniform regulations, whereas this area has generated extensive litigation in other jurisdictions such as England and Wales, as well as in supranational courts such as the European Court of Justice (ECJ).[15]

Uniform regulations imposed by Irish employers, such as a requirement that one's head remain uncovered, or requirements regarding working hours may be characterised as examples of prima facie indirect discrimination contrary to Section 31 of the Employment Equality Acts 1998–2015. If the employee were to find that a uniform or working hour requirement posed a 'particular disadvantage', the employer will have indirectly discriminated unless the requirement can be objectively justified by a legitimate aim, and the means of achieving that aim are appropriate and necessary.

The employer might seek to rely on the Section 37(2) exemption under the Acts, and might argue that 'by reason of the particular occupational activities concerned or of the context in which they are carried out', it is a 'genuine and determining occupational requirement' for employees not to wear headscarves, or to take time off for worship. Again, the objective must be legitimate and the requirement proportionate.

Legal principles have not yet been developed, and we can only await future decisions with interest.

2 The Accommodation of Islam in Irish Education Law

Irish schools present particular challenges for the accommodation of Islam, as there is a monopoly enjoyed by the Catholic Church in education provision. The vast majority of primary or national schools are privately owned by religious denominations, but the Irish State funds and supervises the system of education overall, through the Department of Education and Skills. The system is best described as a State-aided system of education. Statistics for the 2016/2017 school year show that approximately 89% of primary schools are

15 The ECJ recently provided nuanced rulings on headscarf bans in employment for the first time in the cases of *Achbita v G4S Secure Solutions NV* and *Bougnaoui v Micropole SA*, Cases C-157/15 and C-188/15, judgments of 14 March 2017. See also *Dahlab v Switzerland* [2001] ECHR 899, in which the European Court of Human Rights did not find an unjustified or illegitimate interference with the Article 9 freedom of religion right of a Swiss teacher who was banned from wearing a headscarf in the classroom.

Roman Catholic in ethos.[16] A process of divestment of patronage is occurring, but at a slow pace.

There are two Muslim primary schools, both of which are located in Dublin.[17] There are no Muslim secondary schools. It is clear that as a matter of geographical necessity, many Muslim students outside of Dublin will be compelled to attend a school which is likely to be a Catholic one. The accommodation of these students in such schools is therefore the issue which engages us here.

2.1 *The Impact on the Minority of the Ethos of the Majority*

School ethos can be broadly defined as the set of values that informs all aspects of school life. The case of *Campaign to Separate Church and State v Minister for Education* was a key Supreme Court case on the issue of religion and education.[18] The decision recognised the legitimacy of a strong denominational ethos in schools. Article 44.2.4° of the Constitution guarantees the right of a child not to have to attend *religious instruction* at a publicly funded school. The Court noted this right of the child. However, Article 42.2 of the Constitution contemplates children receiving *religious education* in schools recognised or established by the State but in accordance with the wishes of the parents. The judge deduced from these provisions that:

> The Constitution therefore distinguishes between religious 'education' and religious 'instruction' – the former being the much wider term. A child who attends a school run by a religious denomination different from his own may have a constitutional right not to attend religious instruction at that school but the Constitution cannot protect him from being influenced, to some degree, by the religious 'ethos' of the school. A religious denomination is not obliged to change the general atmosphere of its school merely to accommodate a child of a different religious persuasion who wishes to attend that school.[19]

---

16 https://www.education.ie/en/Publications/Statistics/Data-on-Individual-Schools/, accessed 31 January 2018.

17 Sakaranaho notes that Muslims in Ireland have 'managed very smoothly in the establishment of their own national schools, which function in accordance with the Islamic ethos, while adapting to the requirements of the Irish educational system'. Tuula Sakaranaho, *Religious Freedom, Multiculturalism, Islam: Cross-reading Finland and Ireland* (Brill, 2006) 400.

18 [1998] 3 IR 321 (SC). Hereafter referred to as the *Campaign* case.

19 ibid 357–358.

Thus, parents who wish to send their children to denominational schools have a right to religious education and are not obliged to 'settle merely for religious instruction'.[20] It is extremely disappointing that this case did not refer to the protection of minorities, and consider the impact of the religious ethos on the child of a different faith or none.[21]

It is important to note that a Catholic ethos in schools may not necessarily be inimical to Islam. Indeed, the Catholic Schools Partnership professes a model of inclusion:

> Children of other faiths should be invited but not obliged to attend all Catholic religious celebrations in the school. Individual children, with parental consent, can be invited to read special prayers/texts promoting core values such as respect and tolerance, which are common to many faith groups. Parents may decide to excuse their child from school for the duration of any of these celebrations. Appropriate procedures should be in place to facilitate any such request e.g. written notification to the principal teacher. A Catholic school, in a spirit of inclusivity, could incorporate an 'inter-religious' element to these celebrations, where appropriate, without compromising its core values. Consideration may need to be given to the timing of events. All staff should be familiar with the policy and procedures, thereby enabling them to respond positively to parental requests and concerns as necessary.[22]

On the particular issue of the *hijab*, which shall be discussed in greater detail in the next section, schools appear to be permitting Muslim girls to wear the garment, and there has been no litigation to date involving a ban. However, it is questionable as to whether the accommodation of Muslim students should depend on the willingness and capability of the Catholic ethos to embrace students of other faiths. It is clear that the potential for limited or no

20 ibid 358.

21 The *Campaign* judgment was delivered at a time when immigration and population diversity was a novel phenomenon. Glendenning notes that the Supreme Court did not impose any limitations on worship, preparation for the sacraments, or the saying of prayers, which might be regarded as a lack of respect for the freedom of religion principle for religious minorities. Dympna Glendenning, *Religion, Education and the Law* (Tottel, 2008) [9.040].

22 *Catholic Primary Schools in a Changing Ireland Sharing Good Practice on Inclusion of All Pupils* (2015) 27. See also the Irish Catholic Bishops' Conference 2007 publication, *Catholic Primary Schools: A Policy for Provision into the Future* [4.3]: 'The Catholic school welcomes diversity and strives for inclusivity. It is open to people of other denominations and other faiths, welcomes them into its community and respects their beliefs…'.

accommodation exists. There is ample legal scope and protection for schools to decide that a particular Islamic requirement or practice does not cohere with the prevailing ethos, and so to ban it. Moreover, there has been some testimony from Muslim students of a sense of exclusion and pressure resulting from exposure to the Catholic ethos.[23]

Furthermore, it appears that the Catholic Church is keen to make its schools more distinctively Catholic. Most Catholic schools now contain many children who are not from families who are traditional practicing Catholics. Archbishop Diarmuid Martin has stated that the current near monopoly is 'in many ways detrimental to the possibility of maintaining a true Catholic identity in Catholic schools' and that while Catholic schools should be open to all, they should have a 'real Catholic ethos'.[24] It is appropriate in principle that the Catholic Church seeks to ensure that its mission statement is delivered. However, when the lack of choice of an alternative school enters the equation, concerns relating to discrimination are heightened. A new initiative to celebrate annually 'Catholic Schools Week' began in 2009. One can only guess as to the sense of exclusion the Muslim primary or secondary student feels when the suggested prayers and activities are held.[25]

Furthermore, the Church has railed against changes brought in by the Government to change the status quo. As a first example, for many years, Rule 68 of the Rules for National Schools 1965 copper fastened the denominational character of the Irish national school system, providing for an integrated curriculum in the following manner:

> Of all parts of the school curriculum, religious instruction is by far the most important ... Religious instruction is, therefore, a fundamental part of the school course and a religious spirit should inform and vivify the whole work of the school.

Rule 68 was abolished by the Minister for Education and Skills Jan O'Sullivan in January 2016, following years of disquiet and protest about its existence amongst a sizeable cohort of the public. The Bishops' Council for Education

---

23 Kate Holmquist, 'Modern Ireland: meet the families' *The Irish Times*, 27 February 2010.

24 Genevieve Carbery, 'Catholic control of schooling not tenable, says archbishop' *The Irish Times*, 17 June 2009. See also Sarah Burns, 'Church has 'stubborn reluctance' on school divestment, Martin says' *The Irish Times*, 10 July 2017, where it was reported Martin said: 'The risk now looms large that effectively it will become more and more difficult to maintain a true Catholic ethos in Catholic schools'.

25 For resources to be used in schools see https://www.catholicschools.ie/resources-for-use-in-catholic-schools/, accessed 31 January 2018.

immediately responded to the news by restating the entitlement to an all-permeating ethos:

> Faith schools exist because there are parents who wish to have their children educated in accordance with their religious convictions. If the ethos of these schools is undermined then the rights of such parents are compromised. We wish to assure parents that the Minister's announcement does not alter the ethos of Catholic schools and that this ethos will continue to find expression in all aspects of the life of the school.[26]

The second example of resistance to change concerns the abolition of the so-called 'baptism barrier'. Section 7(2) of the Equal Status Acts 2000–2015 provides that an educational establishment shall not discriminate in relation to the admission of a student; his or her access to any course, facility or benefit provided by the establishment; any other term or condition of participation in the establishment by a student; or the expulsion of a student from the establishment or any other sanction against the student. However, Section 7(3)(c) of the Acts permitted preferential admissions policies for schools controlled by religious denominations. Essentially, this provision allowed for admissions policies which give preference to those who have been baptised as members of the Catholic Church. The law was amended and the exception abolished with the enactment of the Education (Admissions to Schools) Act 2018. The Catholic Primary Schools Management Association stated that the Minister's plan was part of a 'secularisation agenda aimed mainly at the Catholic Church', and various other Catholic organisations objected and raised the possibility of legal action.[27]

2.2 *Religious Symbols*

In May 2008, it emerged that the principal of a secondary school in the town of Gorey in County Wexford, had sought advice from the Department of Education following the request from a Muslim couple that their daughter be permitted to wear her *hijab* in school. In the face of mounting pressure for the Department to agree on a position on the headscarf, the Minister announced a review of school dress codes as part of an intercultural education strategy.[28]

26 https://www.catholicbishops.ie/2016/01/28/statement-from-the-bishops-council-for-education-in-response-to-ministers-rescinding-of-rule-68/, accessed 31 January 2018.

27 Carl O'Brien, 'Catholic groups warn of legal action over 'Baptism barrier' removal' *The Irish Times*, 3 January 2018.

28 Ruadhán Mac Cormaic, 'O'Keefe says review will look at *hijab* policy' *The Irish Times*, 20 May 2008.

The Government recommendations on school uniform policy, which were issued in September 2008, are as follows:

1. The current system, whereby schools decide their uniform policy at a local level, is reasonable, works and should be maintained.
2. In this context, no school uniform policy should act in such a way that it, in effect, excludes students of a particular religious background from seeking enrolment or continuing their enrolment in a school. However, this statement does not recommend the wearing of clothing in the classroom which obscures a facial view and creates an artificial barrier between pupil and teacher. Such clothing hinders proper communication.
3. Schools, when drawing up uniform policy, should consult widely in the school community.[29]

The Report concluded that despite the generally satisfactory position regarding admission of girls who wear the *hijab* to schools, each school should examine its policy to ensure that the approach it takes does not operate to exclude such pupils. It was stated that where schools have permitted the wearing of the *hijab*, in a color which is similar to the ordinary school uniform, no problems have been encountered, and that the important consideration was that all parties involved are clearly aware of the position of the school.[30]

The Government's decision was welcomed by all the main teacher unions, but criticised by the Irish Council for Civil Liberties (ICCL), which stated that Ministers had abrogated their own responsibility to ensure that education is provided in a non-discriminatory way, leaving the decision-making onus on school principals; in effect the Report amounted to 'a policy not to have a policy'.[31]

The complete delegation of uniform policy to schools has led to a lack of certainty, and in light of the headscarf cases which have been litigated elsewhere in Europe,[32] it is to be regretted that the government did not clarify the scope of discretion conferred on schools. However, it should be noted that there have been no disputes which have escalated to litigation.

---

29 *Report by the Minister for Integration, Conor Lenihan TD, on the need for a Guidance Note to Schools when reviewing their policies on School Uniforms*, http://www.sdpi.ie/other_des_publications/DES_school_uniform_policy_recommendations.doc, accessed 31 January 2018.

30 ibid [2.6].

31 Ruadhán Mac Cormaic, 'No directive on *hijabs* in classroom to be issued' *The Irish Times*, 24 September 2008.

32 See generally Dominick McGoldrick, *Human Rights and Religion: The Islamic Headscarf Debate in Europe* (Hart, 2006). In particular, the case of *Şahin v Turkey* (2007) 44 EHRR 5 (Grand Chamber), forms the keystone of ECtHR thinking on the matter.

2.3 *Homework for the Department of Education and Skills*

A group called the Irish Muslim Board recently made a submission in a Department of Education consultation process over school admission policies in which it made several recommendations for change.[33] The group stated that Muslim children can feel alienated at school, particularly in activities that revolve around Christmas such as nativity plays and carol services. It was recommended that school uniforms should accommodate Islamic dress codes by allowing girls to wear full-length skirts, long-sleeved shirts and headscarves. Furthermore, there was a call for school uniforms which have crucifix symbols or images of saints to be made optional in the interests of creating greater inclusivity. In addition, the group said school assemblies in faith-based schools should recognise aspects of the Muslim faith, by introducing Ramadan-based themes such as a communal breaking of the fast, when pupils, teachers and community members could eat together.

In another submission, the Muslim Primary Education Board, which represents Dublin's two Muslim primary schools, stated that parents were finding it increasingly difficult to secure school places for their children at second level. It stated that while the number of children refused from schools because of the lack of a baptismal certificate might be small on paper, this does not take into account the parents who do not apply for admission into schools that they know may ask for a certificate. In other words, Muslim parents are gravitating towards 'tried and tested' schools. The Board concluded that the status quo did not favour integration and that it was unfair and exclusionary.

The spirit of co-operation and compromise which is clearly at play between school authorities and Muslim parents is to be lauded. However, it appears to be under stress, and it looks likely that there will be future litigation over issues such as deviations from school uniform, opt-outs from certain subjects, time off for religious observance and the right to avoid the integrated curriculum.

3 Islam in Healthcare Law

The Irish health system is a relatively complex hybrid one, characterised by a mix of public and private health service funding and provision.[34] The Department of Health provides funding to the Health Service Executive and to hospitals, including what are described as 'voluntary hospitals', traditionally run by

33 Carl O'Brien, 'Islamic dress code should be accommodated in schools–group' *The Irish Times*, 6 January 2018.

34 Deirdre Madden, *Medicine, Ethics and the Law* (2nd ed, Bloomsbury, 2011) [1.14].

the religious. There are also private hospitals and clinics in the health system, which are run as businesses.

The following description of the Catholic ethos which exists in many Irish hospitals is relevant to the issue of accommodation of religious minorities generally, as it colours the experience which those who do not share the Catholic faith may have in some of our institutions.

3.1 *The Impact of Ethos in Hospitals*

Despite the common perception of secularisation, many modern Irish hospitals are still run according to Catholic mores. As was the case with the education system, the running of the Irish health service was largely undertaken by religious orders in the past.[35] Orders of nuns were responsible for the setting up of many of Ireland's hospitals in the 19th and 20th centuries.[36]

In 1978, the then Archbishop of Dublin, Dr Dermot Ryan asked all Catholic hospitals to set up ethical committees which would 'set out clearly ethical policy, both for the day to day running of the hospital and for the problem cases'.[37] This request was accompanied by an 'Ethical Code for Hospitals' which outlined general guidelines. According to these guidelines:

> The concern of the hospital for the good of the patient is not confined to his bodily and mental welfare but extends to the spiritual wellbeing which is inseparably connected with bodily and mental welfare.[38]

The guidelines stated that those who accepted appointments in a hospital could not violate the ethical policies and practices of that hospital. The sanctity of life was stressed. The 1980s marked a difficult period between Church and State on the issue of negotiation of the 'common contract' pursuant to which the State was established as the employer of hospital consultants, including those working in Catholic voluntary hospitals. A concern of these hospitals was that the contract did not bind doctors to a Catholic ethos.[39] In later

35 For a comprehensive account of the history of health services in Ireland, see Ruth Barrington, *Health, medicine and politics in Ireland, 1900–70* (Dublin, Institute of Public Administration, 2000).

36 For example, in Dublin, the Sisters of Mercy operated the Temple Street and the Mater hospitals, while the Sisters of Charity operated St Vincent's and St Michael's hospitals.

37 'I resented…that we were not treated as adults' *The Irish Times*, 11 June 1990.

38 ibid.

39 See Orla McDonnell and Jill Allison, 'From biopolitics to bioethics: church, state, medicine and assisted reproductive technology in Ireland' (2006) 28(6) *Sociology of Health & Illness* 817, note 11.

years, there followed a change in ownership of some of the voluntary hospitals. Nonetheless, it is clear that the influence of religious orders was preserved in many cases. For example, in 2001 the Sisters of Mercy sold the Mater Hospital to the State with the contingency that its Catholic ethos, first espoused by the order's founder Catherine McAuley, be retained.[40] Several nuns remain on the board of directors, and before doctors commence employment at the hospital, they must sign contracts promising adherence to the ethos of the hospital. Finally, it should be noted that several private hospitals and clinics, such as the Blackrock and Galway Clinics, are also run in keeping with a Catholic ethos.

The effects of Catholic doctrine in Irish hospitals are wide-ranging. Perhaps the most obvious and tangible effect is the presence and prominence of Catholic icons and prayer books throughout hospital wards. Furthermore, on a fundamental level, Catholic doctrine often affects the way in which healthcare is provided, particularly in matters pertaining to reproductive health. Both the Mater and St Vincent's hospitals, two of the largest predominantly State-funded hospitals, prohibit female sterilisation, a standard procedure which is not illegal, and which is carried out in non-Catholic-run institutions, as well as other fertility treatment centres.[41]

The focus here is on the accommodation of Muslim patients in Irish healthcare settings. When discussing the care that a Muslim patient can expect to receive in Irish hospitals, the effect of the Catholic ethos existing in many hospitals is a matter that must be taken into account. On the one hand, the protection afforded to Catholicism may intimidate Muslim patients, or increase the feeling of being in the minority. On the other hand, the religiosity of hospitals may mean that doctors and ethics committees will be more attuned to the religious accommodation requests of Muslim patients.

3.2 *Muslim Healthcare Needs*

Medico-legal issues involving Islam in particular have yet to achieve prominence in Ireland; the exception being the issue of the circumcision of baby boys, discussed below. Ali Selim of the Islamic Cultural Centre of Ireland has discussed the demands of religious observance which Islam poses in the healthcare context. He remarks: 'A visit to the local doctor, a consultation with a specialist or a short-stay in a hospital may cause anxiety to Muslim patients.

40 Eithne Donnellan, 'Sisters Plan £22m Sale of Private Hospital' *The Irish Times*, 4 October 2000; Elaine Edwards, 'Blackrock Clinic founder critical of selling Catholic-run hospitals' *The Irish Times*, 16 August 2001; Elaine Edwards, 'Sisters of Mercy defend selling private hospitals after surgeon's criticism' *The Irish Times*, 17 August 2001.

41 Maev-Ann Wren, 'Future of Private Hospitals Depends on Election' *The Irish Times*, 2 May 2002.

The impact on a Muslim who is anxious not to violate Islamic injunctions can be quite disturbing'.[42] Some of these healthcare requirements shall be outlined in light of the low levels of awareness of the nature of requests made in the healthcare context.[43]

3.2.1 Death

There are particular Muslim rituals associated with the end of life. The face of the person who has died should be turned towards Mecca, but in hospital turning the face towards the right is sufficient. All clothes should be removed by a person of the same sex and the body covered with a sheet. The corpse should be ritually bathed by respected elders experienced in rules of Muslim burial, and draped in a simple white cloth. Postmortems are not permitted by Islam. However, where the law of the country demands it, most Muslims accept that it must occur.[44] Muslims are always buried, never cremated, and it is a religious requirement that the body be buried as quickly as possible. Delay in issuing death certificates can lead to difficulties in complying with this commandment.[45]

3.2.2 Modesty

Islam places a high value on modesty, and therefore many Muslims believe that whenever possible any medical examination should be carried out by same sex clinicians.[46] Only if there is no alternative should examinations be carried out by opposite sex medical personnel.[47] Furthermore, many Muslims object to traditional hospital gowns, and females may request to remain as covered up

---

42 Patsy McGarry, 'When Modesty is an Obligation' *The Irish Times*, 10 July 2007. Selim states that as hospitalisation for Muslims in Ireland can be a particularly isolating experience due to religious and cultural differences, fellow Muslims tend to visit in numbers. This is encouraged by the fact that visiting the sick is a Muslim duty.

43 See generally, Aziz Sheikh, Abdul R. Gatrad eds, *Caring for Muslim patients* (2nd ed, Radcliffe Publishing, 2008).

44 Abdul R. Gatrad, 'Muslim customs surrounding death, bereavement, postmortem examinations, and organ transplants' (1994) 309 *British Medical Journal* 521.

45 Sheikh comments that Muslims in the UK often face 'unacceptable delays' in having the bodies of deceased relatives released for burial. He argues that training and reform of coroners' services is needed. Aziz Sheikh, 'Should Muslims have faith based health services?' (2007) 334 *British Medical Journal* 74.

46 Ilkilic remarks, 'From a handshake through to a gynaecological examination by a physician of the opposite sex, each such action can represent a violation of varying nature'. Ilhan Ilkilic, 'Bioethical Conflicts Between Muslim Patients and German Physicians and the Principles Of Biomedical Ethics' (2002) 23 *Medicine and Law* 243, 245.

47 Selim comments that 'touching should be within the limits of necessity'. See McGarry (n 44).

as possible during their stay in a hospital. In the UK in 2006, a surgical gown modelled on the *burqa* was designed and introduced in several hospitals in order to alleviate this modesty concern.[48]

3.2.3 Medicinal and Dietary Requirements

A Muslim patient must avoid all pork and alcohol products. This can pose problems connected with certain medicines that may be prescribed to him or her.[49] In a study carried out on a group of patients in the US[50] it was found that 84% were unaware that their medications could contain pork – and/or beef-derived ingredients.[51] Finally, Muslim hospital patients may require *halal* meals. Furthermore, Ramadan affects the treatment regimes of Muslim patients. Fasting rules dictate that the intake of medicines may be prohibited.[52]

3.2.4 Prayer Requirements

The issue of facilitation of prayer in hospital is also very important for the Muslim patient. Prayer must be carried out five times a day and involves kneeling and prostration in a clean and quiet area. It is important that there are facilities for ablution before prayer. Many hospitals contain either a chapel or some sort of prayer room. The prayer space may be filled with iconography which accords with the ethos of the hospital. With regard to this phenomenon, Muslims may have difficulty praying in the presence of symbols from other religions.[53] Furthermore, many argue that Muslim chaplaincy services ought to be established to provide spiritual care.[54] A final issue is timetabling appointments and medical procedures so as to avoid religious holidays.

48 'Modesty gowns for female patients" http://news.bbc.co.uk/2/hi/uk_news/england/lancashire/5315306.stm accessed 31 January 2018.

49 Sheikh (n 45) 74, laments the fact that in the UK, national or local formularies do not routinely flag potentially objectionable drugs or provide advice on suitable alternatives.

50 S Pirzada Sattar, Mohammed Shakeel Ahmed, James Madison, Denise R Olsen, Subhash C Bhatia, Shahid Ellahi, Farhan Majeed, Sriram Ramaswamy, Frederick Petty, and Daniel R Wilson, 'Patient and Physician Attitudes to Using Medications with Religiously Forbidden Ingredients' (2004) 38 *The Annals of Pharmacotherapy* 1830.

51 In addition, approximately 70% of physicians were unaware that more than 1,000 medications contained ingredients that might be against their patients' religion, and most thought that this was important information which should be provided to patients. ibid 1832–1833.

52 See Ilkilic (n 46) 246.

53 McGarry (n 44).

54 See Sheikh (n 45).

3.2.5 Circumcision

3.2.5.1 *Male Circumcision*

Circumcision is routinely carried out on male Muslim infants, and it is seen as a Muslim tenet. The question arising for consideration in most countries is whether this religiously-motivated circumcision should be available in the public hospital service.

A Circuit Court criminal case in October 2005 focused attention on the issue of non-therapeutic or 'ritual' circumcision occurring in Ireland.[55] A jury at Waterford Circuit Court found a Nigerian circumcisionist not guilty of the reckless endangerment of a 29-day old baby boy, Callis Osaghae, born in Ireland to Nigerian parents.[56] The baby had died of severe bleeding from the circumcision wound. It was clarified for the jury that the carrying out of a circumcision by a non-medical person is not an offence in Ireland. The State's case was that when the defendant undertook the circumcision, he recklessly engaged in conduct that caused serious harm to the child. In his direction to the jury, Haugh J described the case as a 'clash of two cultures' and warned them not to bring their 'white Western values' to bear when deciding the case. He added:

> This is a relatively recent matter which Ireland will have to deal with now that we have a significant migrant population. You are not asked whether this form of procedure is acceptable in Ireland. If you start thinking along those lines you are doing [the circumcisionist] a great injustice.[57]

Haugh J stated that the defendant did not have the benefit of being juried by peers who would understand his actions. The possibility of a religious or cultural exception at Irish law that was raised by Haugh J was objectionable to some.[58] The case is of limited precedential value. However, it does beg the question; what is Ireland's best solution to cases that turn on a clash between minority cultural and/or religious values and constitutional dictates regarding the treatment of children?[59]

---

55 Olivia Kelleher, 'Nigerian Cleared in Circumcision Case' *The Irish Times*, 8 October 2005.

56 The parents were Christian, not Muslim. However, circumcision on male Muslim children is a mandatory rite.

57 Kelleher (n 55).

58 Kevin Myers, An Irishman's Diary, *The Irish Times*, 11 January 2006: 'So after this case, are we to have two laws in Ireland? May you ineptly circumcise an Irish boy-child and cause him to die if you are African because of your 'culture', but not if you are Irish? It would seem so'.

59 Simon Mills, 'Circumcision: a question of culture or an assault?' *The Irish Times*, 28 August 2003.

Irish courts will intervene to prevent threats to the life of children from eventuating.[60] However, with regard to lesser 'harms', (if circumcision is to be regarded as harmful, and opinions clearly differ on this point),[61] constitutional law suggests that the autonomy and decision-making power of the family will prevail.

The Osaghae case prompted calls for guidelines to be issued for Irish hospitals.[62] In 2004, the Government appointed an expert group chaired by Professor of Paediatrics Denis Gill to explore demand for circumcision. In January 2006, the report of the expert group was presented to Minister for Health.[63] The core recommendations were that cultural/religious male circumcision should be provided in the Irish health service, and that circumcision should be performed by surgeons and anaesthetists who are appropriately trained, and in adequately equipped units.[64] It was stressed that the wellbeing of the infant male being circumcised was paramount, that the procedure should be as safe and pain-free as possible, and that the operation ought to be made available in the first year of life, ideally in the second six months for safety considerations.[65]

Mills comments: 'Male circumcision, whether for reasons of religion or parental preference, brings limited medical benefits at best'. He questions whether the operation can be legitimately justified for a boy who cannot consent, and identifies the core issue: 'Do cultural imperatives that motivate the parental decision to seek a ritual circumcision outweigh a desire to protect the right of the child not to be operated upon unnecessarily?'

60 For example, in blood transfusion cases involving the children of Jehovah's Witnesses. See *In the Matter of Baby AB, Children's University Hospital Temple Street v CD and EF* [2011] IEHC 1.

61 Dr Peter McKenna, of the Rotunda Hospital in Dublin, has expressed his opposition to the procedure being carried out in Irish hospitals for purely cultural reasons, and regards male circumcision in much the same light as female circumcision: 'I don't believe in cutting bits off baby boys or baby girls. I'm a fundamentalist in that regard'. Quoted in Liam Reid and Eithne Donnellan, 'Irish Medical Experts Oppose Operation' *The Irish Times*, 22 August 2003.

62 Sweden had a similar experience in 1966, when a doctor's circumcision of six Bosnian boys without anaesthetic and under unhygienic conditions, resulted in four of these boys being admitted to hospital. The doctor was found guilty of assault, but was later acquitted, mainly on the grounds that circumcision was a socially adequate mild assault. The incident led to regulation of circumcision by law. See Yngve Hofvander, 'New law on male circumcision in Sweden' (2002) 359 *The Lancet* 630.

63 *Cultural Male Circumcision: Report of Committee 2004/2005* (Department of Health and Children, 2006), http://health.gov.ie/wp-content/uploads/2014/06/circumcision.pdf, accessed 31 January 2018. In pursuance of its work, the group consulted with religious bodies.

64 ibid 4. Interestingly, an exemption from the hospital setting requirement was provided for Orthodox Jewish circumcisions.

65 ibid 5.

It was recommended that circumcisions carried out by untrained people should be reported to the HSE and should be investigated. Furthermore, it was suggested that the HSE should provide a regional service capable of performing the requisite number of circumcisions.[66] This was estimated to be up to 2,000 procedures per year.[67]

The Gill Report did not result in a specific legal prohibition on circumcisions by untrained professionals. For now, it appears that male circumcision of Muslim and Jewish babies is carried out in Ireland in both medical and non-medical settings, and that the area is not the subject of specific legal regulation. In 2013 it was reported that the Muslim community in Ireland was putting a proposal before the HSE aimed at tackling the problem of long waiting lists for cultural circumcision for their male children.[68]

3.2.5.2 *Female Circumcision/FGM*

Although the matter has been the subject of confusion, it is widely recognised that female circumcision and/or female genital mutilation (FGM) is not a tenet of Islam.[69] Notwithstanding the general consensus on the point, prominent Muslims based in Ireland have, on occasion, expressed support for the practice.[70]

The Criminal Justice (Female Genital Mutilation) Act 2012 makes it a criminal offence for someone resident in Ireland to perform FGM. The maximum

66 ibid.

67 ibid 17.

68 See Helen O'Callaghan, 'To cut or not to cut' *The Irish Examiner*, 11 August 2013. In 2009 it was reported that more than half those waiting over 12 months for day case surgery at Temple Street were awaiting circumcision. Eithne Donnellan, 'More than 1,500 wait a year for surgery' *The Irish Times*, 19 May 2009.

69 Williamson notes that four observations negate any argument that the practice is Islamic. First, FGM predates Islam. Second, FGM is currently not practised by all Muslims, nor by all Arabs. Third, FGM has been practised by Western doctors in non-Muslim countries, who previously supported its use as a medical cure for a range of (alleged) psychological aliments, such as nymphomania. Fourth, FMG is currently practised by several non-Muslim groups, such as Coptic Christians in Egypt, Ethiopian Jews and African animist tribes. Myra Williamson, 'Islamic Headscarves and Female Circumcision: Unveiling The Threat Posed By Islam To Human Rights' (2005) 2 *The New Zealand Postgraduate Law E-Journal* 1, 8–10. Williamson writes that FGM is often performed in African nations as a rite of initiation into adulthood, rather than for religious reasons.

70 Catherine Reilly, 'Islamic centre in Dublin supports "female circumcision"' *The Medical Independent*, 6 February 2018, http://www.medicalindependent.ie/101214/islamic_centre_in_dublin_supports_female_circumcision, accessed 31 January 2018. See also, Patsy McGarry, 'I condemn FGM. I totally apologise for the confusion' *The Irish Times*, 19 February 2018.

penalty is a fine or imprisonment for up to 14 years or both. It is also a criminal offence for someone resident in Ireland to take a girl to another country to undergo FGM. In December 2017, a couple were charged with FGM of their daughter under the law, the first of such prosecutions. At the time of writing they await trial.[71]

3.3 *Future Developments*

The Equal Status Acts 2000–2015 prohibit direct and indirect discrimination on the religious ground by those who provide health services, and thus provide an avenue of redress for those who are aggrieved about the treatment they receive in the healthcare setting.[72]

Furthermore, the Health Act 1953 is one of the few Irish statutes which deal with patients' rights. Section 4(2) provides:

> Any person who avails himself of any service provided under this Act shall not be under any obligation to submit himself or any person for whom he is responsible to a health examination or treatment which is contrary to the teaching of his religion.

There has not been any significant litigation involving Islam in the healthcare setting, which could suggest that Irish hospitals and clinics are accommodating in practice.

4 Conclusions

The State pledges to guarantee free profession and practice of religion, subject to public order and morality (Article 44.2.1° of the Irish Constitution). As has been mentioned in the introduction, the interpretation of the Irish Constitution which has emerged from case law arguably supports an obligation on the part of the State to make discriminations or distinctions which facilitate the free profession and practice of religion.

71 Tom Tuite, 'Couple in court charged with female genital mutilation', The Irish Times, 21 December 2017.

72 Under Section 16(2), treating a person differently does not constitute discrimination where the person is so treated in the exercise of a clinical judgment in connection with the diagnosis of illness or his or her medical treatment, or is incapable of entering into an enforceable contract or of giving an informed consent and for that reason the treatment is reasonable in the particular case.

In order to allow people to participate on an equal footing in Irish society, must the State come to the assistance of believers in the exercise of certain activities which are carried out in the workplace, classroom, and in hospitals? Must the State refrain from interference in religiously-motivated activities, including non-criminalisation? Must the Oireachtas create exemptions to generally applicable laws?

Existing accommodation of Islam in employment, education and healthcare has been scrutinised in this article. A common theme is that litigation is not as extensive as it is in other jurisdictions, but that the issues are beginning to crystallise.

In carrying out the administration of justice for a continuously changing religious population, the Irish courts are likely to be faced with dilemmas. That the Irish courts have a duty to respect the free practice of religion is an uncontroversial proposition. However, the task of giving life to this respect in a partly religiously diverse and also partly secular society is less straightforward.

The largely unexplored potential of the 'public order and morality' constraint on freedom of religion is likely to grow in prominence in future cases involving accommodation of religion claims. Furthermore, there may be profound clashes between fundamental rights including freedom of religion, the right to life, and the right to gender and sexual orientation equality. These conflicts will require careful balancing and reconciliation. Comparative law from other States and bodies which have encountered similar cases will have an impact. It is to be hoped that a coherent, principled and measured approach to this area of law will be developed.

Bibliography

Bacik, I., 'Future Directions for the Constitution' in E. Carolan and O. Doyle eds, *The Irish Constitution: Governance and Values* (Dublin, Thomson Round Hall, 2008) 135.

Bacik, I., *Kicking and screaming: dragging Ireland into the 21st Century* (O'Brien Press, 2004).

Barrington, R., *Health, medicine and politics in Ireland, 1900–70* (Dublin, Institute of Public Administration, 2000).

Bauman, R.W. and Weingarten, S.L.M., 'Keeping Religious Fundamentalism Under Wraps: The Clothing Controversy In Selected European Countries' (2006) 15(1) *Constitutional Forum* 1.

Belelieu, C.D., 'The Headscarf as a Symbolic Enemy of the European Court Of Human Rights' Democratic Jurisprudence: Viewing Islam through a European Legal Prism in Light of the *Şahin* Judgment' (2006) 12 *Columbia Journal of European Law* 573.

Bennoune, K., 'Secularism and Human Rights: a Contextual Analysis of Headscarves, Religious Expression, and Women's Equality under International Law' (2007) 45 *Columbia Journal of Transnational Law* 367.

Berthou, K., 'The Issue of the *Voile* in the Workplace in France: Unveiling Discrimination' (2005) 21 *International Journal of Comparative Labour Law and Industrial Relations* 281.

Bolger, M., Bruton, C. and Kimber, C., *Employment Equality Law* (Round Hall, 2012).

Bolger, M., 'Discrimination on grounds of religion: theory and practice' (2004) 1(2) *Irish Employment Law Journal* 48.

Brems, E., 'Above Children's Heads The Headscarf Controversy in European Schools from the Perspective of Children's Rights' (2006) 14 *The International Journal of Children's Rights* 119.

Casey, James, 'State and Church in Ireland', in Robbers ed, *State and Church in the EU* (Baden-Baden, 1996) 147.

Coen, M., 'Religious ethos and employment equality: a comparative Irish perspective' (2008) 28(3) *Legal Studies* 452.

Collins, H., 'The Protection of Civil Liberties in the Workplace' (2006) 69 *Modern Law Review* 619.

Daly, E., *Religion, Law and the Irish State* (Clarus Press, 2012).

Dolye, O., 'Article 44: Privileging the Rights of the Religious' in E Carolan and O Doyle eds, *The Irish Constitution: Governance and Values* (Dublin, Thomson Round Hall, 2008) 476.

Doyle, O., *Constitutional Law: Text, Cases and Materials* (Clarus Press, 2008).

Enright, M., 'Whither White Western Values? Comparative Perspectives on Culturally Motivated Decision-making for the Child' (2007) 7(1) *Hibernian Law Journal* 1.

Esmail, A., 'Should Muslims have faith based health services?' (2007) 334 *British Medical Journal* 75.

Evans, C., *Freedom of Religion under the European Convention on Human Rights* (Oxford University Press, 2001).

Gatrad, A.R., 'Muslim customs surrounding death, bereavement, postmortem examinations, and organ transplants' (1994) 309 *British Medical Journal* 521.

Glendenning, D., *Religion, Education and the Law* (Tottel, 2008).

Havers, P. and Neenan, C., 'Impact of the European Convention on Human Rights on medical law' (2002) 78 *Postgraduate Medical Journal* 573.

Hickey, T., 'Domination And The *Hijab* In Irish Schools', (2009) 31 *Dublin University Law Journal* 127.

Hogan, G. and Whyte, G., *JM Kelly: The Irish Constitution*, (4th ed Tottel, 2003).

Hogan, G., 'De Valera, the Constitution and the Historians' (2005) 40 *Irish Jurist* 291.

Hogan, G., 'Law and Religion: Church-State Relations in Ireland from Independence to the present day' (1987) 35 *American Journal of Comparative Law* 47.

Ilkilic, I., 'Bioethical Conflicts Between Muslim Patients and German Physicians and the Principles Of Biomedical Ethics' (2002) 23 *Medicine and Law* 243

Lalor, N., 'Female Genital Mutilation–An Irish Perspective' (2000) 3(1) *Irish Journal of Family Law* 17.

Madden, D., *Medicine, Ethics and the Law* (2nd ed, Bloomsbury, 2011).

Mason, J.K. and Laurie, G.T., Mason and McCall Smith's, *Law and Medical Ethics*, (7th ed, Oxford University Press, 2006).

Mawhinney, A., 'Freedom of religion in the Irish primary school system: a failure to protect human rights?' (2007) 27(3) *Legal Studies* 379.

McCrea, R., 'The Supreme Court and the School Chaplains Case' (1999) 2 *Trinity College Law Review* 19.

McDonnell, O. and Allison, J., 'From biopolitics to bioethics: church, state, medicine and assisted reproductive technology in Ireland' (2006) 28(6) *Sociology of Health & Illness* 817.

McGoldrick, D., 'Muslim Veiling Controversies in Europe' in J.S. Nielsen, S. Akgönül, A. Alibašić, B. Maréchal and C. Moe eds, *Yearbook of Muslims in Europe* (Brill, 2009, Volume 1) 427.

McGoldrick, D., 'Accommodating Muslims in Europe: From Adopting Sharia Law to Religiously Based Opt Outs from Generally Applicable Laws' (2009) 9(4) *Human Rights Law Review* 603.

McGoldrick, D., 'Extreme Religious Dress: Perspectives on Veiling Controversies' in I. Hare and J. Weinstein eds, *Extreme Speech and Democracy* (Oxford University Press, 2009) 400.

McGoldrick, D., Human Rights and Religion The Islamic *Headscarf Debate* in *Europe* (Hart Publishing, 2006).

McHale, J., 'Fundamental Rights and Health care' in E. Mossialos, G. Permanand, R. Baeten, and T.K. Hervey eds, *Health Systems Governance in Europe: The Role of European Union Law and Policy* (Cambridge University Press, 2010) 282.

Mullally, S. and O'Donovan, D., 'Religion in Ireland's "public squares": education, the family and expanding equality claims' (2011) *Public Law* 284.

Sakaranaho, T., *Religious freedom, Multiculturalism, Islam* (Brill: 2006).

Scharbrodt, O., 'Islam in Ireland: Organising a Migrant Religion' in O. Cosgrove, L. Cox, C. Kuhling and P. Mulholland eds, *Ireland's New Religious Movements* (Cambridge Scholars Publishing, 2011) 318.

Sheikh, A. and Gatrad, A.R., eds, *Caring for Muslim patients* (2nd ed, Radcliffe Publishing, 2008).

Sheikh, A., 'Should Muslims have faith based health services?' (2007) 334 *British Medical Journal* 74.

Whyte, G., 'Education and the Constitution: Convergence of Paradigm and Praxis' (1990–1992) 25–27 *Irish Jurist* 69.

Whyte, G., 'Education and the Constitution' in Lane ed, *Religion, Education and the Constitution* (Dublin, 1992).

Whyte, G., 'Protecting Religious Ethos in Employment Law: A Clash of Cultures' (2005) 12(1) *Dublin University Law Journal* 169.

Wicks, E., *Human Rights and Healthcare*(Hart Publishing, 2007).

Williamson, M., 'Islamic Headscarves and Female Circumcision: Unveiling The Threat Posed By Islam To Human Rights' (2005) 2 *The New Zealand Postgraduate Law E-Journal* 1.

CHAPTER 6

Recognition of Muslim Marriage Ceremonies in Ireland

An Analysis

Susan Leahy and Kathryn O'Sullivan

Introduction

In light of the differences between the statutory formalities required for entry into a legally recognised marriage in many common law jurisdictions and traditional Muslim marriage practice, doubts have been raised as to the legal status of a potentially significant number of Muslim marriages undertaken in the Western World. Mounting attention has been drawn to the issue over the past 20 years, particularly in England and Wales.[1] In 2001, Shah-Kazemi reported that approximately 27% of the 287 divorce case files from the Muslim Law (Shariah) Council which she investigated appeared not to have a recognized civil marriage in the UK.[2] Bano's research shortly after again highlighted the extent of the problem in England and Wales. She reported that almost two-thirds of the women she interviewed were not party to a legally recognised marriage.[3]

1 Pursuant to the Marriage Act 1949 (as amended), there are four main categories of marriage ceremony which enjoy legal recognition in England and Wales: civil marriage ceremonies; marriages contracted according to the rites of the Church of England or Wales; marriages contracted according to Quaker and Jewish traditions; and marriages conducted in other non-Anglican religious ceremonies. In this final category, the marriage will not receive legal recognition unless specific preliminaries have occurred and formalities as to the ceremony itself have been complied with. In particular, the marriage must take place in a registered premises and there must be present a registrar of marriages or authorised person. As will be outlined below, many Muslim marriages do not meet these minimum requirements. The consequences of this are particularly severe in a Muslim context as a non-compliant marriage in England and Wales is likely to be considered 'non-existent', see Kathryn O'Sullivan and Leyla Jackson, 'Muslim Marriage (Non)-Recognition: Implications and Possible Solutions' (2017) 39(1) JSWFL 22–41 for more.

2 Sonia Shah-Kazemi, *Untying the Knot, Muslim Women, Divorce and the Shariah* (Nuffield Foundation, 2001) 31. In addition, one in four of those interviewed as part of the project did not appear to have a legally recognised marriage under the law of England and Wales.

3 Samia Bano, *Complexity, Difference and Muslim Personal Law: Rethinking Relationships between Shari'ah Councils and South Asian Muslim Women in Britain* (Warwick University

 | DOI:10.1163/9789004398252_007

Since then, empirical research undertaken by Douglas et al, showed that just over 50% of the hearings observed in the Birmingham Central Mosque, involved couples with an unrecognised Muslim marriage.[4] These studies – and the activity of leading practitioner activists in the field, notably Aina Khan OBE[5] – have resulted in ever greater attention being focused on the issue with the discourse moving from the academic[6] into the public sphere.[7]

Although much of the discussion focused on the civil recognition of Muslim marriages does spring from England and Wales, the issue is by no means confined to that jurisdiction. Research has also been conducted on the extent to which Muslim marriages are securing legal recognition in North America and elsewhere in Europe with similar concerns raised.[8] Unfortunately, however, notwithstanding that Islam is now the third largest and one of the fastest

Doctoral dissertation, 2004) 221. Only 9 of the 25 women she interviewed had a registered civil marriage.

4 Gillian Douglas et al, 'The role of religious tribunals in regulating marriage and divorce' (2012) 24(2) CFLQ 139. This equated to 14 of the 27 hearings observed.

5 See 'Aina Khan and Baroness Warsi kick start Muslim Marriages Project' retrieved from http://www.prweb.com/releases/2014/01/prweb11483339.htm; Aina Khan, 'Register our Marriage Roadshow comes to Birmingham' (2015) retrieved from: http://www.duncanlewis.co.uk/news/Aina_Khan%E2%80%99s_Register_Our_Marriage_Roadshow_comes_to_Birmingham_28th_March_2015_(27_March_2015).html#sthash.oDQGRi2p.dpbs. Based on her engagement with the community, Aina Khan has suggested that as many as 80% of marriages may be unrecognised in certain areas. See also Muslim Marriage Working Group: Final report (2012) retrieved from https://www.whatdotheyknow.com/request/179578/response/444442/attach/7/MMWG%20SUBMISSION%20AND%20FINAL%20REPORT%2011.10.12.pdf.

6 See also John Eekelaar, 'Marriage, A modest proposal' (2013) (1) FLJ 83; Farrah Ahmed and Jane Calderwood Norton, 'Religious tribunals, religious freedom, and concern for vulnerable women' (2012) 24(4) CFLQ 363–388; Rowan Williams 'Civil and Religious Law in England: A religious perspective' (2008) 10 Ecc LJ 262.

7 Harriet Sherwood, 'Most women in UK who have Islamic wedding miss out on legal rights' (The Guardian, 20 November 2017) available at https://www.theguardian.com/world/2017/nov/20/women-uk-islamic-wedding-legal-rights-civil-ceremony-marriage. See also 'The Truth about Muslim Marriage' (Channel 4, 21 November 2017) available at http://www.channel4.com/programmes/the-truth-about-muslim-marriage.

8 For North America, see Julie Macfarlane, *Understanding trends in American Muslim Divorce and Marriage: A Discussion Guide for Families and Communities* (ISPU, 2012). However, note, this research found that the rate at which marriages were recognised varied from community to community, with different practices and awareness as to the importance of securing legal recognition varying considerably. For European research see, for example, the work of Mahmoud Jaraba (Max Planck Institute for Social Anthropology) who presented a paper entitled 'How Local Muslim Communities Dissolve Unregistered Islamic Marriage (nikāh) in Germany?' at the University of Birmingham's *Europe's New Migrants: Marriage Practices and Policies* conference in April 2018.

growing religions in Ireland, there has been no in-depth exploration as to whether, or to what extent, non-state registered marriages – so called *nikah*-only marriages – may be taking place within the jurisdiction.[9]

While some couples may jointly and knowingly chose to enter into a religious Muslim marriage only,[10] particular concerns surround the potential for Muslim 'spouses' to unwittingly be party to a marriage which enjoys no legal status. Concern has also been raised for those who may have been misled by their 'spouse' as to the latter's intention to secure legal recognition for the marriage following the religious ceremony.[11] Whether such issues are liable to arise in Ireland remains under-investigated with little meaningful research conducted on the topic to date. The dearth of knowledge in this area is regrettable not only for the parties to potentially legally invalid marriages but also for the State. As Poulter suggests, '[i]n a modern industrial society it is vitally important for a state to have accurate information about which of its members are married and which are not'.[12]

This chapter attempts to go some way towards bridging the current gap in knowledge in this area by offering an exploration of the recognition of Muslim marriage ceremonies in Ireland. The discussion is informed by available, albeit limited, data on Muslim marriage practice in Ireland and an investigation of both the legal formalities for marriage in Ireland and the consequences of non-compliance with such formalities. The chapter is broken into five main parts. Providing the broader context for the discussion which follows, Part 1 highlights the importance of marriage and the marital family under Irish law. It considers the way in which marriage law has evolved in the jurisdiction and the different types of marriage which may now be entered into. Part 2 details the formalities required for entry into a legally recognised *religious* marriage in Ireland and the implications of failure to meet these formalities. Considering this legislative framework in light of traditional Muslim marriage practice, Part 3 then seeks to gauge the likelihood of Muslim marriages conducted in Ireland securing legal recognition. In light of the emerging potential for a marriage to

9 The only contribution to date broadly referencing Muslim marriage in Ireland was Mairead Enright, '"Preferring the Stranger?" Towards an Irish Approach to Muslim Divorce Practice' (2013) Ir Jur 49(1) 65. Little specific analysis has emerged in the interim.

10 See Rajnaara C. Akhtar 'Unregistered Muslim Marriages: An Emerging Culture of Celebrating Rites and Conceding Rights' in Joanna Miles, Perveez Mody and Rebecca Probert (eds) *Marriage Rites and Rights* (2015 Hart) 193–210 which focuses on the reasons why parties might be consciously party to an unregistered marriage.

11 See O'Sullivan and Jackson (n 1).

12 Sebastian Poulter, *English law and ethnic minority customs* (Butterworths, 1986) p33.

be unrecognised, Part 4 briefly considers the implications of failing to secure legal status for a marriage under Irish law before Part 5 asks where to next.

1 Marriage and the Marital Family in Irish Law

At a constitutional level, marriage and the marital family enjoy a privileged position in Ireland. Article 41.3.1° of the Irish Constitution of 1937, *Bunreacht na hÉireann,* specifically provides, 'The State pledges itself to guard with special care the institution of Marriage, *on which the Family is founded*, and to protect it against attack'.[13] Moreover, through Article 41.1.1°, the State recognises this constitutional marital family, 'as the natural primary and fundamental unit group of Society, and as a moral institution possessing inalienable and imprescriptible rights, antecedent and superior to all positive law'. It further 'guarantees to protect the Family in its constitution and authority, as the necessary basis of social order and as indispensable to the welfare of the Nation and the State'.[14] Given this importance attributed to marriage, it is perhaps unsurprising that the right to marry has been recognised as an unenumerated right under the Irish Constitution.[15] The Constitution does not, however, provide any detail on the precise formalities required for entry into a legally recognised marriage leaving such matters to the legislature.

Historically, Irish laws regulating the formalities for marriage have been notoriously convoluted. Indeed, commenting in the mid-1990s, Shatter described the law in this area as 'complex and obscure, being contained in a labyrinth of statutes stretching from 1844'.[16] Until the passing of the Family Law Act 1995, the formalities for civil marriage or religious marriage – *other than Roman Catholic marriage* – hailed primarily from the Marriages (Ireland) Act 1844, as amended by the Registration of Marriages (Ireland) Act 1863.[17] The legal

13 Emphasis added. Following the 34th Amendment to the Constitution, Article 41.4 now also provides 'Marriage may be contracted in accordance with law by two persons without distinction as to their sex'.

14 Article 41.1.2°.

15 This constitutional right was first recognised in *Donovan v Minister for Justice* [1951] 85 ILTR 134. For more on the history of the right to marry, see *O'Shea and O'Shea v Ireland and the AG* [2007] 2 IR 313. Note, in the absence of a constitutional or statutory definition of marriage, it has been left to the courts to define. Although the *Inter-Departmental Committee on Reform of Marriage Law* (Discussion Paper No. 5-September 2004) recommended the introduction of a legislative definition of marriage, none has been forthcoming.

16 Alan J. Shatter, *Family Law* (Bloomsbury, 1997) 157.

17 Although Ireland secured its independence from Britain in 1922, the pre-existing marriage law was carried over. As Deirdre McGowan, 'Governed by Marriage Law' (2016) 25(3)

validity Roman Catholic marriages, specifically, was governed by the common law.[18] It was not until the enactment of the Family Law Act 1995 that the formal requirements for *all* marriages solemnised in the State were finally codified.[19] The Civil Registration Act 2004 ultimately repealed and replaced all of the existing rules relating to marriage formalities, creating a more stream-lined and straightforward process.

Pursuant to the Civil Registration Act 2004 (as amended), three types of marriage are recognised under Irish law. First, parties may enter into a civil marriage. Civil marriages are conducted by the Irish State, specifically by registrars employed by the Health Service Executive. Second, as will be discussed below, parties may enter into a religious marriage solemnised by registered members of religious bodies. Although as originally enacted, civil and religious marriages were the only categories of marriage recognised, the Civil Registration (Amendment) Act 2012, extended the categories to three to include secular marriages.[20]

2 Marriage Registration Formalities

To be legally married in Ireland, both parties must be eighteen years of age.[21] The preliminaries for legal marriage in Irish law centre upon compliance with

---

Soc and Leg Stud 311, 314 explains: 'When Ireland gained independence from Britain in 1922, it inherited a body of marriage law built upon the political concerns of a colonial power, and the ecclesiastical rules of a church with few Irish adherents'.

18 Shatter notes that canon law (decree of the Council of Trent 1563) governed the Roman Catholic's recognition of a marriage as valid but it was not relevant to the formalities required by common law, canon law and common law having 'gone their separate ways' after the Reformation: Shatter (n 16) 158. Notwithstanding that Article 41 pledged to protect the institution of marriage 'upon which the Family is founded', McGowan (n 17) at 314 notes that 'in practice the regulation of the marriage relationship itself was left entirely within the authority of the various churches'.

19 For more detail on the framework introduced by the 1995 Act, see Louise Crowley, *Family Law* (Round Hall, 2013), 52–53.

20 In effect, the 2012 amendment recognised a third category of solemniser, one who is neither a registrar employed by the HSE nor a member of a religious body. Secular marriages, in particular, have seen a rapid growth in popularity in Ireland. For more, see Susan Leahy and Kathryn O'Sullivan, 'Changing Conceptions of Marriage in Ireland: Law and Practice' (2018) 30(3) CFLQ 279–300.

21 Section 31(1) of the Family Law Act 1995. It is possible for individuals under the age of eighteen to marry if they obtain a court exemption to do so. Such an exemption can be granted where the applicant(s) show that the exemption from the age requirements is justified by serious reasons and is in the interests of the parties to the intended marriage:

the formal notice requirements. Section 46(1)(a) of the 2004 Act provides that a marriage solemnised in the State, after the commencement of the Act,[22] between persons of any age shall not be valid in law unless the intending spouses provide written notice of their intention to marry not less than three months prior to the date on which the marriage is to be solemnised.[23] This notice must be delivered by both parties in person.[24] The parties must also present themselves at the registrar's office not less than five days (or such lesser number of days as may be determined by that registrar) before the date of the marriage and make and sign a declaration in the presence of the registrar that there is no impediment to the marriage.[25] These requirements are 'substantive requirements for marriage',[26] meaning that their non-observance will legally invalidate the marriage.

Once the registrar is satisfied that the requirements of Section 46 have been complied with, a marriage registration form (MRF) will be completed by the registrar[27] and issued to the parties to the intended marriage.[28] The marriage cannot be solemnised unless the parties present the MRF to the individual who will solemnise the marriage so that s/he may examine it.[29] Immediately after the solemnisation of a marriage, the MRF must be signed by: (a) each of the parties to the marriage; (b) two witnesses to the solemnisation of the marriage, and; (c) the person who solemnised the marriage.[30] The MRF must be returned to the registrar by either one of the parties to the marriage within one month of the ceremony.[31] The registrar will then enter the marriage on the official register.[32]

---

ibid, Section 33(1). Section 39(1)(e) of the Domestic Violence Bill 2017 proposes to remove the facility for the grant of exemptions to the age requirements for marriage by repealing Section 33 of the Family Law Act 1995.

22 The Act commenced on 5th November 2007: Civil Registration Act 2004 (Commencement) Order 2007 (S.I. No. 736 of 2007).

23 It is possible to get a court exemption from the notice requirement prior to the marriage under Section 47 of the Act. Such an exemption 'shall not be granted unless the applicants show that its grant is justified by serious reasons and is in their interests': Section 47(2).

24 Section 46(2). The notice must be accompanied by the prescribed fee ad such (if any) documents that are specified by an tArd-Chláraitheoir (Registrar General): Section 46(3).

25 Section 46(1)(b).

26 Section 46(4).

27 Section 48(1).

28 Section 48(2),.

29 Section 48(3).

30 Section 49(1).

31 Section 49(2).

32 Section 49(3). Once the marriage is registered, a civil marriage certificate may be issued.

In relation to the ceremony itself, there are certain requirements which must be adhered to. First, the marriage must be solemnised by a registered solemniser.[33] Where the solemniser is not a civil registrar, s/he must not solemnise a marriage unless s/he is a recognised by the relevant religious or secular body.[34] A registered solemniser must not solemnise a marriage unless: both parties to the intended marriage are present;[35] two persons over the age of 18 years are present to act as witnesses;[36] the solemnisation takes place in a suitable venue[37] and; the solemniser is satisfied that the parties to a marriage understand the nature of the marriage ceremony and the relevant declarations which must be made as part of the ceremony.[38] With regard to the venue requirement, to be suitable for a marriage ceremony a venue must be a 'place that is open to the public', that is, a building that is open to the public, or a courtyard, garden, yard, field or piece of ground that is open to the public and lying near to and usually enjoyed with such a building.[39] Within these limits, the venue for the ceremony is a matter for the religious body concerned and the parties themselves. There is no requirement that a venue for a religious marriage be registered with or approved by the civil authorities.[40] A solemniser must ensure that the ceremony is in a form which is approved by an *tArd-Chláraitheoir* (Registrar General).[41] The ceremony must also include certain declarations made by each of the parties in the presence of each other,[42] the solemniser and the witnesses, namely that: neither party knows of any impediment to the marriage and; each accepts the other as his/her spouse.[43] These requirements for the marriage ceremony are further stated to be 'substantive requirements for marriage':[44] that is, they must be adhered to if the marriage is to be legally valid.

The instinctive response to a marriage where the formalities have been breached would seem to be that the marriage is void as it has not complied with the legal requirements for civil marriage. If this were to occur, the marriage is

33 Section 51(1).
34 Section 51(3)(c).
35 Section 51(2)(a).
36 Section 51(2)(b).
37 Section 51(2A).
38 Section 51(2)(d). These declarations are set out in Section 51(4) and are described below.
39 Section 51(2A). See Leahy and O'Sullivan (n 20) for more.
40 For more general information, see http://www.welfare.ie/en/Pages/Getting_Married.aspx (accessed 31 March 2018).
41 Section 51(3)(a).
42 Section 51(3)(b).
43 Section 51(4).
44 Section 51(5).

deemed never to have existed. Under Irish nullity law, this would necessarily mean that the parties to this void marriage would not be entitled to any ancillary relief such as maintenance or property division.[45] In Ireland, however, it is not fully settled that breach of formalities will always lead to a marriage being declared void. This supposition is based on the judgment in *IE v WE*,[46] a case which was decided on the pre-2004 law. In that case, the parties married in a Lutheran church in Dublin which, at the date of the ceremony, was not registered for the celebration of marriages. In addition, no statutory licence or certificate was issued to authorise the ceremony and no banns were published. Unbeknownst to the parties to the marriage, their marriage had not complied with the legal formalities for marriage which prevailed at the time under Section 49 of the Marriages (Ireland) Act 1844. Murphy J, however, held that this would not render the marriage void, noting that:

> 'It seems...settled law that to invalidate a marriage for non-compliance with any of the provisions contained in s. 49....it is necessary to establish not only that there should have been a conscious disregard of the provisions of the section but that both parties to the apparent marriage should have been aware of the defect'.[47]

Thus, it would seem that, under the pre-2004 law at least, non-compliance with the legal formalities for marriage will only render a marriage void where both parties were aware of the defect. This rule was subsequently approved in the later case of *DC v NM (falsely known as NC)*.[48]

The prevailing view amongst Irish commentators on family law is that the precedent set in *IE* remains good law. Crowley suggests that whilst non-compliance with age or notice requirements renders and marriage null and

45 See below for more.

46 [1985] ILRM 691.

47 Ibid, at 695.

48 [1997] 2 IR 218. However, interestingly in that case, the judge distinguished IE on the facts. The couple in *DC* had married relying on a forged consent from the bride's father. She was under 21 years of age and, under the law at the time, thus required the consent of her father to marry. Geoghegan J held that the relevant section was 'directory only' and the mere absence of a father's consent could not invalidate a marriage. Consequently, this case suggests a certain hierarchy within the formalities of marriage under the regime which prevailed prior to the enactment of the 2004 legislation such that even a knowing breach of certain formalities may not have had any impact on the legal validity of a marriage. Commenting on the old law, Shatter (n 16) p. 174 suggested that '[a]s a general rule, it is submitted that unless a defect is said expressly to invalidate a marriage, the marriage is completely valid'.

void (unless the relevant exemptions have been obtained from the courts), '[t]he general principle outside these requirements is that the non-observance of or a defect in any of the other prescribed formalities does not invalidate a marriage unless both parties were aware of it at the time of the ceremony'.[49] However, there are problems with this line of argument. The age and notice requirements are rightly exempted from what we might call the 'knowledge rule' as Section 46(4) clearly states that they are substantive requirements for marriage and a court exemption must be obtained to depart from them. However, Section 51(5) similarly states that the requirements for solemnisation of marriages listed above (i.e. that the ceremony be performed by a registered solemniser, with both parties and witnesses present, in a public venue, where the relevant declarations are made) are also substantive requirements for a marriage. Thus, it would seem that the 'knowledge rule' similarly cannot apply where these requirements are not met. Ultimately, this question cannot be properly settled until a relevant case comes before the courts under the new law. Intuitively, it would seem that since the nomenclature 'substantive' is applied to all of these formalities, the legislative intent would appear to have been that they should all be treated equally and that non-compliance with any of these requirements would render a marriage void. Indeed, it is even open to question whether the 'knowledge rule' would be applied to a consideration of non-compliance for the formalities in the 2004 Act (as amended). The legal rules which prevailed at the time of the judgment in *IE* were notoriously more complex than the current legal position. Thus, judges may have less sympathy with a failure to comply with the formalities should a similar case fall for consideration under the current legal rules.

Consequently, for Muslim marriages which do not comply with the legal formalities for marriage, it is difficult to state with certainty whether they would be declared null and void or not. Certainly, there can be no doubt that where age or notice requirements were not met, the marriage could not be valid. However, there is potential for the same outcome where the solemnisation of the marriage does not comply with the formalities for solemnisation of marriage, for example, where a marriage is solemnised by an imam who was not a registered solemniser or where the venue used was not open to the public. Much here would depend on whether the courts opted to apply the precedent in *IE* or not. If *IE* were to be applied in this instance, it would offer some protection to Muslims who were not aware of the fact that their marriage ceremony did not comply with the formal legal requirements. However,

49 Crowley (n 19) 58.

at present, unfortunately, much uncertainty prevails in this area and it is difficult to predict what stance a court would take in this situation.

3 Muslim Marriage in Ireland – Likelihood of Compliance with Formalities

While it may not be possible to answer definitively what the implications of failure to comply with the formalities will be, it is worthwhile considering the extent to which such formalities are being adhered to – insofar as such analysis is possible in the absence of empirical evidence.

It is clear that at least *some* Muslim marriages are securing legal status and the numbers, while small, were – at least until very recently – showing an upward trend. Although in 2012, 28 Muslim marriages were registered, 48 were registered in 2013.[50] Forty-two were registered in 2014 with 89 registered in 2015.[51] Inexplicably, a mere 22 Muslim marriages were registered in 2016.[52] It must also be remembered that a Muslim couple could have a religious marriage ceremony either preceded or followed by a separate civil ceremony, and thus be recorded on official statistics as a civil ceremony only. How many such civil marriages take place within the Muslim community is impossible to state. Thus, while it would appear from the statistics that, at least until 2016, there was evidence of a positive trend in the registration of marriages, it may reasonably be questioned as to whether, in line with the experience of a number of jurisdictions, most notably in England and Wales, more marriages are being conducted which are, knowingly or otherwise, not securing legal recognition.[53]

On one hand, the statutory formalities required in Ireland for legal entry into marriage are more user-friendly in a multicultural society than those in

50 Registrar General, Annual Report 2013, at point 39 available at https://www.welfare.ie/en/downloads/Registrar-General-Report-2013. Islamic marriage represented less than 0.25% of all religious marriages registered in the state in 2013. Figures were included in the Registrar General's report for 2013 but not for 2014.

51 Source: CSO request. There were only 114 Islamic marriages registered in Ireland between 2010 and 2013, see Registrar General, Annual Report 2013, at point 39, available at https://www.welfare.ie/en/downloads/Registrar-General-Report-2013.pdf. It is interesting to note that the Central Statistics Office, Marriages and Civil Partnership Statistical Reports, do not provide details of Islamic marriages undertaken. These marriages fall into the 'other religious ceremonies' category.

52 Source: CSO request. With sincere thanks to Ms. Margaret Hurley, Vital Statistics Section, Central Statistics Office for providing these figures.

53 Anecdotally, mediation practitioners in Ireland have reported experiences of couples party to a *nikah*-only marriage approaching them on the breakdown of the relationship.

other jurisdictions.[54] Seeking to be more inclusive of different marriage ceremonies, the legislation allows much more freedom to various religious bodies to conduct the ceremony according to the rites of their own religion. Unlike other jurisdictions including England and Wales, Muslim mosques in Ireland do not need to be registered for marriage ceremonies.[55] Pursuant to the 2004 Act, the venue for the ceremony is a matter for the religious body. Where the marriage takes place in a mosque, it is unlikely to create any difficulties. Equally, as per Muslim marriage practice, a marriage conducted in another public place such as a restaurant or hotel may also be considered to have met the formalities with the location being considered as within the providence of the religion. Moreover, although the legislation stipulates that, notwithstanding the religious bodies' freedom to control the location of the ceremony, the location where the solemnisation takes place must be open to the public – thus appearing to render any ceremony in a private house, religiously acceptable as *per* Muslim tradition, in contravention of the formalities – where all other formalities are met, such a marriage *might* nevertheless be upheld using the precedent in *IE v WE*.

However, while the legislature ought to be commended on the modernisation of the legislation governing legal entry into marriage, difficulties do nevertheless remain. Intuitively, it stands to reason that public awareness of the formalities required for entry into marriage is of the utmost importance to ensure compliance.[56] Nevertheless, doubts may be raised as to whether such awareness exists within the Muslim community. A cursory investigation of the leading websites of the Islamic community in Ireland highlights a serious lack of information pertaining to the requirements for a legally recognised Muslim marriage: none of the major websites appear to carry any information in

54 Serious concerns have been raised in England and Wales in relation to the Marriage Act 1949 (as amended) and its appropriateness in a multicultural society see the Law Commission for England and Wales, *Getting Married: A scoping paper* (2015). See also John Eekelaar, 'Marriage, religion and gender equality' in Fareda Banda and Lisa Fishbayn Joffe (eds), *Women's Rights and Religious Law* (Routledge 2016); Eekelaar (n 6) above.

55 In England and Wales, this requirement has proven quite problematic. Eekelaar (n 6) 84 citing Office of National Statistics, *Marriages in England and Wales 2010, Area of Occurrence, Type of Ceremony and Denomination*, Tables 6 and 7 notes 'that Muslims are unwilling to seek registration of their premises. For example, in 2010, there were 899 Certified Muslim Places of Worship, but only 198 registered for marriage'. He notes 'for other denominations the discrepancy is much smaller'.

56 See for example the awareness-raising initiatives in England and Wales such as Khan (n 5) above.

relation to the legal formalities for marriage.[57] Worse still is the extent to which false and misleading information appears online. According to the Central Statistics Office of Ireland website,[58] the website of the US Embassy in Ireland[59] and various other marriage information websites:[60] 'There is at present no provision for the civil registration of Muslim marriage ceremonies solemnised in the State'.

Within many religions, whether minority religions or otherwise, the solemniser due to conduct a marriage ceremony is likely a major source of information to prospective spouses on the formalities to be completed to ensure legal recognition. The likelihood of religious solemnisers providing such information in relation to civil recognition appears, at first blush, to be bolstered by the legislation. Section 69(10)(c) of the 2004 Act provides that it is an offence for a person who is a registered solemniser to solemnise a marriage without a MRF having been given to him or her before the solemnisation for examination by him or her. However, it appears that at least six out of seven imams in Ireland are not legally registered to solemnise a Muslim marriage. While the Irish Council of Imams estimates that there are approximately 35 imams in Ireland,[61] the official Register of Solemnisers records only five imams in the jurisdiction: two in Dublin, two in Cork and one in Galway.[62] Moreover, although

57 A number of websites carry sections on marriage and the availability for marriage ceremonies but do not mention any reference to the civil requirements for example Islamic and Educational Centre of Ireland website http://www.islamiccentre.ie/services/marriage-nikah/ (01 February 2017); The Islamic Cultural Centre of Ireland website http://www.islamireland.ie/facilities-services/matrimonial/ (01 February 2017). The main Catholic websites do carry such information for their followers, eg http://www.accord.ie/services/getting-married/getting-married-in-the-catholic-church (01 February 2017).

58 For example when perusing table VSA51 on the Stat Bank, see http://www.cso.ie/px/pxeirestat/Statire/SelectVarVal/Define.asp?maintable=VSA51&PLanguage=0. See also CSO, *Standard Report on Methods and Quality (v1) for Marriages and Civil Partnership Registration* (2013) pt3.4 available at http://www.cso.ie/en/media/csoie/surveysandmethodologies/documents/pdfdocs/marriagesqualityreport13.pdf (accessed 25 January 2017).

59 See http://test3.wgtest3.getusinfo.com/service/other-citizen-services/other-citizen-services/marriage-in-ireland.html (accessed 25 January 2017).

60 See http://irelandnow.com/marriage.html (accessed 25 January 2017).

61 Although anecdotal evidence suggest the figure is likely to be higher as not all imams or Islamic associations are linked to the Irish Council of Imams.

62 See Register of Solemnisers available at https://www.welfare.ie/en/downloads/Register_of_Solemnisers.xls [accessed 27 June 2016]. The geographical clustering of these registered officiants is also interesting in light of the dispersed nature of the Muslim community in Ireland. Approximately, 34 mosques and prayer halls are listed across Ireland on the Islamic Foundation of Ireland website, see http://www.islaminireland.com/services/mosques-and-prayer-rooms/ [accessed 16 August 2016].

four imams were registered in September 2007 on the commencement of the Act, only one extra imam has been registered in the interim (in July 2015) notwithstanding that the community grew significantly during the same period.[63] In addition, although almost half (47.3%) of all Irish Muslims were recorded in County Dublin alone in 2016,[64] only two imams are listed as registered solemnisers for this district.[65]

The limited number of registered solemnisers within the Muslim community presents a number of problems. First, the potential for Muslim marriages to be conducted in the absence of a registered solemniser as required pursuant to the Civil Registration Act 2004 (as amended), whether knowingly or otherwise, would appear high.[66] Second, and arguably more importantly, pursuant to Section 69(10)(b) of the 2004 Act, it is an offence for a person who is not a registered solemniser (within the meaning of Part 6), or the holder of a temporary authorisation under Section 57, to conduct a marriage ceremony in such a way *as to lead the parties to the marriage to believe that he or she is solemnising a valid marriage*.[67] Although, to date, no caselaw has emerged to show precisely what behaviour might constitute 'leading' the parties to believe the marriage would be 'valid', if an unregistered solemniser sought an MRF this might be caught within the behaviour contemplated. On this interpretation, it would be much more advisable for such a solemniser to remain silent as to the formalities required for a religious marriage to secure simultaneous legal recognition. It would appear then reasonable to suggest that where an unregistered solemniser conducts the marriage ceremony, the risk of the marriage securing legal recognition is significantly higher.[68]

63 Between 2006 and 2016, the Muslim community in Ireland almost doubled, increasing by 95%, see CSO, *Census 2016 Profile 8: Religion Ethnicity and Irish Travellers* (Dublin: Stationary Office, 2017), also available to view at http://www.cso.ie/en/releasesandpublications/ep/p-cp8iter/p8iter/p8rnc/.

64 CSO, *ibid.* It noted that the Muslim community in Ireland is 'highly concentrated in urban areas with only 2.1 per cent in rural areas'.

65 Moreover, as referenced elsewhere, the Irish Muslim community is noted for its diversity. Couples within each micro-community would presumably wish an imam from their sect to conduct the ceremony. This further arguably reduces the attractiveness of those imams who are registered from a different sect.

66 As noted above, what the implications of this non-compliance with the formalities would be, remains unclear.

67 Emphasis added. Also the fact it says 'valid' and not 'legal' is interesting – it might be religiously 'valid' if not legally 'valid'.

68 Admittedly, an unregistered solemniser could tell the couple to have a separate civil marriage ceremony before or after the marriage ceremony, see below. However, whether this information is passed on and the extra step is taken by parties or not is unclear. Moreover,

Viewed in this context, it might appear reasonable to suggest that one obvious solution could be to encourage more imams to become registered solemnisers thus better ensuring that spouses do not unwittingly fall foul of the formalities required for legal entry into marriage. However, in achieving this goal, Section 69(10)(c) may actually prove counter-productive. As per Islamic tradition, both spouses may knowingly wish to enter a religious, non-legally binding, marriage. However, where a person who is a registered solemniser conducts such a ceremony they would appear to be left vulnerable to conviction. Their unavailability for such marriages would likely render them less attractive as solemnisers in the community.[69] It is also possible that some imams may wish to avoid registration insofar as such engagement with the Irish State might be viewed with suspicion within some quarters of the community.[70] The likelihood of the number of registered imams increasing significantly in the coming years would therefore appear small.

4 Implications of Non-Recognition

As McGowan explains, the legal consequences of marital recognition 'are so far-reaching as to be virtually impossible to catalogue'.[71] By corollary, the implications of non-recognition are also extensive. Inevitably, the implications of non-recognition will be more severe depending on the particular couple involved and issues such as length of the putative marriage etc. In particular, non-recognition may have more adverse effects on women who may be in a financially vulnerable position on relationship breakdown due to, for example, having taken on a role of home-maker and/or primary caregiver for children, thereby limiting their own earning capacity.[72] For this group, the inability to resort to the typical remedies available on martial breakdown (i.e. ancillary

---

it is unknown to what extent there is in fact knowledge of the provisions of the Civil Registration Act 2004 (as amended) among imams in Ireland.

69 Although, as discussed below, if community expectations focus on registration, the demand for registered solemnisers should outweigh the advantages for imans of non-registration. Nevertheless, the market for unregistered solemnisers which may be likely to be reduced, is unlikely to disappear.

70 Similar suspicion has been highlighted in England and Wales, see Samia Bano, *Exploratory Survey of Shariah Councils in England with Respect to Family Law* (Ministry of Justice/University of Reading, 2012) 24. See also O'Sullivan and Jackson (n 1).

71 McGowan, (n 17) 312.

72 Muslim Marriage Working Group: Final report (2012) Available at https://www.whatdotheyknow.com/request/179578/response/444442/attach/7/MMWG%20SUBMISSION%20AND%20FINAL%20REPORT%2011.10.12.pdf [accessed 15 May 2015] 4.

orders available in judicial separation and divorce proceedings) may have significant financial consequences. Although it is outside the scope of discussion here to fully articulate all the implications which arise when a marriage is deemed void for non-compliance with formalities, it is important to point to the primary effects of such non-recognition.

As noted above, where a marriage is declared legally void, 'the parties are in effect strangers in law'[73] and thus ancillary orders such as maintenance or other property adjustment orders which are typically available on marriage breakdown are not applicable. Parties to a void marriage are also not considered to be spouses for the purposes of the Succession Act 1965. Surviving religious 'spouses' will therefore fail to enjoy an entitlement to a guaranteed legal right share or share on intestacy.[74] Further, important protections against the unilateral disposition of the family home under the Family Home Protection Act 1976 will not apply. Finally, tax credits for married spouses will remain out of reach as will exemptions for spouses from inheritance tax.[75]

Given the availability of legislative rights for cohabitants in Irish law it may appear that a declaration of nullity of marriage is not necessarily as serious a consequence as it would, perhaps, otherwise be thought: parties to a void marriage may, after all, still quality as cohabitants and thus seek ancillary orders under this regime instead. Section 172(1) of the Civil Partnership and Certain Rights and Obligations of Cohabitants Act 2010 defines a 'cohabitant' as 'one of 2 adults (whether of the same or the opposite sex) who live together as a couple in an intimate and committed relationship and who are not related to each other within the prohibited degrees of relationship or married to each other or civil partners of each other'. To be '*qualified* cohabitants' for the purposes of the legislation the couple must have cohabited for five years or, where there are dependent children, for two years.[76] It is likely that many separating

73 Crowley (n 19) 718.

74 On testacy, a surviving spouse is entitled to one-third of the deceased spouse's estate under Section 111 of the 1965 Act. On intestacy, pursuant to Section 67 they are entitled to two-thirds of the estate where the deceased is also survived by children or the entire estate where there are no surviving children. See below regarding the possible protection afforded by the Civil Partnership and Certain Rights and Obligations of Cohabitants Act 2010.

75 Note, however, they may potentially qualify for Family Home Relief under the Finance Act 2000.

76 Section 172(5) (emphasis added). Section 172(2) provides a list of considerations which a judge must take into account when determining whether the parties are qualified cohabitants. Since these are largely to ensure that the relationship is intimate and committed (similar to a marriage-like relationship), it is likely that parties to a legally void marriage will easily satisfy these criteria.

couples whose Muslim marriage is deemed void would quality as 'qualified cohabitants'. However, the scheme provided in the 2010 Act is a 'redress scheme' and, while orders such as maintenance and property adjustment are available to cohabitants,[77] they are not offered on the same terms as they are to spouses. Unlike with spouses who are automatically entitled to access ancillary relief on martial breakdown, a qualified cohabitant seeking orders under the regime in the 2010 Act must prove that they are financially dependent as a result of the relationship if they are to seek relief.[78] Further, any relief granted must go no further than to relieve the financial dependency, thus limiting the extent to which orders may be granted for cohabitants. Consequently, while the cohabitants' legislation may provide a fall-back for parties to a void marriage, the protection available does not equate to that which is available to spouses.

Parties to a void marriage who do not qualify for redress under the cohabitant legislation may pursue a claim in equity (for a beneficial interest under a purchase money resulting trust or relief under proprietary estoppel)[79] or contract law (for enforcement of the mahr if already unpaid). However, such actions are costly and have proven unpopular in other common law jurisdictions, including England and Wales.[80] Depending on the circumstances, relief may also be available under Sharia law on marriage breakdown[81] but in the apparent absence of Sharia Councils in Ireland, the accessibility or otherwise of such remedies in this jurisdiction remains unknown.[82] While it is possible

77 Relief available under the 2010 Act includes orders for: property adjustment (s 174); compensatory maintenance (s 175), and; pension adjustment (s 187). Orders for provision from the estate of a deceased cohabitant are also available: s 194.

78 Section 173.

79 Determinations of questions regarding the ownership of property, for example, the equitable ownership under a purchase money resulting trust, are dealt with under Section 36 of the Family Law Act 1995. Strangely, there is some evidence of ancillary orders being granted on nullity applications despite the absence of jurisdiction for this: Courts Service Annual Reports 2010–2012. However, this would seem to be the exception rather than the rule and an exploration of the extent to which ancillary relief is being granted by judges in this context is beyond the scope of discussion here. For further discussion, see Crowley (n 19) 719.

80 O'Sullivan and Jackson (n 1), 26–27.

81 Ibid, 27–28.

82 Even where a spouse is aware of their civil law rights and is in a financial position to pursue a civil action, they may nonetheless prefer to seek relief under Sharia law for religious reasons. In England and Wales, it has been noted the attraction of obtaining relief under Sharia law extended across the socio-economic spectrum. Shah-Kazemi, (n 2) noted at 18 that the women approaching the Sharia council in her research came from 'a variety of ...backgrounds, ranging from qualified professional women... to those with minimal formal education'. For a recent of religious courts, including discussion of Sharia Councils

local Muslim leaders may be fulfilling this role, there exists an absence of research on the topic to say definitively if such remedies are available in Ireland.

5 A Look to the Future

In this context, the question may legitimately be asked: 'Where to next?'. It is difficult to answer this question in the absence of empirical research on the issue. The gap in knowledge in this field in Ireland is substantial. We do not know the answer to such fundamental questions as what percentage of religious Muslim marriages conducted in Ireland do not secure legal recognition nor the reasons why this may be happening.[83] While it is possible that some members of the Muslim community in Ireland are purposely and jointly eschewing the formalities required for entry into a legally recognised marriage, it is equally possible that other 'spouses' may feel pressurised to enter such marriages in the hope legal recognition will be acquired thereafter. It also unclear to what extent there is even basic awareness of the precise formalities required to be met for a legally recognised marriage and the extent to which 'spouses' may unwittingly be party to an unrecognised Muslim marriage.

Unfortunately, a number of factors appear to militate against the ability to conduct such research in a meaningful and accurate manner. A key difficulty in conducting empirical research in Ireland is the very nature of the Muslim community in the jurisdiction. As has been reported – and as detailed in Chapter 4 – Muslim migration to Ireland has been 'extremely diverse, without any particular ethnic or cultural group being predominant'.[84] Although most Muslims in Ireland are Sunni there are a number of different sects within this grouping, each often with their own mosque.[85] Geographically, the community also come from a very diverse range of regions. Despite originally coming from the Middle East and North Africa, more recent Muslim immigrants have

---

in England and Wales, see Douglas et al, *Social Cohesion and Civil Law: Marriage, Divorce and Religious Courts* (Report of a Research Study funded by the AHRC) (Cardiff University, June 2011).

83 This gap in empirical research leaves Ireland a long way behind jurisdictions such as England and Wales which have been conducting such research for approximately 20 years.

84 Oliver Scharbrodt, 'Muslim Immigration to the Republic of Ireland:Trajectories and Dynamics since World War II' (2012) 47(1) *Éire-Ireland* 221, 231. See also Oliver Scharbrodt et al (eds) *Muslims in Ireland: Past and Present* (Edin Uni Press, 2015) 49–72.

85 Adil Hussain Khan et al 'Mosque communities and Muslim organisations in Dublin and other Cities' in Scharbrodt et al (eds) *Muslims in Ireland: Past and Present* (Edin Uni Press, 2015) 113–138.

originated in South and South-east Asia, sub-Saharan Africa and the Balkans.[86] Moreover, although traditionally the Muslim community in Ireland composed 'middle – and upper-class educated professionals – most of whom immigrated for educational reasons', a 'major transformation' of the community has been observed with the arrival of labour migrants, refugees, and asylum seekers.[87] On this point it has been observed:

> 'This gap [between long established professionals and newly arriving refugees] is … visible in various mosque communities where class distinctions based on social background and educational level are often maintained, with the communal mosque space providing the only forum for limited social interaction'.[88]

Cognisant of these divisions, Scharbrodt explained:

> 'The term "Muslim community" is … problematic. The actual diversity of Muslims in Ireland in terms of their ethnic, national, cultural, and linguistic backgrounds, their sectarian and ideological orientations, their different degrees of religious commitment, their educational levels, and their socioeconomic status would suggest the existence of various "Muslim communities"'.[89]

From a practical perspective, the diverse nature of the community poses a number of challenges for researchers keen to gain a better understanding of Muslim marriage practice in the Irish context. Research in various jurisdictions has highlighted that awareness of and compliance with statutory formalities is heavily influenced by community expectations.[90] Where the community is

86 See Oliver Scharbrodt, 'Muslim Immigration to Ireland after World War II' in Scharbrodt et al (eds) *Muslims in Ireland: Past and Present* (Edin Uni Press, 2015) 49–72. See also Scharbrodt, (2012) (n 84) 231.

87 Scharbrodt, (2012) (n 84) 222. See also Scharbrodt et al (eds) *Muslims in Ireland: Past and Present* (Edin Uni Press, 2015). See also the Special Issue of the *Journal of Muslim Minority Affairs*, 'Islam and Muslims in the Republic of Ireland' (2011) 31(4).

88 Scharbrodt, (2012) (n 84)241.

89 Scharbrodt(2012) (n 84) 222. Consequently, he referenced the 'Muslim population' in Ireland. See also, Patsy McGarry, 'What is it like to grow up Muslim in Ireland?' *Irish Times* (Saturday, 28 January 2017) where Third Level Muslim student respondents also highlighted the diversity of the community.

90 See Julie Macfarlane, *Understanding trends in American Muslim Divorce and Marriage* (ISPU 2012) discussed below. See also Shaheen Sardar Ali, 'Authority and Authenticity: Sharia councils, Muslim women's rights and the English courts' (2013) CFLQ 109.

as fractured as appears to be the case in Ireland, Muslim marriage practice is likely to vary significantly micro-community to micro-community as differing norms, socio-legal and socio-economic considerations, as well as different normative religious influences, play an influential role.[91]

However, it is arguable that the most appropriate answer to the 'Where to next' question may lie in this realisation of the nature of the Irish Muslim community and the role of community expectations. It is strongly arguable that much greater efforts need to be made to raise awareness within the Muslim communities themselves of the legal formalities for a legally recognised marriage and the benefits of securing such recognition. Conscious of the disadvantages of not marrying under civil law,[92] it has been observed that 'the USA is witnessing increasing numbers of mosques and Muslim communities requiring imams to have proof of the civil marriage document of the couple before performing the nikah'.[93] Reflecting this, on the basis of her research in North America, Macfarlane found:

> 'In 95% of cases ... both a nikah and a civil license were included in the marriage formalities (not necessarily at the same time). Most considered legal registration to be an obvious step, in order that they would be regarded as husband and wife in their jurisdiction. *A significant number of imams will not officiate at a nikah ceremony until the couple has already obtained a civil marriage license*'.[94]

On the other hand, highlighting that *nikah*-only marriages were more common in certain communities, Macfarlane noted this was attributed to 'widespread alienation from and mistrust of the legal system' while for others, it was considered more 'passive' than 'reactive' with 'members of this community suggest that there is *little advantage* to registering a marriage, and *that this is not*

91 In this context, painting an accurate picture of the various norms and expectations in relation to Muslim marriage practice existing within each micro-community would represent a major undertaking. It would also necessarily require the co-operation of and engagement with a large number of different Muslim communities in Ireland, a feat which has so far failed to be achieved. There is a sense that the Muslim community in Ireland is not merely diverse, but in some cases actually somewhat polarised, see Khan et al (n85) 113–138. See also McGarry (n 89) where Third Level Muslim student respondents highlighted the lack of unity within the community; see the comments of Shaykh Dr. Umar Al-Qadri on RTÉ television show *The Meaning of Life* (Season 13, Episode 5) (2016).

92 See below.

93 Sardah Ali (n 90) 119. It was noted 'Such trends do not appear apparent in the UK'.

94 Macfarlane, (n 90) 12 (emphasis added).

generally a community expectation'.[95] The perceived lack of understanding as to the importance and advantages of civil registration were also recently highlighted by Akhtar in England.[96]

The need in an Irish context for increased efforts to raise awareness for the formalities required for legal entry into marriage, with an expectation of registration being set by the Muslim communities themselves, appears undeniable. As awareness of the formalities grow and community expectations around registration become embedded, the demand for more imams to register as solemnisers would likely rise – thus ensuring that more marriages would meet the statutory formalities laid down in the 2004 Act (as amended).[97]

Admittedly, this solution is no silver bullet. Where such expectations are not encouraged by a particular micro-community, the vulnerability of parties (particularly women) to a *nikah*-only marriage will continue. Moreover, even where the expectations are set, although the market for unregistered marriages may fall, it is unlikely to disappear entirely. As a result, at least some imams will wish to remain unregistered to meet the needs of this particular cohort. However, even here, good practice can be encouraged. For example, where an unregistered imam is suspicious of coercion or any other situation where one spouse wishes to have legal recognition and the other does not, they could demand a civil marriage be undertaken before they celebrate the religious-only marriage.[98] Equally, although there appears to be no positive legislative obligation placed on unregistered solemnisers to highlight to prospective spouses that the marriage will not be deemed legal, the adoption of such practice would also aid in ensuring spouses are well informed of their status.[99] Indeed, when considered in light of the rapidly growing nature of the Muslim community in Ireland and, especially, its young demographic, the need for such expectations and norms to be set would appear to be vital as we look to the future.

6 Conclusion

Despite the intense discussion on the topic in various common (and, increasingly, civil) law jurisdictions, issues regarding the status of Muslim marriages

95 Macfarlane, ibid, 12–13 (emphasis added). See also Julie Macfarlane *Islamic Divorce in North America* (OUP, 2012) p44–45; 197–198.

96 Akhtar (n 10) 193–210.

97 See above.

98 Arguably, in light of religious and cultural context, the ability of those couples who jointly and knowingly wish to secure a religious marriage only to do so should continue.

99 A legislative amendment to this effect could equally be introduced to encourage such transparency.

conducted within Ireland have attracted minimal attention. Notwithstanding the reasonably straight forward legislative framework applied in the jurisdiction under the Civil Registration Act 2004 (as amended), there appears to be a relatively small number of Muslim marriages registered over the past five years with the Central Statistics Office and a worrying lack of imams registered on the official Register of Solemnisers. The lack of easily accessible information and the abundance of misinformation in relation to the legal position of Muslim marriages in Ireland are major causes for concern. While in the absence of comprehensive empirical evidence on the issue, it appears likely that a potentially significant minority of Muslim marriages conducted in Ireland may not be securing legal status, it appears equally clear that the consequences for such Muslim 'spouses', particularly financially weaker 'spouses' whose marriages remain unrecognised, are severe. It is to be hoped that community awareness of the formalities is promoted and community expectations for the registration of marriages is encouraged.

Bibliography

Accord, 'Getting Married in the Catholic Church', available at: https://www.accord.ie/services/getting-married/getting-married-in-the-catholic-church.

Ahmed, F. and Calderwood Norton, J., 'Religious tribunals, religious freedom, and concern for vulnerable women' (2012) 24(4) CFLQ 363–388.

Akhtar, R. C. 'Unregistered Muslim Marriages: An Emerging Culture of Celebrating Rites and Conceding Rights' in J. Miles, P. Mody and R. Probert (eds) *Marriage Rites and Rights* (Hart, 2015) 193–210.

Al-Qadri, U., *The Meaning of Life* (Season 13, Episode 5) (RTÉ 2016).

Bano, S., *Complexity, Difference and Muslim Personal Law: Rethinking Relationships between Shari'ah Councils and South Asian Muslim Women in Britain* (Warwick University Doctoral dissertation, 2004).

Bano, S., *Exploratory Survey of Shariah Councils in England with Respect to Family Law* (Ministry of Justice/University of Reading, 2012).

Central Statistics Office, *Standard Report on Methods and Quality (v1) for Marriages and Civil Partnership Registration* (Dublin: Stationery Office, 2013).

Central Statistics Office, *Census 2016 Profile 8: Religion Ethnicity and Irish Travellers* (Dublin: Stationery Office, 2017).

Crowley, L., *Family Law* (Round Hall, 2013).

Douglas, G., et al., 'The role of religious tribunals in regulating marriage and divorce' (2012) 24(2) CFLQ 139.

Douglas, G., et al., *Social Cohesion and Civil Law: Marriage, Divorce and Religious Courts* (Cardiff University, 2011).

Eekelaar, J., 'Marriage, A modest proposal' (2013) (1) FLJ 83.

Eekelaar, J., 'Marriage, religion and gender equality' in F. Banda and L. Fishbayn Joffe (eds), *Women's Rights and Religious Law* (Routledge 2016).

Enright, M., '"Preferring the Stranger?" Towards an Irish Approach to Muslim Divorce Practice' (2013) 49(1) Ir Jur 65–97.

Inter-Departmental Committee on Reform of Marriage Law, *Discussion Paper No. 5* (Dublin: Inter-Departmental Committee on Reform of Marriage Law, 2004).

Khan, A H., et al. 'Mosque communities and Muslim organisations in Dublin and other Cities' in O. Scharbrodt, et al (eds) *Muslims in Ireland: Past and Present* (2015, Edin Uni Press) 113–138.

Law Commission for England and Wales, *Getting Married: A scoping paper* (2015).

Leahy, S. and O'Sullivan, K., 'Marriage in Ireland: Current Law and Practice' (2018) CFLQ (forthcoming).

McGarry, P., 'What is it like to grow up Muslim in Ireland?' *Irish Times* (Dublin, 28 January 2017).

McGowan, P., 'Governed by Marriage Law' (2016) 25(3) Soc and Leg Stud 311–331.

Macfarlane, J., *Understanding trends in American Muslim Divorce and Marriage* (ISPU 2012).

Macfarlane, J., *Islamic Divorce in North America*(OUP, 2012).

Muslim Marriage Working Group, Muslim Marriage: *Report of Working Group* (2012), available at: https://www.whatdotheyknow.com/request/179578/response/444442/attach/7/MMWG%20SUBMISSION%20AND%20FINAL%20REPORT%2011.10.12.pdf.

O'Sullivan, K. and Jackson, L., 'Muslim Marriage (Non)-Recognition: Implications and Possible Solutions' (2017) 39(1) JSWFL 22–41.

Poulter, S.M., *English law and ethnic minority customs* (Butterworths, 1986).

Registrar General, *Annual Report 2013*, available at https://www.welfare.ie/en/downloads/Registrar-General-Report-2013.pdf.

Sardar Ali, S., 'Authority and Authenticity: Sharia councils, Muslim women's rights and the English courts' (2013) CFLQ 109.

Scharbrodt, O., 'Muslim Immigration to the Republic of Ireland: Trajectories and Dynamics since World War II' (2012) 47(1) *Éire-Ireland* 221–243.

Scharbrodt, O., et al. (eds) *Muslims in Ireland: Past and Present* (Edi Uni Press, 2015).

Scharbrodt, O., 'Muslim Immigration to Ireland after World War II' in O. Scharbrodt, et al. (eds) *Muslims in Ireland: Past and Present* (Edi Uni Press) 49–72.

Shah-Kazemi, S., *Untying the Knot, Muslim Women, Divorce and the Shariah*, (Nuffield Foundation 2001).

Shatter, A.J. *Family Law* (4th edn, Bloomsbury Professional, 1997).

Sherwood, H., 'Most women in UK who have Islamic wedding miss out on legal rights', *The Guardian*, (London, 20 November 2017).

'The Truth about Muslim Marriage' (Channel 4, 21 November 2017) available at http://www.channel4.com/programmes/the-truth-about-muslim-marriage.

Williams, R., 'Civil and Religious Law in England: A religious perspective' (2008) 10 Ecc LJ262.

CHAPTER 7

Overseas Marriage and Divorce in Islamic Form

A Critical Perspective on the Development of Irish Private International Law

Máire Ní Shúilleabháin

1 Introduction

Private international law mediates the interaction of different legal systems affecting marital status. It assumes a particular significance in the immediate aftermath of significant migration, where persons who have married and divorced within one legal system, become settled within another legal system. Its role is also commensurately affected by the degrees of normative difference between the legal systems at issue. The more varied the domestic norms of the connected legal systems, the greater the reluctance to accept an overseas marital status at face value, and the more critical the role of private international law.

The past 25 years have seen huge increases in immigration from Muslim-majority countries into Ireland.[1] The most recent (2016) census indicates a Muslim population of 63,400.[2] In 1991, the Muslim population stood at 3,875.[3] There is evidence of substantial migration to Ireland from countries including Pakistan, Egypt, Algeria and Saudi Arabia.[4] In this context of *very recent* migration from countries which apply religious 'personal law' in family law matters,[5] it seems probable that there are many Muslims now living in Ireland who have previously married or divorced in a legal system based on Islamic law (also known as 'Sharia' law). As will be illustrated below, Irish and Islamic law express radically different views on the appropriate regulation of marriage and divorce. With this clash of norms, many Irish-resident Muslims will experience

1 Oliver Scharbrodt and others, *Muslims in Ireland, Past and Present* (Edinburgh University Press 2015) 56.

2 See <http://www.cso.ie/en/media/csoie/releasespublications/documents/population/2017/Chapter_8_Religion.pdf> accessed 20 December 2017.

3 Scharbrodt and others (n 1) 56.

4 Scharbrodt and others (n 1) 56.

5 See Dawoud Sudqi El Alami and Doreen Hinchcliffe, *Islamic Marriage and Divorce Laws of the Arab World* (Kluwer 1996) 38–62; Judith Tucker, *Women, Family, and Gender in Islamic Law* (Cambridge University Press 2008) 71–72.

 | DOI:10.1163/9789004398252_008

legal uncertainty in establishing their marital status – unless appropriate private international law frameworks are put in place.

Whilst it is likely that for many Muslim immigrants, at a personal level, the religious standing of their marriage (under Islam) may be at least as important as its Irish civil law status,[6] nonetheless, the significance of the latter (as determined by private international law) should not be underestimated.[7] A migrant's official marital status determines access to a myriad of practical rights in the country of settlement, including, for example, rights relating to inheritance, pensions, social security, immigration and ancillary relief on divorce.

1.1 *A Comparative Overview of Domestic Requirements*

1.1.1 Marriage

Irish domestic law insists on public celebration of marriage before a registered solemniser, with both spouses present, and with subsequent registration.[8] Countries applying Islamic law, on the other hand, tend to apply fewer formalities.[9] Private unregistered ceremonies may give rise to a valid marriage (*nikah*)[10] – and proxy ceremonies (conducted in the absence of one of the parties) are widely accepted.[11]

The substantive conditions of marriage are also markedly different. As will be discussed below, Irish domestic law insists on monogamy, while Islamic law permits of polygamy and allows men to have up to four wives. Islamic law imposes restrictions on inter-faith marriage,[12] whereas Irish law

6 See Ann Black, 'In the Shadow of our Legal System: Shari'a in Australia' in Rex Ahdar and Nicholas Aroney (eds), *Shari'a in the West* (Oxford University Press 2010) 243–244; also Ayelet Shachar, 'State, Religion and the Family: The New Dilemmas of Multicultural Accommodation' in Ahdar and Aroney, 120–121, 124–127.

7 See Mathias Rohe, 'Family and the Law in Europe: Bringing Together Secular Legal Orders and Religious Norms and Needs', in Prakash Shah with Marie-Claire Foblets and Mathias Rohe (eds), *Family, Religion and Law: Cultural Encounters in Europe* (Ashgate 2014) 68; Jørgen Nielsen, *Muslims in Western Europe* (3rd edn, Edinburgh University Press 2004) 111–115.

8 Civil Registration Act 2004, ss 49 and 51.

9 Prakash Shah, 'Inconvenient Marriages, or What Happens When Ethnic Minorities Marry Trans-jurisdictionally' (2010) 6(2) Utrecht Law Review 17, 24–25; El Alami and Hinchcliffe (n 5) 5–6.

10 Shah, 'Inconvenient Marriages' (n 9) 24–25, 27; Tucker (n 5) 71.

11 Shah, 'Inconvenient Marriages' (n 9) 26; El Alami and Hinchcliffe (n 5) 6; Tucker (n 5) 61.

12 Under traditional Islamic law, Muslim women are not permitted to marry non-Muslim men: see Rohe (n 7) 68; Edwige Rude-Antoine, 'Muslim Maghrebian Marriage in France: A Problem for Legal Pluralism' in Ann Laquer Estin (ed), *The Multi-Cultural Family* (Ashgate 2008) 71; Javaid Rehman, 'The Sharia, Islamic Family Laws and International Human

does not.[13] Irish domestic law allows same-sex marriage,[14] whereas Islamic law envisages only heterosexual marriage.[15] In traditional Islamic law, there is no minimum age for marriage,[16] while Irish law sets a minimum age of eighteen years.[17] Consent requirements are also disparate.[18]

Of course, Islamic law is not a single monolithic entity.[19] Traditional standards have been modified by statute and custom in many countries applying Islamic law[20] – and in some specific cases, the applicable rules will match Irish domestic requirements.[21] It is also important to acknowledge that there are discrete 'schools' of Sharia,[22] and differing interpretations of the Quranic injunctions relevant to marriage and divorce.[23] One must also recognise that traditional interpretations permitting of polygamy, child marriage and deemed consent are often challenged by scholars offering revisionist interpretations

Rights Law: Examining the Theory and Practice of Polygamy and Talaq' (2007) 21 International Journal of Law, Policy and the Family 108, 114.

13 The Irish Law Reform Commission has suggested that such a restriction would offend public policy under Irish law, and is therefore incapable of recognition: Law Reform Commission, 'Report on Private International Law Aspects of Capacity to Marry and Choice of Law in Proceedings for Nullity of Marriage' (LRC-19, 1985) 69.

14 Art 41.4 *Bunreacht na hÉireann* (Constitution of Ireland).

15 See <http://ilga.org/maps-sexual-orientation-laws> accessed 20 December 2017.

16 Tucker (n 5) 43; El Alami and Hinchcliffe (n 5) 6.

17 Family Law Act 1995, s 31. Marriage at a younger age can be sanctioned by the court (s 33) – but s 45(1)(e) Domestic Violence Act 2018 will repeal this exception when it comes into force.

18 On Irish law, see Alan Shatter, *Shatter's Family Law* (4th edn, Butterworths 1997) 186–209; *PF v GO'M* [2001] 3 IR 1. On Islamic law, see Tucker (n 5) 42–45; El Alami and Hinchcliffe (n 5) 6.

19 See Black (n 6) 245.

20 Nielsen (n 7) 108–109; Michael Nazir-Ali, 'Islamic Law: Fundamental Freedoms, and Social Cohesion: Retrospect and Prospect' in Ahdar and Aroney (n 6) 84–85; Tucker (n 5) 71–72. Also it is important to note that in some Muslim-majority countries, traditional Islamic law has been entirely displaced by a secular civil code, eg in Turkey: see Amira Mashhour, 'Islamic Law and Gender Equality – Could There be a Common Ground?: A Study of Divorce and Polygamy in Sharia Law and Contemporary Legislation in Tunisia and Egypt' (2005) 27(2) Human Rights Quarterly 562, 587.

21 For example, Moroccan law requires parties to be 18 years of age to marry: see Abdullah Saeed, 'Reflections on the Establishment of Shari'a Courts in Australia' in Ahdar and Aroney (n 6) 236–237. In Tunisia, polygamy is prohibited: Tucker (n 5) 75; Mashhour (n 20) 585.

22 Nazir-Ali (n 20) 73–75; Tucker (n 5) 59; El Alami and Hinchcliffe (n 5) 3–5.

23 Nielsen (n 7) 108–109; Erich Kolig, 'To Shari'aticize or Not to Shari'aticize: Islamic and Secular Law in Liberal Democratic Society' in Ahdar and Aroney (n 6) 264–268; Máiréad Enright, 'Preferring the Stranger? Towards an Irish Approach to Muslim Divorce Practice' (2013) 49 Irish Jurist 65, 66–67.

which would bring aspects of Islamic law into closer alignment with Irish norms.[24] Nonetheless, it remains clear that the domestic requirements for marriage vary considerably as between Irish law and the laws of those countries deriving their family codes from Islam.

1.1.2 Divorce

Similar patterns of divergence exist with respect to divorce. In Ireland, a decree of divorce must be obtained from a civil court, and only after four years of separation.[25] The gender of the applicant has no bearing on the procedure or grounds.[26]

Whilst traditional Islamic law also makes provision for judicial divorce,[27] this is offered in parallel to other forms of private dissolution which can terminate the marriage with immediate effect.[28] Men have a general entitlement to pronounce a repudiation (*talaq*) and this is thought to be the most common method of dissolution in Islamic countries.[29] Women are entitled to pronounce *talaq* only where the right has been delegated by the husband.[30] Islamic law also makes provision for other forms of private dissolution (including the *khul* divorce by mutual consent[31]); however, it is clear that women are much more restricted than men in their access to divorce – and even in the event of divorce by *khul*, the wife may be obliged to forego her *mahr* (a financial settlement agreed at the time of marriage).[32]

In recent times, additional formalities have been imposed on those availing of private divorce mechanisms, and civil and religious authorities have assumed a much greater role in most countries applying Islamic divorce law.[33] Whilst there is therefore a clear pattern of increased regulatory control of

24 See, eg Mashhour (n 20); Rehman (n 12) 114–117; Niaz Shah, 'Women's Human Rights in the Koran: an Interpretative Approach' (2006) 28(4) Human Rights Quarterly 868; Tucker (n 5) 67–70, 78.

25 Art 41.3.2° *Bunreacht na hÉireann* (Constitution of Ireland); Family Law (Divorce) Act 1996, s 5(1).

26 ibid.

27 Lucy Carroll, 'Muslim Women and "Islamic Divorce" in England' in Estin (n 12) 192–196; El Alami and Hinchcliffe (n 5) 29–32; Tucker (n 5) 92–95.

28 Carroll (n 27) 190; El Alami and Hinchcliffe (n 5) 23 referring to the triple *talaq*.

29 El Alami and Hinchcliffe (n 5) 22, 24; *H v S* [2011] EWHC B23 (Fam) [18].

30 El Alami and Hinchcliffe (n 5) 25; Tucker (n 5) 91–92.

31 El Alami and Hinchcliffe (n 5) 27–28; Tucker (n 5) 95–100.

32 Carroll (n 27) 200–201; Black (n 6) 244; Rehman (n 12) 118. Judicial divorce is generally confined to specific fault-based grounds, although these vary from one 'school' to another and between different countries: see Rehman (n 12) 118–121; Tucker (n 5) 92–95, 107–109, 119–120; El Alami and Hinchcliffe (n 5) 29–32: Black (n 6) 244.

33 Nielsen (n 7) 111; Carroll (n 27) 190; Tucker (n 5) 116–117; El Alami and Hinchcliffe (n 5) 24.

divorce in Sharia law countries, the official intervention is often of a limited administrative nature[34] – and even in the event of court involvement, there may be no adjudication as such, simply a responsibility to record the fact of pronouncement of *talaq*.[35]

1.2 *Irish Private International Law: Overview of Current State of Play*

With such stark regulatory divergence, there is an obvious necessity for clear and well-developed private international law rules on recognition of Islamic marriage and divorce. This chapter examines the extent to which Irish law satisfies this need.

As far as overseas marriage recognition is concerned, substantial progress was achieved in the landmark Supreme Court judgment in *HAH v SAA*.[36] While this judgment is problematic in certain respects, it still takes the Irish law common law much further along the path towards a rational and coherent private international law regime. These developments (and their shortcomings) will be discussed below.

By contrast with the advances in the sphere of marriage recognition, Islamic divorce recognition has received very little attention, and, as will be explained below, divorced migrants may face a legal vacuum in their quest for clarity on their marital status. For such persons, legislative intervention appears to offer the only viable solution.

1.3 *Reasons for Differing Levels of Development in Marriage and Divorce Recognition*

The strikingly different levels of development of (a) Islamic marriage recognition and (b) Islamic divorce recognition can be attributed to a number of factors. First, this is a reflection of the long era of indissolubility of marriage under Irish law. While marriage has always been a recognised (and constitutionally-cherished) institution,[37] civil divorce was constitutionally-prohibited until 1995 and then permitted only on very restrictive terms.[38] Consequently, whilst there was never any difficulty in accepting the common law criteria for overseas marriage recognition,[39] Irish law diverged sharply from English law as far as divorce recognition was concerned, and has always been much more

34 See, eg the description of Section 7 of the Pakistan Muslim Family Laws Ordinance in Carroll (n 27) 190.
35 Tucker (n 5) 116; *H v S* [2011] EWHC B23 (Fam) [19, 59–61].
36 [2017] IESC 40.
37 Shatter (n 18) 16 ff.
38 Shatter (n 18) 369 ff.
39 William Binchy, *Irish Conflicts of Law* (Butterworths 1988) 218 ff.

conservative.[40] Second, while marriage recognition has remained largely a matter for the common law[41] (and is therefore amenable to organic, judge-led development), divorce recognition has been subsumed into statutory regulation, both in Ireland[42] and in the United Kingdom.[43] Moreover, the Irish statutory rules pre-date the 1995 constitutional referendum sanctioning domestic divorce, and were adopted at a time when the immigrant Muslim population was comparatively tiny.[44] Third, the development of the marriage recognition rules is an incidental by-product of the use of 'marriage' as a gateway for immigration rights[45] and of the burgeoning litigation on 'family reunification'.[46] This has resulted in the Irish courts being presented with questions of recognition of overseas Islamic marriages in a number of recent cases, and being given an opportunity to develop and modernise the law.

2 Recognition of Overseas Islamic Marriages under Irish Law

Whilst there have been some tentative suggestions of alternative approaches,[47] Irish law has generally remained faithful to the traditional common law criteria for foreign marriage recognition.[48] The common law allows for recognition of an overseas 'marriage' provided: (a) the overseas institution is sufficiently analogous to Irish conceptions of marriage as to be capable of being characterised as 'marriage' under Irish law (the 'characterisation' test); (b) the formality rules of the law of the place of celebration were complied with (the so-called *lex loci celebrationis* test for 'formal validity'); and (c) each party complied with the substantive or capacity rules of his or her own domiciliary law (the so-called

40 Binchy (n 39) 269 ff; Máire Ní Shúilleabháin, 'Foreign Divorce Recognition and Residence: A Critical Analysis of *H v H*' (2017) 57 Irish Jurist 162.

41 See Binchy (n 39) 218 ff; Máire Ní Shúilleabháin, 'Marriage, Divorce and Stagnation in the Irish Conflict of Laws' (2014) 52 Irish Jurist 68, 79 ff; Paul Torremans (ed), *Cheshire, North and Fawcett: Private International Law* (15th edn, Oxford University Press 2017) 891 ff.

42 Domicile and Recognition of Foreign Divorces Act 1986.

43 Family Law Act 1986.

44 Scharbrodt and others (n 1) 216.

45 Refugee Act 1996, s 18.

46 See Ní Shúilleabháin, 'Marriage, Divorce and Stagnation' (n 41) 79–87.

47 See the 'real marital relationships' test, propounded in *Hamza v Minister for Justice, Equality and Law Reform* [2010] IEHC 427 (discussed in Ní Shúilleabháin, 'Marriage, Divorce and Stagnation' (n 41) 79–82) and rejected in *AMA v Minister for Justice and Equality* [2016] IEHC 466 [48–51].

48 *HAH v SAA* (n 36) [2, 6] (O'Malley J).

'dual domicile' test for 'essential validity').[49] In this context, 'domicile' has its traditional common law meaning and refers (broadly) to the law of the country where a person was residing with the intention of remaining permanently or indefinitely.[50]

2.1 *Overview of Impact of Common Law Criteria on Recognition of Overseas Islamic Marriages*

The three-fold common law recognition requirements are generally quite favourable to the recognition of marriages celebrated in a Sharia legal system, and to the avoidance of 'limping marriages' (marriages which are valid under one legal order but invalid under another connected legal order).

As a 'when in Rome' rule, the *lex loci celebrationis* test is accommodating of Sharia law informality. Even if the local law (at the place of celebration of marriage) only prescribes (for example) two witnesses to the ceremony,[51] and lays down no further formality requirement, the marriage will be recognised as formally valid for the purposes of Irish law, once the (minimal) formalities of the *lex loci celebrationis* were observed. An Irish 'presumption of validity of marriage' may also support the recognition of a marriage celebrated overseas in a relatively informal Islamic ceremony.[52] Even if there is some difficulty in *proving* satisfaction of the *lex loci celebrationis* (for example, where the marriage was not registered and no official certificate is available[53]), the Irish judge may assume (in the absence of evidence to the contrary) that the local formalities were duly complied with.[54]

The 'dual domicile' test for essential validity is also broadly favourable to recognition. Where the parties are domiciled in an Islamic legal system (at the time of entry into the marriage), the marriage is entitled to recognition in Ireland (at least in principle) even if the Irish substantive conditions for marriage were not met. However, the fact that only essentials and not formalities are referred to the domiciliary law may sometimes result in the non-recognition

49 Binchy (n 39) 211, 218–235; Jonathan Hill and Máire Ní Shúilleabháin, *Clarkson and Hill's Conflict of Laws* (5th edn, Oxford University Press 2016) 354 ff.

50 See further Binchy (n 39) 45–96; Clarkson and Hill (n 49) 317–339.

51 See El Alami and Hinchcliffe (n 5) 5: offer and acceptance in the presence of two adult male witnesses are the core formalities prescribed by the Hanafi and Hanbali schools of Islam.

52 *Hassan v Minister for Justice, Equality and Law Reform* [2013] IESC 8 [31], [49]–[50].

53 See Shah, 'Inconvenient Marriages' (n 9) 27–28.

54 In *Hassan* (n 52) it was accepted that the presumption could be applied to facilitate recognition of an Islamic marriage ceremony conducted in Somalia (in the absence of official certification).

of marriages celebrated outside of an Islamic law system by persons domiciled in an Islamic law system: for example, where a Muslim couple celebrate only a religious marriage in a jurisdiction requiring supplementary civil marriage or a form of civil registration;[55] or where migrant Muslims develop a practice of marrying in the consulate of their country of origin, thereby abiding by its formality rules, and not those of the receiving state.[56] It is not suggested here that this outcome reflects a particular flaw in the *lex loci celebrationis* rule (rather it is accepted that the *lex loci* rule – as an internationally accepted standard – which normally corresponds to party expectations, is a sensible one[57]) but it is an observable fact that the *lex loci* doctrine can sometimes serve, in practice, to invalidate the marriages of Muslim minorities and to create limping status.[58]

The stark differences between Sharia and Irish domestic conceptions of marriage can potentially result in overseas Islamic marriages failing the 'characterisation' test. In some instances, this will be relatively uncontroversial. For example, it is likely that the Shia '*muta*' (temporary) marriages will not be considered sufficiently analogous to Irish conceptions of marriage because permanent (or at least long-term) commitment is considered to be a core element of marriage, as understood under Irish law.[59] Thus, even if *muta* is renewable, it is unlikely to satisfy the characterisation test.[60] Whilst some may take the view that this is an excessively 'Eurocentric' approach to characterisation,[61] others – who consider *muta* to be an exploitative practice and a form of

55 See, eg *A-M v A-M* (*Divorce: Jurisdiction: Validity of Marriage*) [2001] 2 FLR 6.

56 See *Dukali v Lamrani* [2012] EWHC 1748 (Fam) where a Muslim couple of dual British and Moroccan nationality married in the Moroccan Consulate in London. The marriage was found to be invalid insofar as it failed to comply with the formalities of the *lex loci celebrationis* (English law). The judgment referred (at [22]) to the fact that many Moroccan couples (including – one would presume – many couples with a Moroccan domicile) had married in the same way.

57 Clarkson and Hill (n 49) 360.

58 This problem of formally-invalid marriages is probably best tackled by internal measures *within* the countries where such marriages are celebrated: see Kathryn O'Sullivan and Leyla Jackson, 'Muslim Marriage (Non) Recognition: Implications and Possible Solutions (2017) 39 Journal of Social Welfare and Family Law 22; John Eekelaar, 'Marriage: A Modest Proposal' [2013] Family Law Journal (1) 83; Sophie van Bijsterveld, 'Negotiating the Unfamiliar: Reflections from The Netherlands on the Archbishop of Canterbury's Lecture' in Ahdar and Aroney (n 6) 214–215.

59 See, eg *DT v CT* (*Divorce: Ample Resources*) [2002] 3 IR 334, 405: '… marriage … is… entered into, in principle, for life. It is not entered into for a determinate period'.

60 This was the view of a UK Asylum Tribunal: *LS* (*Mut'a or sighē*) *Iran* [2007] UKAIT 72 [18]–[19].

61 See Shah, 'Inconvenient Marriages' (n 9) 30–32.

prostitution[62] – are likely to welcome this outcome. Either way, it seems reasonable to refuse to characterise *muta* as marriage when, even in the legal systems from which it originates, it is offered in parallel to permanent marriage and is considered to be a distinct legal institution.[63]

The characterisation of polygamous marriage can also be problematic – and for many years, it was suggested that Irish law might impose a blanket prohibition on recognition of all marriages celebrated in a form permitting of polygamy (even in cases where there was no second spouse), thus casting a shadow of invalidity over the vast majority of marriages celebrated in an Islamic legal system.[64] This aversion to 'potential polygamy' is traceable to the notorious judgment in *Hyde v Hyde* where English matrimonial relief was held to be inapplicable to a factually-monogamous marriage celebrated overseas in accordance with Mormon rites permitting of polygamy: 'a system so utterly at variance with the Christian conception of marriage'.[65] The *Hyde v Hyde* definition of marriage 'as understood in Christendom'[66] was embedded into Irish constitutional jurisprudence[67] ('the voluntary union for life of one man and one woman, to the exclusion of all others'[68]) – and in the 1980s, it was determined in *Conlon v Mohamed* that a common law mechanism for saving a formally defective foreign marriage[69] should not be applied where the marriage

62 See, eg Richa Nagar, 'Religion, Race and the Debate over *Mut'a* in Dar es Salaam' (2000) 26 Feminist Studies 661, 676–683; Shahnaz Khan, 'Race, Gender and Orientalism: *Muta* and the Canadian Legal System' (1995) 8 Canadian Journal of Women and the Law 249,256; Shahla Haeri, 'Temporary Marriage and the State in Iran: an Islamic Discourse on Female Sexuality' (1992) 59 Social Research 201.

63 Tucker (n 5) 58.

64 See Máire Ní Shúilleabháin, 'Accommodating Cultural Diversity under Irish Family Law' (2002) 24 Dublin University Law Journal 175, 184; *HAH v SAA* (n 36) [57] (O'Malley J.). In *HAH v SAA* (n 36) the Irish Attorney General initially sought to maintain this position (that all potentially polygamous marriages should be refused recognition even if they were in fact monogamous) but subsequently accepted that a more nuanced approach was justified where potentially polygamous marriages were concerned: O'Malley J [12], [28].

65 *Hyde v Hyde and Woodmansee* (1865–69) LR 1 P & D 130, 136. See Prakash Shah, 'Attitudes to Polygamy in English Law' (2003) 52 International and Comparative Law Quarterly 369, 374 referring to 'the long shadow cast by the decision in *Hyde v Hyde*' and Sebastian Poulter, 'Hyde v Hyde–A Reappraisal' (1976) 25 International and Comparative Law Quarterly 475, 485 referring to the 'religious bigotry' which characterised the judgment (at least to modern eyes).

66 *Hyde* (n 65) 133.

67 Shatter (n 18) 151; *HAH v SAA* (n 36) [30], [36] (O'Malley J).

68 *Hyde* (n 65) 133.

69 At common law, a formally invalid overseas marriage could be recognised, on an exceptional basis, where it was impossible for the parties to comply with the *lex loci*

was potentially polygamous (in this case a factually-monogamous Islamic marriage celebrated in South Africa).[70]

More recently, the unreasonableness of a blanket prohibition on recognition of potential polygamy has been acknowledged: first, in *Hamza v Minister for Justice, Equality and Law Reform* in 2010 where it was accepted that a potentially polygamous marriage could be recognised provided neither spouse was domiciled in Ireland at its inception;[71] and more definitively, in 2017, in the Supreme Court's judgment in *HAH v SAA* where concerns about 'potential polygamy' were finally laid to rest.

In *HAH v SAA* O'Malley J (with the unanimous agreement of the Supreme Court) expressed the view that *Hyde v Hyde* could no longer 'be considered as defining marriage for the purposes of Irish law'.[72] In her opinion, a judgment which identified legal marriage with Christian marriage, could not fit into the current constitutional landscape.[73] Having decided that the Irish legal institution of marriage 'cannot be described in terms of traditional Christian doctrine',[74] O'Malley J concluded that there was no justification for refusing to recognise the marriage of a couple living in a monogamous relationship purely because 'they married under a system of law that permits polygamy'.[75] In her view, there was 'no principle at stake here' and no risk of harm to the public or to the institution of marriage.[76] Crucially, O'Malley J did not qualify this acceptance of potential polygamy by reference to considerations of domicile[77] (as the High Court had in *Hamza*). This was significant because the approach adopted in *Hamza* imperilled the validity of factually-monogamous marriages contracted by Muslim migrants who have settled in (and have become domiciled in) Ireland but who have chosen to celebrate their marriage (in a form permitting of polygamy) in their original homeland.[78]

---

celebrationis, or where an expectation of compliance would be unreasonable: see further Binchy (n 39) 228–231; Clarkson and Hill (n 49) 361–363.

70 [1987] ILRM 172; [1989] ILRM 523. For a more detailed discussion of *Conlon v Mohamed*, see Ní Shúilleabháin, 'Accommodating Cultural Diversity' (n 64) 181–184; *HAH v SAA* (n 36) [55]–[59] (O'Malley J).

71 *Hamza* (n 47) [42].

72 *HAH v SAA* (n 36) [97] (O'Malley J).

73 ibid.

74 *HAH v SAA* (n 36) [98] (O'Malley J), referring to the introduction of no-fault divorce and same-sex marriage.

75 *HAH v SAA* (n 36) [105] (O'Malley J).

76 *HAH v SAA* (n 36) [104]–[105] (O'Malley J).

77 *HAH v SAA* (n 36) [108]–[109] (O'Malley J).

78 For criticism of this position (which also prevailed in English law in the 1970s and 1980s), see Poulter (n 65) 504–506; also Ní Shúilleabháin, 'Marriage, Divorce and Stagnation' (n 41) 85.

The recognition of overseas Islamic marriages may also be affected by the public policy doctrine.[79] This doctrine can have a validating or an invalidating effect:[80] in other words it may serve to invalidate a marriage which is formally valid under the *lex loci celebrationis* and essentially valid under the dual domicile test (where recognition of the marriage is 'egregious' from an Irish perspective[81]) – or may validate a foreign marriage which fails to satisfy one of those requirements (where one of the foreign invalidating restrictions is considered highly objectionable[82]). The more radical the divergences in domestic standards, the more likely it is that public policy will come into play – and it therefore follows that Islamic marriage recognition is particularly vulnerable to its influence. This is all the more true in recent times where the reach of public policy is expanding, and where support for the radical pluralism inherent in the dual domicile test appears to be wavering.[83]

2.2 *Specific Cases*

Having discussed the more general impact of the common law approach to recognition, this section will consider specific aspects of Islamic marriage and their accommodation within the Irish legal order.

2.2.1 Proxy Marriages

In certain schools of Islam, women absent themselves from the marriage ceremony and are represented by a proxy.[84] The orthodoxy of proxy marriages

79 There is a significant overlap between questions of characterisation and questions of public policy, especially where a particular *category* or *type* of foreign marriage is said to be contrary to public policy. Thus, in *HAH v SAA* O'Malley J used the language of public policy in removing what was effectively a characterisation barrier for potentially polygamous marriage.

80 Law Reform Commission (n 13) 68–69.

81 *HAH v SAA* (n 36) [25] (O'Malley J). The examples given are coerced marriages and marriages which may be equated with slavery (and which are nonetheless considered valid marriages under the applicable foreign law).

82 The Law Reform Commission gives the example of a penal or discriminatory incapacity under the applicable foreign law, including one based on race or religion: Law Reform Commission (n 13) 69.

83 See James Fawcett, Máire Ní Shúilleabháin and Sangeeta Shah, *Human Rights and Private International Law* (Oxford University Press 2016) 645–649. English cases decided in the 1960s indicated a willingness to uphold foreign marriages which were significantly out of step with English domestic norms (see eg *Mohamed v Knott* [1968] 2 WLR 1446); however, with increased emphasis of human rights, there is no longer the same sense of the exceptionality of recourse to public policy (see eg *City of Westminster v IC* [2008] 2 FLR 267).

84 EL Alami and Hinchcliffe (n 5) 6. See also *Aslam v Minister for Justice and Equality* [2011] IEHC 512 [22]; *Hamza* (n 47) [22]. This interpretation of Islam is however contested by Muslim feminists and others: see Tucker (n 5) 67; Mashhour (n 20) 593–594; Samia Bano,

also allows for the celebration of marriage where spouses are in two different countries at the time of the ceremony, and such marriage forms may be considered valid as a matter of Islamic law.[85] Whilst English domestic law, like Irish law, insists on the presence of the spouses at a domestic marriage ceremony, the English common law has, for many years, accepted the validity of overseas proxy ceremonies which are formally valid under the law of the country where the ceremony took place (the *lex loci celebrationis*). According to *Apt v Apt* such marriage forms could be recognised even if the absent party was domiciled and resident in England at the time of the overseas ceremony.[86] Whilst *Apt v Apt* concerned an Argentinian marriage ceremony and the court observed that this was 'clearly a Christian marriage within the definition given by Lord Penzance in *Hyde v Hyde*',[87] it has since been confirmed that the doctrine laid down in *Apt v Apt* can apply to non-Christian proxy marriage ceremonies.[88]

The current status of overseas proxy and absentee marriage ceremonies is however somewhat unclear – particularly in Ireland. In the United Kingdom, there have been some suggestions that where the parties to a marriage are in two different countries at the time of the marriage, the formality rules of *both* countries should be brought to bear (a 'dual compliance' approach).[89] In Ireland, whilst *Apt v Apt* has been approved as good law,[90] it has also been suggested that the proxy marriage form should only be capable of recognition where neither spouse was domiciled in Ireland at the time of the ceremony.[91]

Legitimate concerns arise with respect to the recognition of overseas proxy and absentee marriages. The 1962 UN Convention on Consent to Marriage insists on party presence save 'where the circumstances are exceptional'.[92] Clearly physical presence allows for a better verification of true consent and protects against forced marriage. Proxy and absentee marriage forms are also

---

'In Pursuit of Religious and Legal Diversity: a Response to the Archbishop of Canterbury and the "Sharia Debate" in Britain' (2008) 10 Ecclesiastical Law Journal 283, 294.

85 Shah, 'Inconvenient Marriages' (n 9) 26.

86 [1948] P. 83, 88–89.

87 *Apt* (n 86) 86.

88 See, eg *Awuku v Secretary of State for the Home Dept* [2017] EWCA Civ 178 dealing with recognition of a Ghanaian customary ceremony.

89 In particular, where one of the spouses is in the United Kingdom at the time of the ceremony and participating via the telephone: see EB Crawford and JM Carruthers, 'Dual Locality Events: Marriage by Telephone' [2011] Scots Law Times 227; *City of Westminster v IC* (n 83) [41]–[42]; Fawcett, Ní Shúilleabháin and Shah (n 83) 619–620.

90 *Hamza* (n 47) [26].

91 *Hamza* (n 47) [23].

92 Convention on Consent to Marriage, Minimum Age for Marriage and Registration of Marriages 1962, 521 UNTS 231, art 1(2). Ireland is not party to this Convention.

susceptible to abuse in contracting marriages of convenience[93] and the circumvention of immigration restrictions.[94] Nonetheless, it is far from clear that the use of a 'dual compliance' strategy – or the invalidation of proxy marriages involving an Irish domiciliary – will address these concerns.[95] 'Dual compliance' simply tends towards the invalidation of almost all marriages involving spouses located in different countries[96] (even in circumstances where there is a genuine reason for the bilocation). Likewise, the Irish domiciliary requirement will invalidate the marriages of Muslim migrants settled in Ireland in the event that they return to their country of origin to get married, and marry there in a proxy Islamic form (with the wife absenting herself during the ceremony). Of course, an interpretation of Islam which marginalises women is objectionable from the perspective of Irish gender equality principles. However, it does not follow that a refusal to recognise Islamic proxy marriages (involving Irish domiciliaries) is a proportionate or constructive response – particularly where the departure from Irish human rights standards occurs outside of Ireland and outside of any ECHR Contracting State.

2.2.2 Consent

As has been seen, the method of giving consent (whether in person or by proxy) is a considered to be a question of formal validity governed by the *lex loci celebrationis*. However, the fact of consent is a matter of essential validity, governed by the domiciliary law of each party.[97] Therefore (at least in principle) questions as to the effect of mistake or misrepresentation or duress or unsoundness of mind are referred to the domiciliary law. In practice, however, it seems that an absence of consent according to domestic conceptions is particularly likely to trigger a public policy objection, and to lead to the non-recognition of a marriage considered essentially valid under the domiciliary law.[98] Therefore, insofar as Islamic law allows parental consent to substitute

---

93 *City of Westminster v IC* (n 83) [40].

94 See *MRA v NRK* [2011] ScotCS CSOH 101 [14].

95 See Fawcett, Ní Shúilleabháin and Shah (n 83) 621–622.

96 Because of the unlikelihood of a single ceremony complying with the disparate formalities of two different countries.

97 *Apt* (n 86) 88; *Hamza* (n 47) [24]–[26]. See also Binchy (n 39) 240–241.

98 Clarkson and Hill (n 49) 387. This impression is reinforced by the provisions of the Domestic Violence Act 2018. This Act creates new offences relating to conduct bringing about forced marriage. Conduct within the State will lead to the commission of an offence under ss 38(1) and 38(2) even if a forced marriage occurs abroad and is lawful under the law of the place where it occurs (although conduct outside the State constitutes an offence under s 38(3) only in the event that forced marriage is also proscribed in the place where that conduct occurs).

for party consent[99] (again a highly contested interpretation of Islam[100]), such a consent (even if valid under the domiciliary law) is unlikely to be accepted for Irish recognition purposes[101] – unless there is subsequent approbation by the non-consenting party.[102]

This use of public policy is, in the opinion of this author, appropriate. Free will is considered to be a core component of the right to marry under Article 12 of the European Convention on Human Rights (ECHR)[103] and personal autonomy is a protected interest under Article 8 ECHR which safeguards the right to respect for private and family life.[104] Whilst Article 8 ECHR has also been interpreted as requiring recognition in an ECHR Contracting State of a marital status obtained in a third (non-ECHR) country (*Orlandi v Italy*),[105] it has also been accepted that non-recognition may be justified on grounds of 'community interests'.[106] On this analysis, it is submitted that Irish law strikes an appropriate balance of rights, in allowing for recognition of non-consensual marriages in cases of subsequent approbation but not otherwise.

Leaving aside the situation where a mentally competent adult has been forced into marriage, there have been some suggestions that substituted consent under Islamic law should be tolerated where the marriage is intended to provide a permanent family-based care arrangement for a mentally-incapacitated adult.[107] This situation is clearly more complex[108] – and the European Court of Human Rights (ECtHR) has emphasised that vulnerable adults suffering from serious mental illness should not be unnecessarily deprived of the right to marry.[109] Nonetheless the ECtHR also appears to accept that Contracting

99 See Tucker (n 5) 42–43; El Alami and Hinchcliffe (n 5) 5–7; *City of Westminster v IC* (n 83) [3], [35], [49]; Werner Menski, 'Plurality-Conscious Rebalancing of Family Law Regulation in Europe' in Shah with Foblets and Rohe (n 7) 42.

100 Tucker (n 5) 42, 67; El Alami and Hinchcliffe (n 5) 6.

101 *HAH v SAA* (n 36) [25], [101] (O'Malley J). O'Malley J refers to 'voluntary entry' into marriage and the possession of 'capacity to enter into such commitments' as 'defining characteristic[s] of marriage as envisaged by the Constitution' [101].

102 *HAH v SAA* (n 36) [101] (O'Malley J).

103 See Fawcett, Ní Shúilleabháin and Shah (n 83) 592–593, 595.

104 See Fawcett, Ní Shúilleabháin and Shah (n 83) 584.

105 *Orlandi v Italy* App Nos 26431/12, 26742/12, 44057/12 and 60088/12 (ECtHR, 17 December 2017) concerning *inter alia* same-sex marriages contracted in Canada and the United States.

106 *Orlandi* (n 105) [192], [199] [209].

107 See Menski (n 99) 42.

108 Rebecca Probert, 'Hanging on the Telephone: *City of Westminster v IC*' (2008) 20 Child and Family Law Quarterly 395, 402–404.

109 *Lashin v Russia* App No 33117/02 (ECtHR, 22 January 2013).

State authorities owe a duty of protection in such circumstances.[110] Against this backdrop, it is difficult to disagree with the view of the English Court of Appeal (*obiter*) that public policy must preclude recognition of a foreign marriage involving a person suffering from a very severe mental incapacity (such that personal consent to marriage is impossible), even in the event that the domiciliary law sanctions substituted consent.[111]

2.2.3 Non-Age

The dual domicile test allows (at least in principle) for the recognition of overseas marriages involving young teenagers and children – and in England in the late 1960s, the marriage in Nigeria of a 26 year old man and a 13 year old girl, both domiciled in Nigeria, where the marriage was valid, was held to be entitled to recognition when they arrived in London shortly after the ceremony (*Mohamed v Knott*).[112] In Ireland, the dual domicile test has been partially displaced by a statutory rule which requires non-recognition of a foreign marriage where either party was less than 18 years and where either was ordinarily resident in Ireland at the time of the marriage.[113] In theory, this statutory rule allows *Mohamed v Knott* to be followed in cases where neither spouse was ordinarily resident in Ireland at the relevant time. In practice, however, it is now likely – with an increased human rights emphasis on non-age and on the undesirability of child marriage[114] – that a marriage similar to that in *Mohamed v Knott* would be refused recognition as a matter of public policy.[115] Thus insofar as Islamic law permits marriage at a very young age (a contested interpretation of Islam[116]), differing non-age standards are likely to lead to limping status under Irish law. This outcome is easily justified where the child is very young at the time of the marriage – and at the time when the question of marriage recognition arises. However, it is less defensible in circumstances where there is subsequent approbation upon the child reaching adulthood[117] – or where the underage party is almost eighteen at the time of the marriage. The common

110 See, eg *F v Switzerland* (1988) 10 EHRR 411 [36] where the ECtHR indicated that there was a duty to protect an 'insane' person from marriage.
111 *City of Westminster v IC* (n 83) [32], [59], [101].
112 *Mohamed* (n 83).
113 Family Law Act 1995, s 31.
114 See Fawcett, Ní Shúilleabháin and Shah (n 83) 647–648; Ruth Gaffney-Rhys, 'The Law Relating to Marriageable Age from a National and International Perspective' [2009] International Family Law 228; also *ZH and RH v Switzerland* App No 60119/12 (ECtHR, 8 December 2015) [44].
115 See *HAH v SAA* (n 36) [2.11] (Clarke J).
116 See Tucker (n 5) 69–72.
117 See Fawcett, Ní Shúilleabháin and Shah (n 83) 649.

law rules may allow for validation in such circumstances[118] – however, the statutory rule appears entirely inflexible. Therefore, in the event of either party being ordinarily resident in Ireland, it seems that an overseas Islamic marriage is destined for non-recognition in the event that either spouse was (just) under eighteen years of age – even if the underage party affirms the marriage as an adult.[119]

2.2.4 Actually Polygamous Marriage

As has been discussed above, the longstanding problems with potentially polygamous marriage have now been comprehensively resolved by the Supreme Court judgment in *HAH v SAA*. Nonetheless, characterisation difficulties remain where *actual* polygamy is concerned (in other words where a Muslim man has married two women in a Sharia law system allowing polygamy, in circumstances where all three are domiciled in legal systems permitting polygamy).

In the High Court in *HAH v SAA*, it was concluded that in cases of actual polygamy, neither the marriage to the first wife, nor the marriage to the second wife could be recognised in Irish law.[120] Dunne J reasoned that 'it is impossible to equate polygamous marriage with marriage as understood in the Constitution'. In the Supreme Court, however, it was determined that in cases of actual polygamy, the marriage to the first wife should be recognised,[121] but that the *second* polygamous marriages (as a class) could not. This refusal of recognition was based on the public policy doctrine,[122] but in a sense it represents a determination that second polygamous marriages are incapable of characterisation as 'marriage' in Irish law.

The Supreme Court offered two reasons for the non-recognition of second polygamous marriages. First, it referred to the fact that the Irish Constitution (following the amendments introduced by the Marriage Equality Referendum) makes specific reference to marriage as a union of *two* persons.[123] Second – and more forcefully – the Court invoked the gender equality guarantee enshrined

118 *HAH v SAA* (n 36) [2.11]–[2.12] (Clarke J).

119 For further discussion of the Irish position on non-age, see Ní Shúilleabháin, 'Accommodating Cultural Diversity' (n 64) 176–181.

120 [2010] IEHC 497.

121 *HAH v SAA* (n 36) [111] (O'Malley J).

122 *HAH v SAA* (n 36) [96], [115] (O'Malley J).

123 The Thirty-Fourth Amendment to the Constitution, 2015 added a new art 41.4: 'Marriage may be contracted in accordance with law by two persons without distinction as to their sex'. See *HAH v SAA* (n 36) [69], [100], [113] (O'Malley J). O'Malley J also referred to the fact that prior marriage is an impediment to a second marriage under the Civil Registration Act 2004, s 2(2) and that bigamy is an indictable offence: *HAH v SAA* (n 36) [76]–[77] (O'Malley J).

(implicitly[124]) in the Irish Constitution and in international human rights instruments, including the ECHR.[125] Polygamous marriage was found to entail a structural inequality which was incompatible with the Irish view of marriage as a partnership based on equality of rights[126] – and it was held that recognition of actual polygamy would give legal effect to discrimination and subordination of women.[127]

Notwithstanding this general non-recognition of second polygamous marriages, the Supreme Court envisaged that it would be entirely constitutional for the legislature to afford limited recognition to such marriages for particular practical purposes.[128] It was suggested that the Oireachtas might consider extending maintenance, inheritance and pension rights equivalent to those conferred on recognised spouses.[129]

The reasoning in *HAH v SAA* appears, at first glance, to be somewhat contradictory. If gender equality demands non-recognition of actual polygamy, why should the Supreme Court (in almost the same breath) recommend that the legislature consider conferring certain practical rights on second polygamous wives? The reality is, of course, that while the elimination of polygamy may promote gender equality, for so long as the practice persists, and there are second wives living in polygamous unions, complete non-recognition will exacerbate the position of those women.[130] In this way, what appears to be a contradictory fudge on the part of the Supreme Court, might actually constitute a nuanced and sensitive response to the complexities of gender equality in a particular cultural and religious context,[131] with perhaps an implicit

124 See *HAH v SAA* (n 36) [70]–[74] (O'Malley J) discussing the interpretation of art 40.1.

125 *HAH v SAA* (n 36) [90]–[95], [114], [116] (O'Malley J).

126 See also *HAH v SAA* (n 36) [101] (O'Malley J) where marriage is defined in terms of 'equal partnership'.

127 *HAH v SAA* (n 36) [114]–[115] (O'Malley J).

128 *HAH v SAA* (n 36) [117]–[118], [121]–[122] (O'Malley J); [4.2] (Clarke J).

129 *HAH v SAA* (n 36) [3.1] (Clarke J). Clarke J (in whose judgment 4 out of the other 6 Supreme Court judges concurred) went so far as to suggest that in the event of legislative inaction, such rights might be developed by the courts: *HAH v SAA* (n 36) [3.5] (Clarke J). O'Malley J (whose judgment had the unanimous backing of the Supreme Court) appeared to envisage that such rights would only be created by the Oireachtas.

130 On the complexities of the 'double-edged' gender equality analysis of polygamy, see Patrick Parkinson, 'Taking Multiculturalism Seriously: Marriage Law and the Rights of Minorities' in Estin (n 12) 60–61.

131 See Shachar (n 6) 116–117, 132–133 illustrating (more generally) the ineffectiveness of uncompromising gender equality strategies where immigrant women with multi-layered connections are concerned.

acknowledgement of 'intersectionality' considerations.[132] Nonetheless, it is a pity that the Supreme Court did not elaborate further, and did not take the opportunity to articulate a more developed analytical framework for future cases concerning foreign marriage laws with gender discriminatory elements. Taken in isolation, the public policy analysis in *HAH v SAA* might suggest that structural inequality must necessarily trigger non-recognition.[133] As will be seen, this is a dangerous implication, which might imperil cross-border status recognition in other contexts.

Whilst the spouses in *HAH v SAA* were united in seeking recognition for their polygamous unions,[134] they did not seek to rely on religious or cultural rights under the Irish Constitution[135] or the ECHR.[136] Even if they had, it is unlikely that the outcome would have been different. Whilst religious marriage norms may be protected as 'manifestations of religion' under Article 9 ECHR,[137] polygamy is merely a permitted practice under traditional Islamic law, and as Witte points out, the argument for accommodation is much weaker where penumbral religious practices are concerned.[138] The legitimacy of polygamy is also hotly contested within Islam and revisionist interpretations challenge its permissibility.[139] Arguments for culture rights – and for state recognition

---

132 On 'intersectionality', see Kimberle Crenshaw, 'Mapping the Margins: Intersectionality, Identity Politics, and Violence Against Women of Color' (1991) 43 Stanford Law Review 1241; Sumi Cho, Kimberlé Crenshaw and Leslie McCall, 'Towards a Field of Intersectionality Studies: Theory, Applications, and Praxis' (2013) 38 Signs: Journal of Women in Culture and Society 785. According to Crenshaw et al, intersectionality theory requires the abandonment of simplistic identity categories and the modification of antidiscrimination law to take account of multiple identities and multidimensionality. It aims to challenge the law's myopic, unidimensional conceptualisation of discrimination.

133 It is interesting to note that Clarke J appeared to distance himself from this analysis. He suggested that less fundamental gender inequalities might not justify non-recognition of foreign marriage laws: *HAH v SAA* (n 36) [2.13]–[2.14] (Clarke J).

134 *HAH v SAA* (n 36) [7]–[9] (O'Malley J).

135 Article 44.2.1° guarantees freedom of conscience and the free profession and practice of religion (subject to public order and morality) and art 44.2.3° prohibits religious discrimination.

136 Article 9 ECHR protects religious freedom and art 14 prohibits unjustified discrimination (including on religious grounds) in the exercise of Convention rights. Article 8 ECHR (right to respect for private life) requires Contracting States to show respect for cultural identity: see, eg *Chapman v United Kingdom* App No 27238/95 (ECtHR, 18 January 2001) [96] (and art 27 of the International Covenant on Civil and Political Rights 1966 lays down an explicit obligation to protect the cultural rights of minorities).

137 See Fawcett, Ní Shúilleabháin and Shah (n 83) 674.

138 John Witte Jr, 'The Future of Muslim Family Law in Western Democracies' in Ahdar and Aroney (n 6) 289. See also Fawcett, Ní Shúilleabháin and Shah (n 83) 678–679.

139 See Tucker (n 5) 77–80; Mashhour (n 20) 568–569, 585; Shah (n 24) 890–891.

of religious personal laws – arouse concerns of essentialism[140] and the subordination of individual rights to group rights.[141] In any event, as O'Malley J pointed out in *HAH v SAA*, Article 5 of CEDAW[142] requires the elimination of customary practices based on the idea of the inferiority or superiority of either of the sexes.[143] Literature also suggests that many Muslim women are deeply opposed to any erosion of controls on polygamy.[144] In these circumstances, it is very difficult to see the Irish Supreme Court being swayed towards a wider recognition of polygamy, even in the event that religious and cultural rights had been invoked.

3 Recognition of Overseas Islamic Divorces under Irish Law

3.1 *Divorce Recognition under Irish Domestic Law*

The basic position of Irish law is that all divorces granted by EU Member State courts are automatically entitled to recognition (pursuant to the Brussels II *bis* Regulation[145]) – and that divorces granted by courts outside of the EU are entitled to recognition under the Domicile and Recognition of Foreign Divorces Act 1986 provided at least one of the spouses was domiciled[146] in the country granting the divorce at the time of instituting proceedings.[147] So the law is tolerably clear – if somewhat restrictive – where foreign *courts* grant divorces.

As has been noted above, however, in countries applying Islamic law, many divorces are obtained without recourse to a court – and even where there is

140 Bano (n 84) 286, 296, 309; Maarit Jänterä-Jareborg, 'Cross-border Family Cases and Religious Diversity: What Can Judges Do?' in Shah with Foblets and Rohe (n 7) 148. On the heterogeneity of Muslim immigrants in Ireland and Europe, see Scharbrodt and others (n 1) 7, 9, 49–50, 199–211; and Nielsen (n 7) 27, 54, 117, 158.

141 See Pratibha Jain, 'Balancing Minority Rights and Gender Justice: The Impact of Protecting Multiculturalism on Women's Rights in India' in Estin (n 12) 233–235; Rohe (n 7) 73; John Eekelaar, *Family Law and Personal Life* (Oxford University Press 2017) 168–171.

142 UN Convention on the Elimination of All Forms of Discrimination Against Women 1979.

143 *HAH v SAA* (n 36) [95] (O'Malley J).

144 See, eg Tucker (n 5) 77–79; Black (n 6) 251–252; Mashour (n 20) 580.

145 Council Regulation (EC) No 2201/2003 of 27 November 2003 concerning jurisdiction and the recognition and enforcement of judgments in matrimonial matters and the matters of parental responsibility, repealing Regulation (EC) No 1347/2000 [2003] OJ L338/1. This EU regime applies to divorces granted since 1 March 2001.

146 As in the case of foreign marriage recognition, 'domicile' in this context has its traditional common law meaning – see above text to n 50.

147 S 5(1). Also, under s 5(4), a divorce *recognised* in the jurisdiction or jurisdictions in which the spouses were domiciled is entitled to recognition in Ireland, even if neither spouse was domiciled in the granting jurisdiction.

court involvement, the court's role is often facilitative rather than constitutive. This mode of divorce does not fit comfortably with the language of the 1986 Act. While there is no explicit requirement of court involvement under that Act, the legislation envisages recognition where a divorce has been 'granted' following 'the institution of proceedings', a formula which is ill-adapted to the pronouncement of *talaq* or the agreement of *khul*.

Up until recently, it was understood that the recognition regime laid down in the 1986 Act could potentially be supplemented by common law recognition rules[148] – and if this understanding had prevailed, it would have allowed for some judicial creativity in fashioning a recognition mechanism for extra-judicial Islamic divorces. However, the Supreme Court in *H v H*[149] (a case concerned with an English judicial divorce) ruled out any parallel application of common law recognition rules. Separation of powers considerations weighed heavily on the court and it was assumed that the 1986 Act provided the sole mechanism for recognition of non-EU divorces obtained since 1986. In the view of the Court, any further accommodation of foreign divorces had to come from the legislature. Thus, *H v H* indicates that Islamic divorces obtained outside of the EU must be recognised within the framework of the 1986 Act, if at all – when, as has been seen, the 1986 Act will require a very strained interpretation in order to extend to informal Islamic divorces.

Furthermore, even if it proves possible to construe the pronouncement of *talaq* or the agreement of a *khul* as entailing 'the institution of proceedings' resulting in a 'grant' of divorce, the reasoning in *HAH v SAA* suggests that public policy considerations may still preclude recognition.[150]

As has been discussed, the pronouncement of *talaq* is controlled by men – and even the *khul* may entail a degree of 'structural inequality' insofar as it involves the relinquishment of *mahr*. The Supreme Court in *HAH v SAA* ruled against actual polygamy on the basis that its recognition would 'give legal effect to discrimination and subordination in a relationship where the principle of equality should hold sway'.[151] The recognition of *talaq* (and arguably *khul*) can be condemned in similar terms – although one might reasonably argue that foreign divorce-recognition is different insofar as any discrimination is

148 Ní Shúilleabháin, 'Foreign Divorce Recognition' (n 40) 167–168.

149 [2015] 1 ILRM 453.

150 S 5(6) of the 1986 Act preserves the power to refuse recognition on public policy (or other similar) grounds: Shatter (n 18) 416–419; Binchy (n 39) 284. But see *MY v AA* [2017] IEHC 227 [95].

151 *HAH v SAA* (n 36) [114] (O'Malley J).

in the past. The recognition of an overseas polygamous marriage, by contrast, gives legal effect to an *ongoing* structural inequality within the State itself.[152]

In European continental jurisdictions, it is often suggested that gender equality concerns can be overcome if the wife is herself consenting to the recognition of a *talaq*.[153] Thus one might argue that any 'structural inequality' (as per *HAH v SAA*) can be cured if the wife supports recognition of a *talaq* (or *khul*). The Irish courts' support for this proposition may however be doubted insofar as the wives in *HAH v SAA* favoured recognition of the polygamous union – and yet their consent to recognition was clearly to no avail. In this sense, the gender-equality public policy doctrine articulated in *HAH v SAA* was framed as a public law principle which was not amenable to private waiver.

A blanket refusal to recognise all informal Islamic divorces – even if obtained in the jurisdiction of the spouses' then domicile many years earlier – and even where *both* spouses support recognition, is unreasonable and arguably discriminatory insofar as it creates a mass of limping relationships for one religious group.[154] As Rohe points out, such a blanket policy of non-recognition forces the immigrant Muslim woman, who had ordered her affairs many years earlier in her country of origin, to initiate fresh divorce proceedings with all of the attendant expense.[155] Where she has remarried in reliance on the validity of her Islamic divorce, the validity of her second marriage is in jeopardy.[156]

Ultimately, it seems that legislation is necessary to fill this problematic void in Irish law. As has been noted, the Supreme Court in *HAH v SAA* envisaged that legislation could confer certain entitlements on second polygamous wives despite the general non-recognition of these marriages, so one would assume that a legislative scheme for recognition of *talaqs* – to which wives have consented – would also be constitutionally sound.

3.2 *Automatic Divorce Recognition under EU Law (Brussels II* **bis)**

Within the EU, the only context in which national divorce law accords to Islamic norms is in the Greek province of Western Thrace.[157] In Western Thrace,

152 Clarke J appeared amenable to the view that *some degree* of gender inequality in overseas marriage laws might be tolerated: *HAH v SAA* (n 36) [2.13] (Clarke J).

153 See Rohe (n 7) 64–65; Cristina González Beilfuss, 'Islamic Family Law in the European Union' in Johan Meeusen and others (eds), *International Family Law for the European Union* (Intersentia 2007) 433.

154 Jänterä-Jareborg (n 140) 156.

155 Rohe (n 7) 65.

156 ibid.

157 Rohe (n 7) 58: Evangelos Vassilakakis and Vassilios Kourtis, 'The Impact and Application of the Brussels II bis Regulation in Greece' in Katharina Boele-Woelki and Cristina

family law matters may be dealt with by the Mufti – and divorces may be obtained before the Mufti, by pronouncement of *talaq*, agreement of *khul* or on proof of fault in accordance with Islamic law.[158] The decisions of the Mufti become effective once they have been declared enforceable by the Greek civil courts, following a very limited formal review.[159]

As Member State divorces, one might expect that these divorces would enjoy automatic recognition throughout the EU (pursuant to Brussels II *bis*); however, it appears that the status of these Western Thrace divorces is very uncertain.[160] The Brussels II *bis* Regulation makes explicit provision for the inclusion of (and automatic recognition of) Roman Catholic annulments granted by ecclesiastical tribunals and accorded civil effectiveness under the law of a Member State[161] – and so, in the absence of an equivalent provision for Mufti divorces granted in Western Thrace, it is arguable that these divorces fall outside of the scope of the Regulation (which generally excludes 'purely religious procedures'[162]). The Regulation's inapplicability to Western Thrace Islamic divorces has been accepted by a German court.[163]

González Beilfuss (eds), *Brussels II bis: Its Impact and Application in the Member States* (Intersentia 2007) 137.

158 Aspasia Tsaoussi and Eleni Zervogianni, 'Multiculturalism and Family Law: The Case of Greek Muslims' in Katharina Boele-Woelki and Tone Sverdrup (eds), *European Challenges in Contemporary Family Law* (Intersentia 2008) 215–217. In January 2018, the application of Sharia law became optional for Muslims in Western Thrace: see Apostolos Anthimos, 'Sharia Law in Greece: Blending European Values with Islamic Tradition' (24 January 2018) at <http://conflictoflaws.net/2018/sharia-law-in-greece-blending-european-values-with-islamic-tradition/> accessed 2 November 2018. This legislative change followed the bringing of a challenge before the European Court of Human Rights in *Molla Sali v Greece*, App No 20452/14. The complainant in *Molla Sali* argued that the compulsory application of Sharia law in succession matters violated property and fair trial rights (under art 1 of Protocol 1 and art 6 ECHR). The case was heard by the Grand Chamber on 6 December 2017 but the judgment is still awaited: see <https://www.echr.coe.int/Pages/home.aspx?p=hearings/gcpending&c> accessed 2 November 2018.

159 Tsaoussi and Zervogianni (n 158) 213–214, 219–220.

160 Vassilakakis and Kourtis (n 157) 138; Ulrich Magnus and Peter Mankowski (eds), *Brussels IIbis Regulation* (Sellier 2012) 55–56; Máire Ní Shúilleabháin, *Cross-Border Divorce Law: Brussels II bis* (Oxford University Press 2010) 125–126.

161 Article 63.

162 See Recital (9) to Council Regulation (EC) No 1347/2000 of 29 May 2000 on jurisdiction and the recognition and enforcement of judgments in matrimonial matters and in matters of parental responsibility for children of both spouses [2000] OJ L160/19 (the predecessor to Brussels II *bis*).

163 Magnus and Mankowski (n 160) 55–56.

3.3 *Final Reflections on Recognition of Islamic Divorces*

Both in terms of domestic law, and the applicable EU rules for Member State divorces, Irish law is extremely unclear as to its accommodation of overseas Islamic divorces. It likely follows that there are many Muslims now living in Ireland, who previously divorced in an Islamic form, and are uncertain as to their marital status.

The situation under Irish domestic law appears to be largely accidental: it is the result of legislative choices made prior to the emergence of a substantial immigrant Muslim population, combined with the knock-on effects of judgments concerned with other matters altogether. Even if this legal quandary is inadvertent, however, the need for remedial legislative intervention is now very obvious, and legislative inertia will be justifiably criticised.

The failure to cater for Mufti divorces under Brussels II *bis* is less likely to have been the result of mere inadvertence. Insofar as special consideration was given to Roman Catholic ecclesiastical annulments, one might assume that the Greek authorities must have made a conscious decision not to seek an equivalent protection for the Mufti divorces. The status of the Mufti courts is contentious within Greece (in particular insofar as the application of Islamic law was conceded under an international agreement with Turkey which has itself replaced Islamic law with a secular code).[164] Consequently, any Greek request for a special EU accommodation of Mufti divorces might have been politically controversial at home.

Alternatively, it is possible that resistance to any inclusion of Mufti divorces under Brussels II *bis* came from elsewhere in the EU. The Rome III Regulation[165] (on choice-of-law in divorce) is explicit in precluding the application of any law which 'does not grant one of the spouses equal access to divorce ... on grounds of their sex', even in the event of spousal agreement on the application of that law.[166] Thus, like *HAH v SAA*, Rome III supports a gender equality principle which is not amenable to private waiver, and it is possible that the same policy barrier precluded any specific accommodation of Mufti divorces under Brussels II *bis*.

164 Tsaoussi and Zervogianni (n 158) 210–212, 219–222.

165 Council Regulation (EU) No 1259/2010 of 20 December 2010 implementing enhanced cooperation in the area of the law applicable to divorce and legal separation [2010] OJ L343/10. This is an 'enhanced cooperation' measure which applies only in 17 of the 28 EU Member States. It does not apply in Ireland.

166 Article 10. (Ordinarily – where the spouses chose from the art 5 menu of connected laws – their choice of applicable law will be honoured).

4 Conclusion

Irish law has shifted gear, from a position of unthinking hostility towards overseas Islamic marriage to a policy of rational, tolerant accommodation. The blind adherence to *Hyde v Hyde*, and the orthodoxy of Christian rhetoric in common law jurisprudence, allowed the nonsensical aversion to 'potential polygamy' to go unchallenged for far too long. The Irish courts now appear to be determined to honour their human rights commitments and to avoid limping marriages (as per *Orlandi v Italy*), unless there is a cogent basis for refusal of recognition. The *HAH v SAA* judgment also suggests a willingness to combine an ideological commitment to gender equality with some practical concessions to the 'lived reality' of polygamy – although the court fell short in articulating a theoretical framework for this recognition strategy.

Whilst there has been much progress in developing the law on marriage recognition, the same cannot be said of divorce recognition (and there are some unfortunate echoes of the common law Christian bias in the marginalisation of Mufti divorces under Brussels II *bis*). There is also a clear need for domestic legislative reform, given the inflexibility of the 1986 Act – and its inadaptability to Islamic divorce norms. The existing legal vacuum is indefensible in a context of substantial immigration from Muslim majority countries.

Bibliography

Ahdar, R. and Aroney, N. (eds), *Shari'a in the West* (Oxford University Press 2010).

Apostolos, A., 'Sharia Law in Greece: Blending European Values with Islamic Tradition' (24 January 2018) at <http://conflictoflaws.net/2018/sharia-law-in-greece-blending-european-values-with-islamic-tradition/>.

Bano, S., 'In Pursuit of Religious and Legal Diversity: a Response to the Archbishop of Canterbury and the "Sharia Debate" in Britain' (2008) 10 Ecclesiastical Law Journal 283.

Binchy, W., *Irish Conflicts of Law* (Butterworths 1988).

Boele-Woelki, K. and González Beilfuss, C. (eds), *Brussels II bis: Its Impact and Application in the Member States* (Intersentia 2007).

Boele-Woelki, K. and Sverdrup, T. (eds), *European Challenges in Contemporary Family Law* (Intersentia 2008).

Cho, S., Crenshaw, K. and McCall, L., 'Towards a Field of Intersectionality Studies: Theory, Applications, and Praxis' (2013) 38 Signs: Journal of Women in Culture and Society 785.

Crawford, E.B. and Carruthers, J.M., 'Dual Locality Events: Marriage by Telephone' [2011] Scots Law Times 227.

Crenshaw, K., 'Mapping the Margins: Intersectionality, Identity Politics, and Violence Against Women of Color' (1991) 43 Stanford Law Review 1241.

Eekelaar, J., 'Marriage: A Modest Proposal' [2013] Family Law Journal (1) 83.

Eekelaar, J., *Family Law and Personal Life* (Oxford University Press 2017).

El Alami, D. and Hinchcliffe, D., *Islamic Marriage and Divorce Laws of the Arab World* (Kluwer 1996).

Enright, M., 'Preferring the Stranger? Towards an Irish Approach to Muslim Divorce Practice' (2013) 49 Irish Jurist 65.

Fawcett, J.J., Ní Shúilleabháin, M. and Shah, S., *Human Rights and Private International Law* (Oxford University Press 2016).

Gaffney-Rhys, R., 'The Law Relating to Marriageable Age from a National and International Perspective' [2009] International Family Law 228.

Haeri, S., 'Temporary Marriage and the State in Iran: an Islamic Discourse on Female Sexuality' (1992) 59 Social Research 201.

Hill, J. and Ní Shúilleabháin, M., *Clarkson and Hill's Conflict of Laws* (5th edn, Oxford University Press 2016).

Khan, S., 'Race, Gender and Orientalism: *Muta* and the Canadian Legal System' (1995) 8 Canadian Journal of Women and the Law 249.

Laquer Estin, A. (ed), *The Multi-Cultural Family* (Ashgate 2008).

Law Reform Commission, 'Report on Private International Law Aspects of Capacity to Marry and Choice of Law in Proceedings for Nullity of Marriage' (LRC-19, 1985).

Magnus, U. and Mankowski, P. (eds), *Brussels IIbis Regulation* (Sellier 2012).

Mashhour, A., 'Islamic Law and Gender Equality – Could There be a Common Ground?: A Study of Divorce and Polygamy in Sharia Law and Contemporary Legislation in Tunisia and Egypt' (2005) 27(2) Human Rights Quarterly 562.

Meeusen, J. and others (eds), *International Family Law for the European Union* (Intersentia 2007).

Nagar, R., 'Religion, Race and the Debate over *Mut'a* in Dar es Salaam' (2000) 26 Feminist Studies 661.

Nielsen, J., *Muslims in Western Europe* (3rd edn, Edinburgh University Press 2004).

Ní Shúilleabháin, M., 'Accommodating Cultural Diversity under Irish Family Law' (2002) 24 Dublin University Law Journal 175.

Ní Shúilleabháin, M., *Cross-Border Divorce Law: Brussels II bis* (Oxford University Press 2010).

Ní Shúilleabháin, M., 'Marriage, Divorce and Stagnation in the Irish Conflict of Laws' (2014) 52 Irish Jurist 68.

Ní Shúilleabháin, M., 'Foreign Divorce Recognition and Residence: A Critical Analysis of *H v H*' (2017) 57 Irish Jurist 162.

O'Sullivan, K. and Jackson, L., 'Muslim Marriage (Non) Recognition: Implications and Possible Solutions' (2017) 39 Journal of Social Welfare and Family Law 22.

Poulter, S., 'Hyde v Hyde–A Reappraisal' (1976) 25 International and Comparative Law Quarterly 475.

Probert, R., 'Hanging on the Telephone: *City of Westminster v IC*' (2008) 20 Child and Family Law Quarterly 395.

Rehman, J., 'The Sharia, Islamic Family Laws and International Human Rights Law: Examining the Theory and Practice of Polygamy and Talaq' (2007) 21 International Journal of Law, Policy and the Family 108.

Scharbrodt, O. and others, *Muslims in Ireland, Past and Present* (Edinburgh University Press 2015).

Shah, N., 'Women's Human Rights in the Koran: an Interpretative Approach' (2006) 28(4) Human Rights Quarterly 868.

Shah, P., 'Attitudes to Polygamy in English Law' (2003) 52 International and Comparative Law Quarterly 369.

Shah, P., 'Inconvenient Marriages, or What Happens When Ethnic Minorities Marry Trans-jurisdictionally' (2010) 6(2) Utrecht Law Review 17.

Shah, P., with Marie-Claire Foblets and Mathias Rohe (eds), *Family, Religion and Law: Cultural Encounters in Europe* (Ashgate 2014).

Shatter, A., *Shatter's Family Law* (4th edn, Butterworths 1997).

Torremans, P. (ed), *Cheshire, North and Fawcett: Private International Law* (15th edn, Oxford University Press 2017).

Tucker, J., *Women, Family, and Gender in Islamic Law* (Cambridge University Press 2008).

CHAPTER 8

A Comparative Review of the Accommodation of Islamic Finance in Irish Law

Edana Richardson

Introduction

The contemporary Islamic finance industry, which is arranged around financial activity structured to adhere to the financial principles of Islamic law (a term frequently used interchangeably with *shari'ah*),[1] has grown from its rural beginnings in Egypt in the 1960s[2] to become a defined segment of the global financial markets. Though not immune to broader economic crises, geopolitical tensions and unstable oil prices,[3] the Islamic finance industry has matured and diversified over the last two decades, with an expanding range of Islamic finance products progressively coming to market.

In recent years, a number of Muslim-majority countries have developed as active centres for Islamic finance activity.[4] Among these countries some, such as Malaysia, have introduced comprehensive legislative frameworks targeted

1 This chapter will use the term Islamic law unless quoting directly or the context requires. There is no single correct means of expressing Arabic terms and sounds in the Latin alphabet. Throughout this chapter, quotations and the official names of products and organisations, which contain a transliteration of Arabic terms and use of italicisation which are different from that used in this chapter, will be reproduced without adjustment. This chapter reflects the legal position in Ireland as of February 2019.

2 See generally, RK Ready, 'The Egyptian Municipal Saving Bank Project' (1967) 9(2) International Development Review 2; Walid S Hegazy, 'Contemporary Islamic Finance: From Socioeconomic Idealism to Pure Legalism' (2007) 7(2) Chicago Journal of International Law, 581, 585–587.

3 Lauren McAughtry, 'A safe haven in stormy seas: Shariah banks show strength amid global turmoil' 13(2) (2016) Islamic Finance News 1, 3; Mohamed Damak, 'Islamic Finance 2018, Slow Growth Is The New Normal', in Standard & Poor's, 'Islamic Finance Outlook 2018 Edition' (S&P Global Inc 2017) 4, <https://img.en25.com/Web/StandardPoorsRatings/Islamic%20Finance%202018%20Digital.pdf> accessed 25 February 2019.

4 See a breakdown of the share of Islamic banking assets as at 30 June 2017 in Islamic Financial Services Board, *Stability Report 2018* (IFSB 2018) 10. See also Robert Toan, 'Cross-Border *Ijarah*; A Case study in the US Taxation of Islamic Finance', in *Third Harvard Islamic Proceedings* (Harvard Islamic Finance Program 2000) 191, 191.

 | DOI:10.1163/9789004398252_009

directly (and explicitly) at Islamic finance activity and market participants.[5] Coupled with an overtly supportive government attitude,[6] the legislative framework in countries like Malaysia has established a legal environment in which the development of the Islamic finance industry has been actively encouraged. Within some non-Muslim majority countries, steps have also been taken by legislative and regulatory authorities to facilitate Islamic finance activity within their domestic economies.[7] Implementing a comprehensive approach of accommodating Islamic finance activities within the existing legislative framework, the United Kingdom (the 'UK') has, over the past fifteen years, sought to enable the development of the UK as a centre for Islamic finance. It has, however, done so without favouring, or creating a separate legal framework for, such activity.[8] More recently, Irish authorities have also taken some interest in the Islamic finance market. In doing so, they have implemented an approach to the accommodation of certain Islamic finance products that is similar to that put in place in the UK.

This chapter presents a comparative analysis of the accommodation of Islamic finance in Irish law. It begins by introducing the core concepts guiding the development of the contemporary Islamic finance industry. It then presents an overview of the taxation and regulatory reforms introduced into the UK's legislative regime 'to create the right conditions in the UK for Islamic finance to grow'.[9] Legislative guidance and reforms in Ireland with respect to Islamic finance activity have been more modest when compared with accommodative measures implemented in the UK. Nevertheless, accommodations introduced to date in Ireland do suggest a receptive attitude to Islamic finance by the Irish government. Taking Islamic mortgage-alternatives as an example,

5 See, for example, in the context of Malaysia, the Islamic Financial Services Act 2013 (Act 759), which repeals existing Islamic banking legislation in Malaysia (the Islamic Banking Act 1983 (Act 276) and the Takaful Act 1984 (Act 312)) and consolidates Islamic banking legislation into one statute. Islamic capital markets law in Malaysia is set out in the Capital Markets and Services (Amendment) Act 2015 (Act A1499) and the Securities Commission (Amendment) Act 2015 (Act A1489) amending the Capital Markets and Services Act 2007 and the Securities Commission Malaysia Act 1993, respectively.

6 See, for example, Bank Negara Malaysia, 'Malaysia: World's Islamic Finance Marketplace' (1 August 2013) <http://www.bnm.gov.my/index.php?ch=en_press&pg=en_press&ac=616&lang=en>.

7 Toan (n 4) 191.

8 Barry Cosgrave, 'United Kingdom' in *The Islamic Finance and Markets Law Review*, Andrew M Metcalf and Michael Rainey (eds) (Law Business Research Ltd 2016) 68, 68.

9 Howard Davies, 'Islamic Finance in the United Kingdom: Current Initiatives And Challenges' Speech given at the *LSE-Harvard Public Lecture on Islamic Finance*, London School of Economics, London, UK (26 February 2009).

this chapter considers relevant guidance and legislative amendments introduced by Irish authorities and discusses how further legal clarifications and reforms may be needed. Finally, this chapter considers the position under Irish law of religious scholars in Islamic finance institutions.

1 Islamic Finance – An Overview

The remit of Islamic law is not restricted to what may be seen as strictly religious aspects of an adherent's life.[10] As a result, principles of Islamic law form a standard against which private, social and commercial life are to be measured. With respect to Islamic finance, stated adherence to the financial principles of Islamic law represents a defining feature of the industry, and reference within the context of Islamic finance transactions to concepts derived from Islamic law distinguishes Islamic from conventional finance activity.[11]

The rules of Islamic law that have guided and shaped the contemporary Islamic finance industry are derived from a number of sources. Primary among these are the *Qur'an* and *Sunnah*.[12] The *Qur'an*, the holy book of Islam, is considered to be the direct revelation from Allah, as spoken to the Prophet Mohammad.[13] *Sunnah* are composed of the sayings and actions of the Prophet Mohammad in light of revelations in the *Qur'an*.[14] The non-divine, derivative sources of Islamic law are developed through human effort[15] and include *ijmaʿ* (consensus of legal scholars) and *qiyas* (analogy). *Ijmaʿ* and *qiyas* are used as a

10 Mustafa Hussain, 'A general introduction to Islamic Finance' in Rahail Ali (ed) *Islamic Finance: A Practical Guide* (Globe Business Publishing Ltd 2008) 7, 8.

11 Mohammad Shafique, 'Food for thought: role of Shari'ah scholars' (April-June 2010) NewHorizon 24, 24.

12 Noel James Coulson, *Conflicts and Tensions in Islamic Jurisprudence* (The University of Chicago Press 1969) 55–56.

13 Fuad Al-Omar and Mohammed Abdel-Haq, *Islamic Banking Theory, Practice and Challenges* (Zed Books 1996) xvi.

14 *Qur'an* 4:80, 'He who obeys the Messenger (Muhammad), has indeed obeyed *Allah*, but he who turns away, then we have not sent you (O Muhammad as a watcher over them'. All extracts from the *Qur'an* in this chapter are taken from *Interpretation of the Meanings of The Noble Qur'an in the English language, A Summarized Version of At-Tabari, Al-Qurtubi and Ibn Kathir with comments from Sahih Al-Bukhari Summarized in One Volume*, Muhammad Taqi-ud-Din Al-Hilali and Muhammad Muhsin Khan (trans) (Maktba Dar-us-Salam 1996); Al-Omar and Abdel-Haq (n 13) 1.

15 Referred to by some as *ijtihad*. *Ijtihad* is defined by Weiss as 'the process of extracting or deriving (*istinbat, istithmar*) legal rules from the sources of the Law', Bernard Weiss, 'Interpretation in Islamic Law: The Theory of Ijtihād' (1977–78) 26 American Journal of Comparative Law 199, 199–200.

means of extrapolating rules of Islamic law where the *Qur'an* and *Sunnah* are not explicit.[16]

Guided by the sources of Islamic law, four subsisting rules applicable to financial activity have been derived: the prohibition of *riba*[17] (*riba* signifies increase or growth, but it is often translated simply as interest), the avoidance of *maysir* (gambling and speculation),[18] the need to limit *gharar* (risk and uncertainty)[19] and the unlawfulness of *haram* (forbidden) activities, such as the making or selling of alcohol, pork products and pornography.[20] This connection between Islamic law and Islamic finance remains central to the development of the Islamic finance industry. Islamic finance products offered in a contemporary financial context are, therefore, specifically structured to show their compatibility with the financial principles of Islamic law. At the same time, in order to operate alongside non-Islamic, conventional finance products, these Islamic finance products will often be designed to function as alternatives to conventional finance products and in doing so, to replicate the economic substance of their conventional alternatives.[21]

Like much of Islamic law, there is not unwavering unanimity over the contemporary meaning of every aspect of Islamic finance or the finer details of

---

16 Potter LJ in the UK Court of Appeal noted that 'most of the classical Islamic law on financial transactions is not contained as 'rules' or 'law' in the *Qur'an* and *Sunnah* but is based on the often divergent views held by established schools of law formed in a period roughly between 700 and 850 CE', *Shamil Bank of Bahrain v Beximco Pharmaceuticals Ltd* [2004] 1 Lloyd's Rep 1 [30] (Potter LJ).

17 See, amongst others, *Qur'an* 4:161, 'that they took *Ribā* (usury) though they were forbidden from taking it and their devouring of men's substance wrongfully (bribery). And We have prepared for the disbelievers among them a painful torment'. Though the area is not without disagreement, Saleh suggests that enough Islamic scholars now interpret the *Qur'an* as prohibiting all forms of bank interest that *ijma'* may have been reached on the issue, Nabil A Saleh, *Unlawful Gain and Legitimate Profit in Islamic Law* (2nd edn, Graham & Trotman 1992) 15.

18 *Qur'an* 5:90, 'O you who believe! Intoxicants (all kinds of alcoholic drinks), and gambling… are an abomination of Shaitan's (Satan) handiwork. So avoid (strictly all) that (abomination) in order that you may be successful'.

19 One tradition notes that the Prophet Mohammed forbade the 'sale by means of pebbles' (*Bay' al-Hast*) and the *gharar* sale (*Bay' al-Gharar*), *Sahih Muslim*, Book 10, Introduction, Abdul Hamid Siddiqui (trans) <http://www.documentacatholicaomnia.eu/03d/0834-0893,_Sahih_Muslim,_Hadith,_EN.pdf> accessed 25 February 2019. See also, Frank E Vogel and Samuel L Hayes, *Islamic Law and Finance, Religion, Risk and Return* (Kluwer Law International 1998) 87.

20 For example, the *Qur'anic* prohibition of pork; *Qur'an* 2:173: 'He hath forbidden you only Maitah (dead animals), and blood, and the flesh of swine…'.

21 Jonathan Ercanbrack, 'The Regulation of Islamic Finance in the United Kingdom' (2011) 13 Ecclesiastical Law Journal 69, 70.

every Islamic finance product.[22] Nevertheless, while differences of opinion remain, contemporary Islamic finance activity often displays a broad level of consistency with respect to the key features of the applicable rules.[23] It is suggested that within Ireland, any Islamic finance products offered by financial institutions and any Islamic finance activity accommodated within the legislative framework will be unlikely to deviate from broad market standards followed in other (particularly western) financial markets. This chapter will not, therefore, consider the correctness of any interpretation of Islamic law. It will instead proceed on the basis that there are certain distinguishing characteristics that are commonly found in finance products that have been structured to be compatible with Islamic law.

2 The Accommodation of Islamic Finance in non-Muslim Majority Countries – The Case Study of the UK

Guided by the financial principles of Islamic law, while also striving to maintain competitiveness within global financial markets, Islamic finance products combine nominate contracts from classical Islam with structures used in conventional finance.[24] This approach to product engineering facilitates adherence to Islamic finance principles, while offering finance products to market participants that function as economic substitutes for certain conventional finance products.

In countries where the legislative framework has not been designed or modified to support the contractual structures used in Islamic finance activity, Islamic finance transactions, institutions and market participants may be subject to regulatory and tax regimes based on the legal structure of the finance products used, rather than those products' economic substance. As a result, legal treatment of Islamic finance activity may differ from that imposed on economically similar conventional finance activity. Where Islamic finance products have been specifically structured to function economically like conventional finance products, differing tax and regulatory treatment may make the Islamic finance products uncompetitive.

22 Werner Menski, 'Accommodating religious needs in relation to marriage: Flying kites and navigating state law and other forms of law', paper presented for *Diritto & Religione, Prima giornata di studio 'Edoardo Dieni', Il riconoscimento civile dei matrimoni religiosi: conflitto di leggi o di culture?*, Università degli Studi dell'Insubria, Facoltà di Giurisprudenza, Como, Italy (28–29 November 2008) noting that Islam is itself 'internally plural'.

23 Scott Morrison, *The Law of Sukuk: Shari'a Compliant Securities* (Sweet & Maxwell 2017) 32.

24 Ercanbrack (n 21) 70.

In order to facilitate Islamic finance within domestic economies, a number of non-Muslim majority countries have taken steps to clarify the legal position of certain structures commonly found in Islamic finance activity.[25] The stated purpose of these reforms has generally not been to provide Islamic finance products, or those involved in Islamic finance activity, with preferential treatment, but rather to level the playing field between the legal treatment of certain Islamic finance transactions and their conventional alternatives.[26] Consistent with this, the UK has taken a pioneering role in legislating to accommodate Islamic finance activity.[27] The initial aim of this accommodation was said to be one of social inclusion to provide British Muslims with financial products and services that are compatible with their religious belief.[28] More recently, the focus of the UK government's accommodative policy has been to reinforce London's position as a leading international financial centre.[29] Reforms introduced to date in the UK have been religiously-neutral and UK authorities have maintained a no obstacles, no special favours[30] approach to accommodating Islamic finance. In order to achieve this, UK authorities have

25 See for example in the case of Luxembourg, Luxembourg for Finance, 'Islamic finance' January 2017 <www.alfi.lu/sites/alfi.lu/files/LFF_brochure_islamic_finance.pdf>; in the case of France, Direction Générale des Finances, Bulletin Officiel Des Impôts, No 78 of 24 August 2010, 'Régime Applicable aux Sukuk d'investissement' (Direction Générale des Finances Publiques 4 FE/S2/10, 2010). For more details on the approach of French authorities with respect to Islamic finance see Ibrahim-Zeyyad Cekici, 'Managing Islamic finance vis-à-vis *laïcité*: the case of France' in Valentino Cattelan (ed) *Islamic Finance in Europe, Towards a Plural Financial System* (Edward Elgar 2013) 192. While these (and other) countries in Europe have sought to engage with Islamic finance, a less interventionist approach has generally been taken with respect to amending existing legislative provisions.

26 See, for example, HM Treasury, *The Development of Islamic Finance in the UK: The Government's Perspective* (HM Treasury 2008).

27 Cosgrave (n 8) 68.

28 Callum McCarthy, 'Regulation and Islamic Finance', Speech given at the *Muslim Council of Britain Islamic Finance and Trade Conference* (13 June 2006) <http://www.fsa.gov.uk/pages/Library/Communication/Speeches/2006/0613_cm.shtml> accessed 25 February 2019. See also, Speech given by The Rt Hon Sir Edward George, Governor of the Bank of England, Islamic Home Finance Seminar, London (27 March 2003) in Bank of England *Quarterly Bulletin 0A42/12* (May 2003) 240.

29 HM Treasury, *The Development of Islamic Finance in the UK: The Government's Perspective* (n 26) 13.

30 Michael Ainley and others, *Islamic Finance in the UK: Regulation and Challenges* (Financial Services Authority 2007) 11. See also Mohammed Amin, 'The Taxation of Islamic Finance in Major Western Countries' (2007) 1st Quarter Arab Banking Review 129.

built upon the legal and regulatory framework already in place in English law and have sought to assimilate Islamic finance produces and services into that framework.[31] Where some aspect of the existing framework inadvertently inhibits Islamic finance activity, UK authorities have been prepared to adapt tax and regulatory law to treat certain contractual structures according to their economic substance, rather than their legal form. The purpose of this approach has been to reduce legal hurdles that would otherwise make it difficult for Islamic finance to compete on an equal footing and a level playing field with economically comparable conventional finance.[32]

The primary focus of UK legislative reforms relating to Islamic finance has been in the context of taxation. Starting with tax issues associated with Islamic mortgage-alternatives in 2003 and subsequently addressing the taxation of other retail and wholesale Islamic finance products, successive Finance Acts in the UK have categorised structures used in certain Islamic finance transactions as 'alternative finance arrangements' and have expanded the existing tax regime to include these arrangements.[33] By including alternative finance arrangements in existing tax legislation, amendments introduced by the Finance Acts have sought to ensure that features of Islamic finance activity that arise from that activity's compliance with principles of Islamic law – such as multiple transfers of an asset in the context of a single financial product and the payment of a return characterised as profit rather than interest – do not place Islamic finance market participants in a worse (or indeed a better) tax position than their conventional counterparts.[34]

Regulation of Islamic finance activity in the UK has sought to maintain consistency with relevant tax reforms by using similar religiously-neutral terminology while facilitating equality of treatment between Islamic and conventional finance transactions and participants. The Financial Conduct Authority (the 'FCA') is responsible for the oversight and supervision of the UK financial

---

31 Jonathan Ercanbrack, *The Transformation of Islamic Law in Global Financial Markets* (Cambridge University Press 2015) 146.

32 Ken Eglington, remarks made at the 'The Future of Islamic Finance in Britain Panel', *Islamic Finance: The Way Forward Conference*, The London School of Economics and Political Science (27 February 2016).

33 See, for example, Finance Act 2003, Part 4, ss 72 and 73, Finance Act 2005, Part 5, Finance Act 2006, ss 95 to 98 and s 168, Finance Act 2007, ss 53 and 75, Finance Act 2008, ss 154 to 157 and Schedule 46, Finance Act 2009, s 123 and Schedule 61, Finance Act 2013, s 157, Finance Act 2015, s 68, Finance Act 2016, s 136 (dealing with land in Scotland), Finance Act 2018, s 41.

34 Cosgrave (n 8) 68.

services industry and the institutions operating within it.[35] Provision within the UK of certain financial services that constitute 'regulated activities' will, therefore, require the provider of such services to obtain an exemption or authorisation from the FCA.[36] To avoid Islamic finance activity falling outside the supervisory oversight of the FCA, or being subject to a level of supervision that is not appropriate to the economic substance of the activity, UK authorities have modified the list of regulated activities within the purview of the FCA. As a result, Islamic mortgage-alternatives and *sukuk* (Islamic bonds) have now been brought into the existing regulatory regime under the titles of 'home purchase plans'[37] and 'alternative finance investment bonds',[38] respectively.

In conjunction with the FCA's supervisory function, the Prudential Regulatory Authority (the 'PRA') is responsible for the prudential regulation of certain financial institutions in the UK.[39] The FCA and the PRA together oversee financial firms offering Islamic finance products and services in the UK, including standalone Islamic banks. Regulatory authorities in the UK have emphasised that Islamic banks and financial institutions will be held to the same standard as conventional banks and financial institutions and have noted that 'all financial institutions authorised by the FSA [now the FCA] and operating in the UK, or seeking to do so, are subject to the same standards. This is true regardless of their country of origin, the sectors in which they wish to specialise, or their

35 Financial Services Act 2012, s 6 amending s 1 to 18 of the Financial Services and Markets Act 2000.

36 Financial Services and Markets Act 2000, s 19.

37 The UK authorities extended secondary legislation (primarily the Financial Services and Markets Act 2000 (Regulated Activities) Order 2001 ('RAO') but also the Terrorism Act 2000, (UK), the Proceeds of Crime Act 2002 (UK), and The Financial Services and Markets Act 2000 (Financial Promotions) Order 2005 (UK)), to create a new category of regulated activity relating to 'Home Purchase Plans'. In order to ensure a more comparable playing field the FCA's 'Mortgage and Home Finance: Conduct of Business Sourcebook' ('MCOB') has also been amended to provide guiding rules relating to the provision of Islamic mortgage-alternatives.

38 In order to clarify the regulatory position of *sukuk* and to prevent them from being subject to the more restrictive regulatory regime applying to collective investment schemes, a new category of regulated activity was introduced by means of the Financial Services and Markets Act 2000 (Regulated Activities)(Amendment) Order 2010, No. 86 of 2010. This amendment resulted in the creation of s 77A in the specified investments section of the RAO 2001, which has now been extended to include 'Alternative Finance Investments'. Consequential amendments were also made to the Financial Services and Markets Act 2000 (Carrying on Regulated Activities by Way of Business) Order 2001 and the Financial Services and Markets Act 2000 (Financial Promotion) Order 2000.

39 Laura Cox and others, 'United Kingdom regulatory reform: emergence of the twin peaks' (2012) 95(Apr) Compliance Officer Bulletin 1, 15.

religious principles'.[40] Based on this non-discriminatory approach, UK authorities now regulate five standalone Islamic banks[41] and over 20 conventional institution offering Islamic finance products and services.[42]

Notwithstanding strong political support for Islamic finance in the UK, the FCA has stated that it is 'a secular and not a religious regulator'.[43] Noting that '[i]t would not be appropriate, even if it were possible, for the [FCA] to judge between different interpretations of Sharia law',[44] UK authorities have not adopted any publicly articulated interpretation of the financial principles of Islamic law.[45] As a result, the UK government has not appointed its own religious supervisory board, nor has it published guidelines or regulations on the religious compatibility of any Islamic finance products. Indeed, there is no legal requirement that institutions engaged in Islamic finance in the UK establish their own Islamic governance structure.[46] Any institutions that have appointed a religious supervisory board (*Shari'ah* supervisory board or 'SSB') or a religious adviser have done so on a voluntary basis, with those religious supervisory entities subject to no tailored government oversight.[47] The FCA has, however, expressed concern regarding the proper categorisation of religious

40 Ainley and others (n 30) 11.

41 These are currently: Gatehouse Bank, Al Rayan Bank, Bank of London and the Middle East, Abu Dhabi Islamic Bank and QIB UK, a unit of Qatar Islamic Bank.

42 Bank of England, 'Topical article, Islamic banks and central banking' *Quarterly Bulletin 2017 Q3* <https://www.bankofengland.co.uk/-/media/boe/files/quarterly-bulletin/2017/islamic-banks-and-central-banking.pdf?la=en&hash=15D94BD65C2EFA6962989D10E21543B7B7013C1C> 156, 157, accessed 25 February 2019.

43 Ainley and others (n 30) 13.

44 ibid.

45 Michael Foot, 'The Future of Islamic Banking in Europe', Speech given at the *Second International Islamic Finance Conference*, Dubai, United Arab Emirates (22 September 2003) <http://www.fsa.gov.uk/Pages/Library/Communication/Speeches/2003/sp150.shtml> accessed 25 February 2019, noting that 'we shall have neither the ability nor the desire to monitor a bank's actual sharia'a compliance. That has to be something for the sharia'a board and for the institution itself'. As Ercanbrack notes, however, by putting in place a legislative framework to accommodate Islamic finance activity, the UK government has in a way facilitated certain Islamic finance activities that 'reflect a specific understanding of Islamic commercial law', the UK government, however, adopts no stated position on the meaning of the structures used in that Islamic finance activity. Jonathan Ercanbrack, 'Regulating Islamic financial institutions in the UK' in Valentino Cattelan (ed) *Islamic Finance in Europe, Towards a Plural Financial System* (Edward Elgar 2013) 157, 164.

46 Zulkifli Hasan, 'Regulatory Framework of *Sharī'ah* Governance System in Malaysia, GCC Countries and the UK' (March 2010) 3–2 Kyoto Bulletin of Islamic Area Studies 82, 103.

47 Antony Hainsworth, 'Governance rules for Islamic financial institutions: the new frontier?' (2007) 9 Journal of International Banking and Financial Law 515, 515.

supervisors within institutions,[48] and each institution offering Islamic finance products and services within the UK must consider (together with the FCA) whether any Islamic scholar advising that institution occupies a position of director within the institution or merely one of advisor.[49]

UK authorities, then, have adopted a consistent approach to accommodating Islamic finance activity within the existing legislative framework. Guidance and reforms introduced have been relevant to retail and wholesale Islamic finance activity and have sought to mitigate tax and regulatory obstacles that could otherwise hinder the development of a level playing field between Islamic and conventional finance. An articulated government commitment to growing the Islamic finance market in the UK has been strengthened by recent innovative steps taken by UK authorities, such as the 2014 UK sovereign *sukuk*,[50] the 2015 issue of *sukuk* certificates guaranteed by UK Export Finance (the *sukuk* market's first issuance guaranteed by an export credit agency)[51] and the 2017 confirmation by the Bank of England of its intention to establish a deposit facility designed for Islamic banks.[52]

3 The Accommodation of Islamic Finance in Ireland

3.1 *Guidance and Legislative Amendments*

Sukuk certificates and *sukuk* programmes have been listed on the Irish Stock Exchange plc. trading as Euronext Dublin ('Euronext Dublin')[53] regularly since 2006,[54] with Euronext Dublin's first listing of *sukuk* certificates taking place only weeks after the first listing of *sukuk* certificates on the London Stock

48 Ainley and others (n 30) 13.

49 ibid.

50 HM Treasury UK Sovereign Sukuk PLC, £200,000,000 Certificates due 2019.

51 Khadrawy Limited, U.S.$913,026,000 2.471 percent Certificates due 2025 with the benefit of a guarantee by Her Britannic Majesty's Secretary of State acting by the Export Credits Guarantee Department (UK Export Finance).

52 Bank of England, 'Shari'ah compliant liquidity facilities: establishing a fund based deposit facility' (6 April 2017) <https://www.bankofengland.co.uk/paper/2017/shariah-compliant-liquidity-facilities-consultation-paper> accessed 25 February 2019.

53 For consistency, this chapter refers to the Irish Stock Exchange plc as Euronext Dublin, including when referring to listings of bonds and *sukuk* certificates that occurred prior to Euronext's acquisition of the Irish Stock Exchange plc in March 2018.

54 NICBM Sukuk Limited, U.S.$100,000,000 Trust Certificates due 2011 (the '2006 NICBM *sukuk*'). Some commentators have indicated that the first *sukuk* was listed in Ireland in 2005, however, the author has found no concrete evidence of this. The 2006 NICBM *sukuk* referenced above is the earliest listed *sukuk* on Euronext Dublin that the author is aware of, see also, Gerard Scully, 'Sector set for continued growth' Finance-Magazine (2007)

Exchange.[55] It took a further three years, however, for Irish authorities to publicly engage with the structural aspects of Islamic finance activity and the interaction between certain Islamic finance products and Irish law.

In October 2009, the Irish Revenue Commissioners (the 'Revenue') published a Tax Briefing outlining the tax position in Ireland of certain Islamic finance products (the 'Tax Briefing 2009').[56] This non-binding briefing note represented a public statement by the Revenue and sought to clarify the taxation of a number of Islamic finance products, without amending any provisions of Irish law. Instead, the Tax Briefing 2009 confirmed that three Islamic finance products – *takaful* (Islamic insurance), *ijarah* (Islamic leasing) and Islamic investment funds (similar to conventional investment funds, but with an investment strategy that aligns with Islamic finance principles) – would be subject to the same tax regime as conventional insurance, leasing and investment funds, respectively.[57] The clarifications set out in the Tax Briefing 2009 were important optically and provided an indication to domestic and international financial market participants that the Irish government was open to the idea of Islamic finance activity within the Irish economy. In practice, the three particular Islamic finance products covered by the Tax Briefing 2009 – *takaful*, *ijarah* and Islamic investment funds – can be structured such that even without the Revenue's Tax Briefing 2009, they would be taxed in Ireland in a manner that is consistent with their economic substance and that aligns with the tax treatment of economically comparable conventional finance products. The Tax Briefing 2009, therefore, simply confirmed the existing position under Irish law.

As in the UK, tax liability in Ireland is determined on the basis of a product's legal form.[58] In the case of the Islamic finance products covered in the Tax Briefing 2009, their contractual structures operate so as to allow the application of Ireland's tax laws in a manner that reflects the products' respective economic substance. However, the contractual structure of certain other Islamic

---

<http://www.finance-magazine.com/supplements/abs2007/display_article.php?i=7477> accessed 25 February 2019.

55 Tabreed 06 Financing Corporation U.S.$200,000,000 Trust Certificates due 2011.

56 Irish Revenue Commissioners, 'Islamic Finance, Tax Briefing Issue 78' (Revenue Commissioners, October 2009) <http://www.revenue.ie/en/tax-professionals/historic-material/tax-briefing/2009/tax-briefing-78-2009.pdf> accessed 27 November 2018.

57 ibid.

58 *McGrath v McDermott* [1988] IR 258, 276 (Finlay CJ), 277 per McCarthy J who noted that the substance over form approach to determining tax liability was 'attractive in equity but it is wrong in law'. See also, *Inspector of Taxes v Kiernan* [1981] IR 117 (SC), *O'Sullivan (Inspector of Taxes) v P Ltd* (1962) 2 ITC 464 (HC), *Revenue Commissioners v Doorley* [1933] IR 750 (SC).

finance products not covered in the Tax Briefing 2009 meant that without legislative amendment, these products would be subject to a tax treatment that did not reflect their economic substance and which was inconsistent with the taxation of conventional finance products.[59] This disparity of tax treatment would, according to the Irish Department of Finance (the 'Department of Finance'), act as a 'disincentive to such Islamic transactions occurring or being sited in Ireland'.[60] As a result, shortly after the publication of the Tax Briefing 2009, the Finance Act 2010 introduced amendments to Ireland's existing tax laws: the Taxes Consolidation Act 1997 (the 'TCA 1997') and the Stamp Duties Consolidation Act 1999 (the 'SDCA 1999'). These amendments were designed to facilitate greater equality of tax treatment between certain conventional and Islamic finance products,[61] and to address the tax position of Islamic finance products whose legal structure would otherwise have resulted in the application of Ireland's tax laws in a manner that did not reflect their economic substance.

Ss 39 and 137 of the Finance Act 2010 deal with 'specified financial transactions'[62] and insert Part 8A[63] into the TCA 1997 and s 85A[64] into the SDCA 1999, respectively. Neither Part 8A TCA 1997 nor s 85A SDCA 1999 refer to Islam or Islamic finance. As a result, any finance transaction that falls within the structures provided for in Part 8A TCA 1997 and s 85A SDCA 1999 may elect to be treated for tax purposes as a specified financial transaction.[65] However,

59 Irish Revenue Commissioners, 'Tax Treatment of Islamic Financial Transactions', *Tax and Duty Manual* (Part 08A-01-01) (Irish Revenue Commissioners 2018) [1.3]. See also, Irish Revenue Commissioners, *Guidance Notes on the Tax Treatment of Islamic Financial Transactions* (Irish Revenue Commissioners 2010) 6 (the *Tax and Duty Manual* (Part 08A-01-01) replicates almost exactly the content of the *Guidance Notes on Tax Treatment of Islamic Financial Transactions*).

60 Department of Finance, 'Section 1 of Finance Act 2010, Report on Tax Expenditures', *PRN A10/0776* (July 2010) [9.3] <http://taxpolicy.gov.ie/wp-content/uploads/2011/03/Section1ofFA2010ReportonTaxExpenditures.pdf> accessed 25 February 2019.

61 For more recent Irish government discussions on Islamic finance in Ireland, see Department of Finance, *IFS2020: A Strategy for Ireland's International Financial Services sector 2015–2020* (The Stationery Office 2015) 20, in which it was noted that 'Islamic Finance will continue to feature in the sectoral and regional strategies outlined in IFS2020'.

62 Defined in Part 8A TCA 1997 as meaning a 'credit transaction', a 'deposit transaction' or an 'investment transaction'.

63 Inserted by Finance Act 2010, s 39. See also, Oireachtas, 'Finance Bill 2010, Explanatory Memorandum' 10 < https://data.oireachtas.ie/ie/oireachtas/bill/2010/9/eng/memo/b0910d-memo.pdf> accessed 25 February 2019.

64 Inserted by Finance Act 2010, s 137.

65 This does need to be a positive election and the provisions dealing with specified financial transactions will not apply unless the election is made – see, TCA 1997, s 267U, as amended by Finance 2012, s 37.

the Irish government has confirmed that the aim of these legislative provisions is to 'extend tax treatment applicable to conventional finance transactions to Shari'a compliant or Islamic financial products which achieve the same economic result in substance as comparable conventional products'.[66] As a result of the Finance Act 2010, three Islamic finance structures are now addressed in religiously neutral terms in Irish tax law: 'deposit transactions' (Islamic deposits); 'credit transactions' (covering a number of Islamic financing arrangements); and 'investment transactions' (*sukuk*). Minor clarifications to the specified financial transactions regime have been introduced in subsequent Finance Acts[67] although the scope of the accommodations has remained unchanged since their introduction in 2010.

To date, the focus of legislative accommodation of Islamic finance activity in Ireland has been with respect to the taxation of this activity. Unlike in the UK, where both the tax *and* regulatory aspects of Islamic finance transactions have been addressed under English law, the regulation of Islamic finance transactions and institutions that engage in Islamic finance activity has not been the subject of tailored legal accommodation in Ireland.[68] As a result, the Central Bank of Ireland (the 'Central Bank') as Ireland's financial services regulator, must continue to apply existing regulatory rules to Islamic finance activity and institutions.

3.2 *Islamic Finance in Practice – the Case of Islamic Mortgage-Alternatives under Irish Law*

When discussing the introduction of guidance and legislative amendments aimed at accommodating Islamic finance in Ireland, the Department of Finance outlined certain 'opportunities' for Ireland: (a) encouraging investment into Ireland in the form of wholesale Islamic finance activity and the establishment of Islamic finance institutions; (b) the provision of ethical investment opportunities for Irish investors; and (c) the opportunity for Muslims to participate in the financial sector in a manner that is consistent with their religious beliefs.[69] These perceived benefits for Ireland, which can be broken

66 Department of Finance, *Islamic Finance in Ireland; An Information Note* (Department of Finance, Dublin, March 2010) 5.

67 See Finance Act 2012, s 37 and Finance Act 2013, ss 24 and 75.

68 Central Bank (Supervision and Enforcement) Act 2013, s 73 introduced an amendment to the Central Bank Act 1971 to allow banks established in non-EEA countries to open branches in Ireland. This could potentially assist with the opening of a branch of an Islamic bank in Ireland, but does not go towards the regulation of those banks.

69 Department of Finance, *Islamic Finance in Ireland; An Information Note* (n 66) 4.

down into economic benefits associated primarily with the wholesale Islamic finance sector and social benefits arising from the availability of Islamic finance products domestically, are consistent with the aims outlined by UK authorities when introducing corresponding reforms under English law. Like the UK, then, the legislative amendments and guidance introduced in Ireland cover financial structures that could be used in retail and wholesale Islamic finance transactions.

The tangible growth to date of Islamic finance in Ireland's economy has, however, been largely limited to wholesale Islamic finance activity.[70] In practice, there remain gaps in the legislative regime applicable to Islamic finance activity in Ireland, particularly at retail level. As a result, remaining taxation issues, uncertainty surrounding the regulation of Islamic finance activity and institutions, and questions of consumer protection are still to be addressed by the Irish authorities. The position of Islamic mortgage-alternatives under Irish law illustrates the relevance of a comprehensive legislative approach when accommodating Islamic finance activity.

Islamic mortgage-alternatives have been developed by the Islamic finance industry to provide an alternative to a conventional mortgage.[71] Three main forms of these mortgage-alternative products exist. The first is structured around a *murabaha* contract and involves the sale of property by the financial institution to the customer, with the purchase price for the property paid by the customer to the financial institution on a deferred and marked-up basis.[72] The second structure incorporates an *ijarah wa-iqtina* contract involving a lease of property by the financial institution to the customer in return

70 For example, a press release published on 5 April 2018 indicated that an Irish-incorporated company issued a *sukuk*. However, no publicly available information on this issuance is available as at the date of publication of this chapter, Matheson, *News and Insights,* 'Matheson Advises on the First Irish Issuance of a Sukuk Bond Under Irish Tax Law' (5 April 2018), <https://www.matheson.com/news-and-insights/article/matheson-advises-on-the-first-irish-issuance-of-a-sukuk-bond-under-irish-ta> accessed 25 February 2019. From a retail perspective, anecdotal evidence suggests that money received from informal sources, such as a co-operative model implemented within the Muslim community, is being used to provide capital to some in that community, thereby avoiding or reducing reliance on conventional non-Islamic finance products. This informal approach, however, exists outside of the formal banking system and the oversight of regulatory and tax authorities.

71 Rodney Wilson, 'Islamic Finance in Europe' RSCAS Policy Papers No 2007/02 (European University Institute for MUSMINE 2007) 10–11, for a discussion about the development of Islamic mortgage-alternatives.

72 Under the *murabaha* model, the financier buys the property and sells it immediately to the borrower for the original purchase price plus an agreed mark-up (the financier's profit) to be paid in instalments.

for payment of rent (which includes a repayment and a profit element) and ultimately a transfer of the property's title to the customer.[73] Finally, the third structure is based on a diminishing *musharaka* contract and involves shared ownership of the property between a financial institution and customer, the lease of that property to the customer in return for payment of rent and ultimately purchase of full title to the property by the customer.[74] Although the legal structure of these three Islamic finance products does not involve any loan of capital by the financial institution or payment of interest by the customer, the economic substance of each Islamic mortgage-alternative is consistent with an interest-based mortgage. As a result, each structure allows a customer to purchase property with the financial assistance of a financial institution on the basis that the amount of this financial assistance, together with an element of profit, will ultimately be returned to the financial institution.

As a result of the amendments to Ireland's tax legislation introduced by the Finance Act 2010, the TCA 1997 now provides for a number of 'credit transactions' that are structurally similar to the *murabaha*[75] and diminishing *musharaka*[76] structures used in some Islamic mortgage-alternatives. If certain conditions are met,[77] the provisions of Part 8A TCA 1997 now deem these credit transactions to have established a loan relationship between a financial institution and a customer (even though in legal substance no such relationship exists).[78] The periodic returns paid by the customer to a financial institution pursuant to a credit transaction will, therefore, be treated under Irish tax law as if it were interest paid on a loan.[79] From the perspective of the parties involved in an Islamic mortgage-alternative based on a *murabaha* contract, this means that the amount of the customer's periodic payments above the

73 Under the *ijarah wa-iqtina* model, the borrower undertakes to purchase the property at the end of the rental period with the purchase price spread out over the duration of the lease – the bank remains owner of the property for the lease term and the rent paid by the borrower represents the banks profit, Humayon A Dar, 'Islamic House Financing in the United Kingdom: Problems, Challenges and Prospects' (2002) 12 Review of Islamic Economics 47, 51.

74 Under diminishing *musharaka* model, the financier and the customer enter into a joint ownership of a property, the financier leases its share back to the borrower who also progressively purchases the financier's equity in the property until the financiers share in the property is reduced to zero. Ainley and others (n 30) 20.

75 Paragraph (a) of the definition of 'credit transaction', s 267N TCA 1997.

76 Paragraph (c) of the definition of 'credit transaction', s 267N TCA 1997.

77 Definition of 'credit transaction', s 267N TCA 1997 and s 267O TCA 1997.

78 *Global Islamic Finance Report 2011*, Humayon Dar and Mufti Talha Ahmad Azami (eds) (BMB Islamic UK Limited 2011) 208–209.

79 TCA 1997, s 267O(1).

consideration paid for the property will be treated for tax purposes as interest paid on a loan.[80] In the case of an Islamic mortgage-alternative based on a diminishing *musharaka* contract, the rental portion of the customer's periodic payments will be treated for tax purposes as interest paid on a loan.[81]

These amendments to Ireland's existing tax framework seek to align the taxation of certain Islamic and conventional home financing products by removing some of the obstacles that would have prevented these Islamic and conventional financing transactions from being subject to the same tax regime. In this way, such amendments are a noteworthy step towards the establishment of a level playing field between Islamic and conventional finance. They also reflect similar accommodations introduced in UK tax law.[82]

However, there remain limitations with respect to the applicable legal framework in Ireland that may restrict the viability of some Islamic mortgage-alternatives within the Irish economy. While the amendments introduced by the Finance Act 2010 did not address the tax position of Islamic mortgage-alternatives based on an *ijarah wa-iqtina* contract,[83] the Tax Briefing 2009 outlined the tax treatment of *ijarah* leasing arrangements, including those 'used for a finance lease'.[84] These leasing arrangements bear clear similarities to an *ijarah wa-iqtina* structure. However, this is the extent of the Tax Briefing 2009's usefulness with respect to Islamic mortgage-alternatives as the Tax Briefing 2009 and the November 2018 update of the Tax and Duty Manual (Part 08A-01-01) (the 'Tax and Duty Manual')[85] specifically limit their application to 'the leasing of plant and machinery and other chattels'[86] rather than leases of immovable property. This removes the relevance of the Tax Briefing 2009 for market participants trying to determine the tax regime applicable to Islamic

80 *Global Islamic Finance Report 2011* (n 78) 208–209.

81 ibid.

82 HM Land Registry, 'Practice guide 69: Islamic financing' (updated 16 March 2018) <https://www.gov.uk/government/publications/islamic-financing/practice-guide-69-islamic-financing> accessed 25 February 2019.

83 While the Irish Revenue Commissioners' *Tax and Duty Manual* (Part 08A-01-01) suggests that *ijarah wa-iqtina* structures would fall within the provisions of the Finance Act 2010, it acknowledges that the provisions do 'not apply to a lease *of immovable property*'. (Irish Revenue Commissioners, 'Tax Treatment of Islamic Financial Transactions', *Tax and Duty Manual* (Part 08A-01-01) (n 59) [3.3.2], emphasis added).

84 *ijarah muntahia bittamleek* – Irish Revenue Commissioners, *'Islamic Finance', Tax Briefing* (n 56).

85 Irish Revenue Commissioners, 'Tax Treatment of Islamic Financial Transactions', *Tax and Duty Manual* (Part 08A-01-01) (n 59).

86 Irish Revenue Commissioners, *Islamic Finance, Tax Briefing* (n 56), Irish Revenue Commissioners, 'Tax Treatment of Islamic Financial Transactions', *Tax and Duty Manual* (Part 08A-01-01) (n 59) [3.3.1].

mortgage-alternatives based on an *ijarah wa-iqtina* contract. Without an expansion of the definition of credit transaction in Part 8A TCA 1997 to include transactions where a financial institution acquires sole ownership of property that it then leases to a customer, it remains unclear how the Irish authorities will tax returns paid to a financial institution in the form of rental payments under an *ijarah wa-iqtina* contract. It also remains unclear how such authorities will distinguish between the portion of the rent paid by the customer for occupation of the property and the portion of the rent that will eventually go towards the acquisition of the property.

In addition to uncertainties with respect to the tax position of *ijarah wa-iqtina* contracts involving immovable property, the accommodations introduced into Irish law have not addressed the multiple impositions of stamp duty that will be relevant to all forms of Islamic mortgage-alternatives. Unlike a conventional mortgage, which only involves one property sale, *murabaha*, diminishing *musharaka* and *ijarah wa-iqtina*-based transactions all technically involve two sales of the underlying property, the first when the financial institution acquires ownership of the property from the original vendor and the second when the financial institution transfers ownership of that property to the customer.[87] In the absence of some structural engineering of an Islamic mortgage-alternative contract,[88] these two property sales within the same financial arrangement may result in a double imposition of stamp duty.[89] UK authorities addressed this double stamp duty issue early in their legislative accommodation of Islamic finance activity by eliminating the double stamp duty land tax imposed on *murabaha*-based transactions in 2003[90] and on diminishing *musharaka* and *ijarah wa-iqtina*-based transactions in 2005.[91] Through these UK accommodations, the points at which the first and second property transfers take place in a single Islamic finance transaction are identified, and the imposition of stamp duty land tax is limited to only one of these transfers. As such, in the UK there is now only one imposition of stamp duty land tax

87 Fahim Uz-Zaman, *Shariah-Compliant Financial Services: A Guide to Products, Markets and Trends* (VRL KnowledgeBank Ltd 2006) 37; Reinhard Leopold Klarmann, *Islamic Project Finance; a Legal Study with Particular Reference to the Laws of Switzerland and the United Arab Emirates* (Schulthess 2003) 252.

88 Such as, for example, the use of a sale and trust structure, rather than two separate sales transactions.

89 The Tax and Duty Manual issued by the Irish Revenue Commissioners, while referring to the stamp duty issue, reiterate that 'stamp duty will arise under normal rules'. Irish Revenue Commissioners, 'Tax Treatment of Islamic Financial Transactions', *Tax and Duty Manual* (Part 08A-01-01) (n 59) [6.3.8].

90 Finance Act 2003, s 73.

91 Finance Act 2003, s 71A, inserted by the Finance Act 2005, s 94, Schedule 8 [1]-[2].

on Islamic mortgage-alternatives.[92] In Ireland, the Revenue may be reluctant to open up any possibility of tax avoidance or an unintended reduction in tax liabilities. However, without some re-engineering of either the stamp duty liability within Islamic property-based transactions or the structure of Islamic mortgage-alternative contracts themselves, inconsistency between the stamp duty position of Islamic and conventional finance products in Ireland could result in certain Islamic finance products being prohibitively expensive.

Finally, the regulatory treatment of Islamic mortgage-alternatives under Irish law remains unchanged by legislative accommodation. In Ireland, the Land and Conveyancing Law Reform Act 2009 (the '2009 Act') defines a mortgage as including 'any charge or lien on any property for securing money or money's worth'.[93] It then goes on to restrict legal mortgages over real property in Ireland to those created by means of a charge by deed on the land.[94] Complementing this regime, consumer protection in the context of mortgages is established in the Consumer Credit Act 1995 (the 'CCA 1995').[95] The CCA 1995 defines a 'housing loan' as an agreement for the provision of credit (or refinancing credit) on the security of a mortgage of a freehold or leasehold estate or interest in land for the purpose of the construction, improvement or purchase of a house,[96] and a mortgage is defined as including a charge.[97] In order to ensure

92 Cosgrave (n 8) 73.

93 Land and Conveyancing Law Reform Act 2009, s 3. Irish courts have defined 'money's worth' as not simply 'something for which people are willing to pay money but something for which they are able to get money', *The Attorney General (at the Prosecution of Superintendent J.P. Hynes) v Casino Amusement Theatres Limited* [1957] 91 ILTR 41 (SC) 49–50 (Kingsmill Moore J). A 'housing loan mortgage' is defined by the 2009 Act as 'a mortgage to secure a housing loan', Land and Conveyancing Law Reform Act 2009, s 3.

94 Land and Conveyancing Law Reform Act 2009, s 89(1). From a strictly legal point of view a charge and a mortgage remain distinct structures under which a mortgage involves a transfer of estate and a charge merely a transfer of an interest. Mokal has suggested that this difference may have a practical impact in liquidation, Riz Mokal, 'Liquidation Expenses and Floating Charges – the Separate Funds Fallacy' [2004] Lloyd's Maritime and Commercial Law Quarterly 387. Nevertheless, the Land and Conveyancing Law Reform Act 2009, amongst others, now establishes a confluence in terminology with mortgage and charge often used interchangeably. This chapter assumes that any Islamic mortgage alternative would be created after 1 December 2009 (the date from which the regime set out in the 2009 Act applies).

95 Consumer Credit Act 1995, No. 24/1995.

96 Consumer Credit Act 1995, Interpretation as amended by the Central Bank and Financial Services Authority of Ireland Act 2004 (21/2004), s 33 and sch 3 pt 12 item 1(b), (ba), (d), SI 455/2004.

97 Consumer Credit Act, 1995, s 2(1), as amended by the Central Bank and Financial Services Authority of Ireland Act 2004 (21/2004), s 33 and sch 3 pt 12 item 1(b), (ba), (d), SI 455/2004.

Ireland's property and consumer protection regimes apply consistently to Islamic mortgage-alternatives, the structures developed by the Islamic finance industry must be brought within the existing regulatory provisions.

In the case of Islamic mortgage-alternatives based on a *murabaha* contract, bringing these financial structures within the regulatory regime applying to mortgages would seem to be relatively straightforward. Like a conventional mortgage,[98] *murabaha*-based arrangements often result in title to the property being transferred to the customer almost immediately upon the commencement of the transaction.[99] This structure then allows the customer to grant a charge over the property to the financial institution for the remainder of the transaction as security for payment of the purchase price. Reflecting this, Community Finance Ireland is developing a *murabaha*-based product to be used to finance the acquisition of property by Muslim community groups or social enterprises in Ireland.[100] Islamic mortgage-alternatives based on *ijarah wa-iqtina* and diminishing *musharaka* contracts raise more difficulties from a regulatory perspective. In both of these Islamic mortgage-alternatives, the financial institution assumes full or partial ownership of the property and only at maturity of the transaction will full title to the property be transferred to the customer. As such, the legal structure of these arrangement means that the financial institution maintains all or some ownership interest in the property for the duration of the transaction. There is, therefore, not only limited scope for the customer to grant a charge over the property in the financial institution's favour, but legally no debt owed by the customer the repayment of which can be secured.[101]

It is arguable that other than in the case of structures based on a *murabaha* contract, Islamic mortgage-alternatives may fall outside of Ireland's property and consumer protection regimes. As a result, a number of the Islamic mortgage-alternatives could be classified by Irish law as leases, or at least as including a lease, rather than as mortgages. This classification reflects the legal form of these Islamic finance products, but may impact on the manner in which these

98 Kevin Gray and Susan Frances Gray, *Land Law* (Oxford University Press 2007) 216.

99 Mahmoud El-Gamal, *Islamic Finance; Law, Economics and Practice* (Cambridge University Press 2006) 67.

100 Philip Lee, 'Ireland's First Islamic Financing Product: The First Of Many' (2018), <https://www.philiplee.ie/irelands-first-islamic-financing-product-the-first-of-many/> accessed 25 February 2019 although Community Finance Ireland's Islamic mortgage-alternatives are offered to community groups and social enterprises, rather than to consumers.

101 *Secretary of State for Work and Pensions v UP* [2011] AACR 12 [13].

products are treated under Irish law.[102] Unlike lessors of real estate, residential mortgage lenders[103] and mortgage intermediaries[104] in Ireland are subject to regulatory oversight by the Central Bank.[105] Residential mortgage lenders are also subject to the consumer protection standards set by the CCA 1995 and conduct standards established by the Consumer Protection Code 2012. It is this direct institutional authorisation and indirect consumer protection-centred regulation that could result in a distinction in the protections offered to Islamic and conventional customers using economically comparable finance products. From a consumer protection and policy perspective, Islamic customers need the same level of information, the same protection from exploitation and the same types of safeguards as conventional customers. A similar divergence in regulatory oversight prompted UK authorities to establish a tailored regulatory regime for Islamic retail mortgage-alternatives. By creating a new category of regulated activity relating to 'home purchase plans'[106] and by amending the Financial Conduct Authority's 'Mortgage and Home Finance: Conduct of Business Sourcebook' ('MCOB') to cover Islamic mortgage-alternatives, UK authorities addressed some of the key regulatory obstacles faced by these Islamic finance products.[107] As part of this regulatory accommodation, provisions of

102 Department of Finance, 'Section 1 of Finance Act 2010, Report on Tax Expenditures' (n 60) [9.15].

103 Consumer Credit Act 1995, s2(1) as amended by the Central Bank and Financial Services Authority of Ireland Act 2004 (21/2004), s 33 and sch 3 pt 12 item 1(b), (ba), (d), SI 455/2004 defines a 'mortgage lender' as a person who carries on a business that consists of or includes making housing loans.

104 Consumer Credit Act 1995, s 2(1) as amended by the Central Bank and Financial Services Authority of Ireland Act 2004 (21/2004), s 33 and sch 3 pt 12 item 1(c), SI 455/2004 defines a 'mortgage intermediary' as 'any person (other than a mortgage lender or credit institution) who, in return for commission or some other form of consideration – (a) arranges or offers to arrange the provision of a housing loan by a mortgage lender, or (b) introduces a consumer to an intermediary who arranges, or offers to arrange, for a mortgage lender to provide the consumer with such a loan'.

105 Either as a credit institution, building society, credit union or retail credit firm. Central Bank Act 1997, s 28 as amended by Markets in Financial Instruments and Miscellaneous Provisions Act 2007, s 19. See also, Consumer Credit Act 1995, s 116(1). In certain circumstances, if they are classified as a 'Property Services Providers', certain entities involved in the lease of any estate or interest in land may need to be licensed and regulated by the Property Services Regulatory Authority pursuant to the Property Services (Regulation) Act 2011.

106 Financial Services Authority (now the Financial Conduct Authority) *Regulation of Home Reversion and Home Purchase Plans* (London 2006) 6.

107 MCOB 1.2.1 (1) noting that: '(a) carries on a home finance activity (subject to the business loan and loans to high net worth mortgage customers application provisions); or (b) communicates or approves a financial promotion of qualifying credit, of a *home purchase*

MCOB dealing with disclosure, responsible lending, treatment of arrears and repossessions[108] were extended to cover Islamic mortgage-alternatives.

If the Irish government decides to accommodate structures used in Islamic mortgage-alternatives into Ireland's regulatory framework, and seeks to do so in a manner that acknowledges the economic substance of these structures, then tailored adjustments would need to be made to the scope of established legislative provisions. These adjustments should deal with regulation, consumer protection and the classification of these Islamic finance arrangements under Irish law. An extension of the existing legislative framework to include *ijarah wa-iqtina* and diminishing *musharaka*-based property transactions, and subjecting such transactions to a regulatory regime that is comparable to that imposed on conventional interest-based mortgages, could allow Islamic mortgage-alternatives to be brought under the regulatory oversight of the Central Bank,[109] subsumed within the consumer protection regime[110] and conferred a status in Irish law that reflects their economic substance. Using religiously-neutral terminology such as 'Specified Home Purchase Arrangements',[111] Irish authorities could establish a new finance product under Irish law that is subject to a regulatory regime that is comparable to that of interest-based mortgages. These accommodative measures would be consistent with the Irish government's approach to legislative accommodation introduced to date and the precedent set in the UK. Such amendments would not alter the definition of a mortgage under Irish law, nor would they be suggesting that Islamic mortgage-alternatives are mortgages. They would, instead, acknowledge that the risks faced by Islamic customers, and the economic similarities between Islamic mortgage-alternatives and conventional mortgages, justify an extension of existing regulatory, disclosure and transparency requirements found in Irish law.[112]

---

plan, of a home reversion plan or of a regulated sale and rent back agreement'. (emphasis added).

108 MCOB 4.10 (advertising and selling standards), MCOB 5.8 (pre-application disclosure), MCOB 6.8 (Disclosure at the offer stage), MCOB 7.8 (Disclosure at start of contract and after sale), MCOB 11 (Responsible lending and responsible financing of home purchase plans), MCOB 12.7 (charges), MCOB 13.8 (arrears and repossessions).

109 By expanding the definition of 'regulated business' in the Central Bank Act 1997 to include 'Specified Home Purchase Arrangements', Central Bank Act 1997, s 28 as amended by Markets in Financial Instruments and Miscellaneous Provisions Act 2007, s 19 and as further amended by Central Bank (Supervision and Enforcement) Act 2013, s 59(d).

110 By expanding Part 9 of the Consumer Credit Act 1995.

111 Or similar religiously-neutral terminology.

112 Dan Waters, 'Home reversions and Islamic mortgages get new consumer protections' (FSA/PN041/2006) (27 April 2006) <http://www.fsa.gov.uk/pages/Library/Communication/PR/2006/041.shtml> accessed 25 February 2019, discussing the UK amendments.

3.3 *Supervision of Religious Compliance*

While the Irish government may have sought to accommodate structures that reflect financial principles of Islamic law, Irish authorities have not adopted an interventionist role in determining the compatibility of Islamic finance activity with those financial principles. As is the case in the UK, amendments to Ireland's tax framework introduced by the Finance Act 2010 are ideologically neutral and do not require a financial product to comply with Islamic law in order to benefit from the specified financial transactions regime.[113] As a result, beyond compliance with Irish law, the manner in which any Islamic finance activity in Ireland is used, and the extent to which a transaction's overall structure adheres to Islamic law, are beyond the purview of the legislation and the concern of the Irish authorities. As the Irish Government has noted, it is 'not legislating for the express enactment of Sharia law in Ireland',[114] it has simply expanded the types of contracts provided for under Irish law. Consistent with this, the Central Bank has confirmed (in the context of Islamic investment funds) that it will not look to determine whether Islamic finance activity is carried out in accordance with the financial principles of Islamic law.[115] In Ireland, supervision of compliance with Islamic law has, therefore, been left to individual institutions offering Islamic finance products and services.[116]

In accordance with recommendations of standard setting bodies, institutional-level religious supervision in the form of SSBs has become commonplace within the Islamic finance industry.[117] In Ireland, Islamic investment funds (being examples of Irish-incorporated institutions offering Islamic finance products) have followed this approach. The investment activities of Oasis Crescent

113 Irish Revenue Commissioners, 'Tax Treatment of Islamic Financial Transactions', *Tax and Duty Manual* (Part 08A-01-01) (n 59) [1.3], noting that; '[a]lthough designed to cover certain Shari'a compliant structures, the legislation applies to any financing arrangement falling within the meaning of the term "specified financial transaction" regardless of whether the arrangement is, in fact, Shari'a compliant'.

114 Brian Lenihan, *Dáil Eireann Debate*, Vol. 704 No. 4; 'Finance Act 2010: Report Stage (Resumed) and Final Stage' (10 March 2010).

115 Central Bank of Ireland, 'Address by Head of Markets Policy, Martin Moloney at the IFLC at the UCD School of Law' (14 May 2015) <https://www.centralbank.ie/news-media/press-releases/martin-moloney-at-iflc-at-the-ucd-school-of-law> accessed 25 February 2019.

116 Something acknowledged by the Islamic Financial Services Board: Islamic Financial Services Board, *Revised Guidance on Key Elements in the Supervisory Review Process of Institutions offering Islamic Financial Services (excluding Islamic Insurance (Takāful) Institutions and Islamic Collective Investment Schemes)* (IFSB 2014) 17.

117 *Shari'ah* consultancy services or individual Islamic advisers can also be appointed. Hennie Van Greuning and Zamir Iqbal, *Risk analysis for Islamic banks* (World Bank Publications 2008) 192.

Global Investment Fund (Ireland) plc are, for example, 'reviewed and audited by the Investment Manager's [Oasis Crescent Capital (Proprietary) Limited] Shari'ah Advisory Board',[118] while CIMB-Principal Islamic Asset Management (Ireland) Plc and its investment manager 'have each appointed CIMB Islamic Bank Berhad ('CIMB Islamic') as their Shariah Adviser pursuant to Shariah Advisory Agreements'.[119] CIMB Islamic is in turn 'backed by [it]'s Shariah Committee'.[120]

Although there is no single model of SSB,[121] institutional SSBs frequently carry out a number of core functions that can be broken down into *ex-ante* review and authorisation of the religious conformity of financial instruments, advising interested parties on issues of religious compliance and *ex-post* auditing of an institution's activities to confirm adherence to Islamic finance principles.[122] Such oversight aims to legitimate Islamic finance activity from a religious perspective[123] and is an overt acknowledgement to stakeholders of the additional religious standards to which Islamic finance activity should adhere. These SSBs typically operate simultaneously with the board of directors and other supervisory and administrative organs of an institution, and constitute an extra limb in the corporate governance framework of that institution.[124] As a unique moral filter within an institution involved in Islamic finance activity,[125] the practical impact that SSBs can have on the actions of an

118 Oasis Crescent Global Investment Fund (Ireland) plc, Prospectus dated 15 March 2018, 13.

119 CIMB-Principal Islamic Asset Management (Ireland) Plc, Prospectus dated 7 September 2016, 13.

120 ibid.

121 Islamic Financial Services Board (n 116) 17.

122 Wafik Grais and Matteo Pellegrini, 'Corporate Governance and Shariah Compliance in Institutions Offering Islamic Financial Services' *World Bank Policy Research Working Paper 4054* (World Bank 2006) 4; Accounting and Auditing Organization for Islamic Financial Institutions ('AAOIFI'), 'Governance Standard for Islamic Financial Institutions No. 1, Shari'a Supervisory Board: Appointment, Composition and Report', in *Accounting, Auditing and Governance Standards for Islamic financial institutions* (AAOIFI 2010) [2]; Islamic Financial Services Board, *Guiding Principles on Sharīʿah Governance Systems for Institutions offering Islamic Financial Services* (IFSB 2009) [3].

123 Yusuf Talal DeLorenzo, 'Shari'ah Compliance Risk' (2006–2007) 7(2) Chicago Journal of International Law 397, 398.

124 Zulkifli Hasan, *Shari'ah Governance in Islamic Banks* (Edinburgh University Press 2012) 25.

125 Hjh Siti Faridah Abd Jabbar, 'The Shari'a supervisory board of Islamic financial institutions: a case for governance' (2009) 30(8) Company Lawyer 243, 243, David Bassens and Ben Derudder and Frank Witlox, 'Setting Shari'a standards: On the role, power and spatialities of interlocking Shari'a boards in Islamic financial services' (2011) 42 Geoforum 94, 94, Rifaat Ahmed Abdel Karim, 'The Independence of Religious and External Auditors: The Case of Islamic Banks' (1990) 3(3) Accounting, Auditing & Accountability Journal 34, 35.

institution could arguably range from one similar to directors of the institution to one more consistent with advisers or auditors.

SSBs and the Islamic scholars who sit on them have, however, traditionally been subject to little or no external oversight in many of the countries in which they operate.[126] In Ireland, the Central Bank has set out three principles guiding its on-going interaction with SSBs. First, the Central Bank has confirmed that it would not be appropriate for it to adopt a view on the quality of different SSBs or their suitability to make the judgements that they make. Second, the Central Bank will not verify any claim that an Islamic finance transaction is compliant with Islamic finance principles or that it has been approved by an SSB. Finally, the Central Bank will not subject Islamic finance activities to surveillance in order to check on-going compliance with the terms of any SSB's approval.[127]

In the absence of specific qualitative standards for Islamic scholars sitting on the SSB of an institution subject to Irish law, such scholars and the boards on which they sit will be subject to the same supervisory framework imposed on conventional institutions. For Islamic scholars advising institutions incorporated in Ireland, principles of Irish company law will apply. Islamic scholars advising institutions operating in the regulated financial sector will also be subject to the Central Bank's rules for regulated entities. Ireland's supervisory and enforcement authorities will, therefore, need to consider the role of an SSB within an institution offering Islamic finance products and services in Ireland and the impact of that board on the direction and activities of the institution.

To date, much of the guidance issued by Irish authorities has indicated that SSBs are generally expected to exercise an advisory function within the institutions that they supervise. The Revenue's Tax and Duty Manual expressly notes that '[t]he Shari'a Board should not be confused with the Board of Directors

---

126 Malaysia, for example, has implemented qualitative standards and registration requirements for Islamic scholars sitting on the SSBs or advising Islamic finance institutions in Malaysia–Islamic Financial Services Act 2013, s29(2)(a)(ii), providing for the implementation of a fit and proper test for Islamic scholars (as codified in Bank Negara Malaysia, Fit and Proper Criteria, BNM/RH/GL 018-5, see also Bank Negara Malaysia, Fit and Proper Criteria for Approved Person Exposure Draft, BNM/RH/EH 029-9 (30 August 2018)) and Islamic Financial Services Act 2013, s 31 requiring compliance with s29(2)(a)(ii) and prior written approval by Bank Negara Malaysia. See also Bank Negara Malaysia, *Shariah Governance Framework for Islamic Financial Institutions*, BNM/RH/GL_012_3 (2011) and Bank Negara Malaysia, *Shariah Governance Exposure Draft* BNM/RH/ED 028-7(2017) s 12, setting out Bank Negara Malaysia's proposed regulatory requirements on *shari'ah* governance for Islamic financial institutions.

127 Central Bank of Ireland, *Address by Head of Markets Policy, Martin Moloney at the IFLC at the UCD School of Law* (n 115).

of a company, as a Shari'a Board only has an advisory role',[128] while an earlier briefing by the Department of Finance also observed that '[t]he Shari'a Board ... only has an advisory role'.[129] The Department of Finance's briefing did, however, go on to note that '[f]rom a company's perspective, the Shari'a Board can be taken as a sub-committee of the company's Board of Directors'.[130] This reference to a 'sub-committee of the company's Board of Directors' adds an unhelpful level of uncertainty to the position of SSBs in Ireland. Committees and sub-committees[131] of companies incorporated in Ireland are often composed of a subset of the board of directors.[132] Indeed the Companies Act 2014 provides that a committee of the board of directors will be constituted 'in whole or in part of members of the board of directors'[133] indicating that at least some of a company's directors should be members of any committee or sub-committee of that company.[134] Similarly, the Central Bank envisages the board of directors of regulated financial institutions delegating authority to 'act on behalf of the board in respect of certain matters'[135] to sub-committees on which non-executive directors in particular are to play a leading role.[136] Where an SSB is constituted as a sub-committee of an institution's board of directors and the SSB's members include Islamic scholars and appointed company directors, the Islamic scholars sitting on that SSB may be faced with a suggestion that they are *de facto* or shadow directors of the company. Company directors in Ireland, including *de facto* and shadow directors (neither of which are formally appointed as directors) are subject to statutory duties set out in the Companies Act 2014, including fiduciary duties such as a duty to act in good faith and in the best interests of the company,[137] a duty to avoid conflicts of interest[138] and

128 Irish Revenue Commissioners, 'Tax Treatment of Islamic Financial Transactions', *Tax and Duty Manual* (Part 08A-01-01) (n 59) [2.1].

129 Department of Finance, *Islamic Finance in Ireland; An Information Note* (n 66) 7.

130 ibid 7. The Tax and Duty Manual provides similar guidance, Irish Revenue Commissioners, 'Tax Treatment of Islamic Financial Transactions', *Tax and Duty Manual* (Part 08A-01-01) (n 59) [2.1].

131 The terms are used interchangeably in legislation and official guidance in Ireland.

132 Thomas Courtney, The Law of Companies (4th edn, Bloomsbury Professional 2016) 978.

133 Companies Act 2014, s 160(9).

134 Unless the relevant company's constitutional documents specifically modify or disapply the provisions of Companies Act 2014, s 260(9), in which case the provisions of the constitutional documents shall prevail.

135 Central Bank of Ireland, *Corporate Governance Requirements for Credit Institutions 2015* (Central Bank of Ireland 2015) [13.4].

136 ibid [19.4].

137 Companies Act 2014, s 228(1)(a).

138 Companies Act 2014, s 228(1)(f).

a duty to exercise due care, skill and diligence.[139] Company directors are also limited in the number of directorships that they can hold at any particular time.[140] In the context of regulated institutions providing financial services, persons occupying senior positions in such institutions are also subject to the Central Bank's fitness and probity standards.[141] These standards apply where a person within a regulated financial services provider has the ability 'to exercise a significant influence on the conduct of the affairs'[142] of that institution and will, among other things, require that the person display competence and capability appropriate to the function performed. To meet the requisite level of competence and capability, a person must have obtained 'qualifications, experience, competence and capacity appropriate to the relevant function'[143] and must not 'allow the conduct of concurrent responsibilities to impair his or her ability to discharge the duties of the relevant function or otherwise allow personal conflicts of interest'.[144] An Islamic scholar treated by Irish authorities as occupying the position of a director in a regulated company may, therefore, be subject to proficiency requirements that are difficult to benchmark as there is no national or international standardised education or competency framework for scholars advising on matters of Islamic finance.[145] A director's fiduciary duties to a company and the need to limit directorships and conflicts

139 Companies Act 2014, s 228(1)(g).

140 Companies Act 2014, ss 142(1), 986 and 1258, limiting the number of directorships to 25 Irish companies (subject to exceptions). See also Central Bank of Ireland, *Corporate Governance Requirements for Credit Institutions 2015* (n 135) [7.8].

141 Central Bank of Ireland, *Fitness and Probity Standards* (Code issued under Section 50 of the Central Bank Reform Act 2010) (Central Bank of Ireland 2014). They may also be subject to the Central Bank's minimum professional standards for persons providing certain financial services, in particular when dealing with consumers, as set out in The Minimum Competency Code 2017 and the Central Bank (Supervision and Enforcement) Act 2013 (Section 48 (1) Minimum Competency Regulations 2017).

142 'CF1' in the definition of 'controlled functions', prescribed by the Central Bank of Ireland. The list of controlled functions is available at <https://www.centralbank.ie/docs/default-source/Regulation/how-we-regulate/authorisation/authorisation/fitness-probity/regulated-financial-service-providers/list-of-11-controlled-functions.pdf?sfvrsn=0> accessed 25 February 2019.

143 Central Bank of Ireland, *Fitness and Probity Standards* (n 141) [3.2].

144 ibid.

145 Matthias Casper, 'Sharia Boards and Sharia Compliance in the Context of European Corporate Governance', lecture given at *The Influence of Islam on Banking and Finance Conference*, Ernst von Caemmerer-Foundation and Commerzbank, Frankfurt, Germany (12 October 2012).

of interest may also be problematic for Islamic scholars who frequently sit on multiple SSBs across a variety of institutions.[146]

In light of the practical difficulties associated with classifying Islamic scholars as company directors, UK authorities have emphasised that they will look to Islamic institutions to successfully show 'that the role and responsibilities of their SSB are advisory and it does not interfere in the management of the firm'.[147] In Ireland, the position of an SSB in individual institutions will equally need to be considered on a case by case basis. To the extent that an SSB's influence over the activities of an institution is explicable by the discharge of the Islamic scholars' professional function within their area of expertise, those Islamic scholars may be treated as exercising an advisory role rather than that of a *de facto* or shadow director.[148] Such Islamic scholars may then only be caught by the regime applicable to company directors if they go beyond their role as paid experts in Islamic law and Islamic finance.[149] Going forwards, a clear statement of policy to this effect from the relevant Irish authorities is needed. SSBs occupy a unique position in institutions offering Islamic finance products and services. Because of this, Irish authorities should adopt a consistent approach to dealing with SSBs and confirm their understanding of the position of SSBs in Islamic finance institutions falling within their remit. If SSBs will, in the absence of evidence to suggest otherwise, be treated by Irish supervisory and enforcement authorities as exercising an advisory role only, this position should be clarified, and Islamic finance institutions should be prepared to affirm this status if required to do so by the relevant authority. This would decrease uncertainty with respect to the legal position of Islamic scholars acting as advisors. At the same time, it would put the onus on Islamic finance institutions to maintain this advisory status and would put Islamic scholars on notice that to the extent they act beyond their responsibility as an advisor they may be subject to the heightened legal regime applicable to company directors.

146 Standard & Poor's, 'Islamic Finance Outlook 2018 Edition' (S&P Global Inc 2017) 32, <img.en25.com/Web/StandardPoorsRatings/Islamic%20Finance%202018%20Digital.pdf> accessed 25 February 2019.

147 Ainley and others (n 30) 13.

148 Companies Act 2014, ss 221 and 222.

149 This interpretation of the government's policy towards SSBs is also held by the Irish Funds Industry Association which has suggested that the Central Bank 'will require confirmation that the Shari'ah Board is acting in an advisory capacity only with no discretionary powers over the assets of the fund. If acting in an advisory capacity only, the Central Bank will not seek to regulate or approve the Shariah Board', Irish Funds Industry Association, *Ireland: Opportunities for Middle Eastern Fund Managers* (IFIA 2010).

This conclusion, admittedly, does leave members of an SSB in an Irish incorporated or regulated institution subject to no external oversight. Unlike an institution's other advisers, such as lawyers and accountants, who are subject to regulation by industry bodies, Islamic scholars in Ireland do not need to be registered, are subject to no tailored competency requirements, no rules of professional conduct and no industry-led supervision of their activities. Addressing this continuing issue that is relevant to the Islamic finance industry more broadly will require coordination between international Islamic finance standard setting bodies. The Accounting and Auditing Organization for Islamic Financial Institutions, one such standard setting body, has suggested that national SSBs should be established in countries in which Islamic finance is available in order to increase standardisation across the industry.[150] While this approach may reduce the scope for SSBs within different institutions to issue inconsistent rulings, it does not address concerns raised by the existence of a national religious body with the power to make binding determinations on matters of religious compliance and potentially the power to influence government policy. Instead, standard setting bodies could work to establish an accreditation model for Islamic scholars sitting on SSBs that provides a minimum competency benchmark. Standardisation of accreditation for Islamic scholars would lessen the need for domestic regulatory authorities, such as the Central Bank, to decide who can and cannot be an Islamic scholar.[151] At the same time, it could help to provide the Islamic finance market with a level of confidence that Islamic scholars are subject to some level of external oversight and are held to a consistent standard.[152]

150 Accounting and Auditing Organization for Islamic Financial Institutions, Exposure Draft, AAOIFI Governance Standard No. 8 'Central Shari'ah Board' (AAOIFI 2017). See discussion of this suggestion in S&P Global Ratings, 'AAOIFI Proposes Recommendations For Central Sharia Boards A Step In The Right Direction' in Standard & Poor's, 'Islamic Finance Outlook 2018 Edition' (S&P Global Inc 2017) <img.en25.com/Web/StandardPoorsRatings/Islamic%20Finance%202018%20Digital.pdf> accessed 25 February 2019.

151 Mushtak Parker, remarks made at the 'The Future of Islamic Finance in Britain' Panel, *Islamic Finance: The Way Forward Conference*, The London School of Economics and Political Science (27 February 2016).

152 The Islamic Financial Services Board has suggested that individual supervisory authorities may consider the establishment of a professional organisation or an industry association for Islamic scholars serving within their respective jurisdictions. Islamic Financial Services Board, *Guiding Principles on Corporate Governance for Institutions offering only Islamic Financial Services (Excluding Islamic Insurance (Takaful) Institutions and Islamic Mutual Funds)* (IFSB 2015) 12. However, it is not within the remit of Irish authorities to determine whether Islamic scholars display an acceptable level of expertise on religious matters. This should be something spearheaded by an industry body.

4 Conclusion

Islamic finance is one of the only aspects of Islam within Irish life that the Irish government has actively sought to address through guidelines and legislative amendments. Positive steps have, therefore, been taken to try to clarify the legal treatment of certain Islamic finance products under Irish law. Legislative amendments have also been introduced to address obstacles that may have prevented Islamic finance products from operating on a level playing field with economically comparable conventional alternatives. These steps reflect a willing attitude to encourage Islamic finance activity by the Irish government and are in line with similar accommodations introduced in other non-Muslim majority countries.

In practice, the domestic Islamic finance industry in Ireland, particularly at a retail level, has been slow to develop. Instead, the growth of Ireland's Islamic finance activity has been with respect to Irish-domiciled Islamic investment funds and the approval and listing of international *sukuk* by the Central Bank and Euronext Dublin. While the slow growth of Ireland's domestic Islamic finance market may be due in part to the level of demand, there also remain certain tax inequalities and uncertainties regarding the regulatory position of Islamic finance activity and SSBs that could hinder future growth of an Irish Islamic finance industry.

The Irish government may, therefore, need to actively consider its approach to future accommodation of Islamic finance activity in Irish law. Should demand for domestic *sukuk* issuances or Islamic retail activity continue to grow, the generally pragmatic and accommodative attitude of the Irish authorities to date indicates that further accommodations may be introduced, building on those already laid down by the Finance Act 2010. At the same time, until comprehensive accommodation is introduced, certain Islamic finance products and services could be seen as unviable within the Irish economy, potentially hindering development of the very demand needed to encourage government action.

Bibliography

Global Islamic Finance Report 2011, Humayon Dar and Mufti Talha Ahmad Azami (eds) (BMB Islamic UK Limited 2011).

Interpretation of the Meanings of The Noble Qur'an in the English language, A Summarized Version of At-Tabari, Al-Qurtubi and Ibn Kathir with comments from Sahih

Al-Bukhari Summarized in One Volume, Muhammad Taqi-ud-Din Al-Hilali and Muhammad Muhsin Khan (trans) (Maktba Dar-us-Salam 1996).

Sahih Muslim, Book 10, Introduction, Abdul Hamid Siddiqui (trans) <http://www.documentacatholicaomnia.eu/03d/0834-0893,_Sahih_Muslim,_Hadith,_EN.pdf> accessed 25 February 2019.

Abdel Karim, R.A., 'The Independence of Religious and External Auditors: The Case of Islamic Banks' (1990) 3(3) Accounting, Auditing & Accountability Journal 34.

Accounting and Auditing Organization for Islamic Financial Institutions, 'Governance Standard for Islamic Financial Institutions No. 1, Shari'a Supervisory Board: Appointment, Composition and Report', in *Accounting, Auditing and Governance Standards for Islamic financial institutions* (AAOIFI 2010).

Accounting and Auditing Organization for Islamic Financial Institutions, Exposure Draft, AAOIFI Governance Standard No. 8 'Central Shari'ah Board' (AAOIFI 2017).

Ainley, M., Mashayekhi, A., Hicks, R., Rahman, A., Ravalia, A., *Islamic Finance in the UK: Regulation and Challenges* (Financial Services Authority 2007).

Al-Omar, F. and Abdel-Haq, M., *Islamic Banking Theory, Practice and Challenges* (Zed Books 1996).

Amin, M., 'The Taxation of Islamic Finance in Major Western Countries' (2007) 1st Quarter Arab Banking Review 129.

Bank Negara Malaysia, 'Malaysia: World's Islamic Finance Marketplace' (1 August 2013) <http://www.bnm.gov.my/index.php?ch=en_press&pg=en_press&ac=616&lang=en> accessed 25 February 2019.

Bank Negara Malaysia, Fit and Proper Criteria for Approved Person Exposure Draft, BNM/RH/EH 029-9 (30 August 2018).

Bank Negara Malaysia, *Shariah Governance Framework for Islamic Financial Institutions*, BNM/RH/GL_012_3 (2011).

Bank Negara Malaysia, *Shariah Governance Exposure Draft* BNM/RH/ED 028-7 (2017).

Bank of England, 'Topical article, Islamic banks and central banking' *Quarterly Bulletin 2017 Q3* <https://www.bankofengland.co.uk/-/media/boe/files/quarterly-bulletin/2017/islamic-banks-and-central-banking.pdf?la=en&hash=15D94BD65C2EFA6962989D10E21543B7B7013C1C> accessed 25 February 2019.

Bank of England, 'Shari'ah compliant liquidity facilities: establishing a fund based deposit facility' (6 April 2017) <https://www.bankofengland.co.uk/paper/2017/shariah-compliant-liquidity-facilities-consultation-paper> accessed 25 February 2019.

Bassens, D., Derudder, B. and Witlox, F., 'Setting Shari'a standards: On the role, power and spatialities of interlocking Shari'a boards in Islamic financial services' (2011) 42 Geoforum 94.

Casper, M., 'Sharia Boards and Sharia Compliance in the Context of European Corporate Governance', lecture given at *The Influence of Islam on Banking and Finance*

Conference, Ernst von Caemmerer-Foundation and Commerzbank, Frankfurt, Germany (12 October 2012).

Cekici, I.-Z., 'Managing Islamic finance vis-à-vis *laïcité*: the case of France' in Valentino Cattelan (ed) *Islamic Finance in Europe, Towards a Plural Financial System* (Edward Elgar 2013) 192.

Central Bank of Ireland, *Fitness and Probity Standards* (Code issued under Section 50 of the Central Bank Reform Act 2010) (Central Bank of Ireland 2014).

Central Bank of Ireland, 'Address by Head of Markets Policy, Martin Moloney at the IFLC at the UCD School of Law' (14 May 2015) <https://www.centralbank.ie/news-media/press-releases/martin-moloney-at-iflc-at-the-ucd-school-of-law> accessed 25 February 2019.

Central Bank of Ireland, *Corporate Governance Requirements for Credit Institutions 2015* (Central Bank of Ireland 2015).

Cosgrave, B., 'United Kingdom' in *The Islamic Finance and Markets Law Review*, Andrew M Metcalf and Michael Rainey (eds) (Law Business Research Ltd 2016) 68.

Coulson, N.J., *Conflicts and Tensions in Islamic Jurisprudence* (The University of Chicago Press 1969).

Courtney, T., The Law of Companies (4th edn, Bloomsbury Professional 2016).

Cox, L., Dorudi, B., Gordon, L., Newsome, J., Stadelmann, G., Strange, A., O'Sullivan, V., 'United Kingdom regulatory reform: emergence of the twin peaks' (2012) 95(Apr) Compliance Officer Bulletin 1.

Dar, H.A., 'Islamic House Financing in the United Kingdom: Problems, Challenges and Prospects' (2002) 12 Review of Islamic Economics 47.

Davies, H., 'Islamic Finance in the United Kingdom: Current Initiatives And Challenges' Speech given at the *LSE-Harvard Public Lecture on Islamic Finance*, London School of Economics, London, UK (26 February 2009).

DeLorenzo, Y.T., 'Shari'ah Compliance Risk' (2006–2007) 7(2) Chicago Journal of International Law 397.

Department of Finance, 'Section 1 of Finance Act 2010, Report on Tax Expenditures', *PRN A10/0776* (July 2010) <http://taxpolicy.gov.ie/wp-content/uploads/2011/03/Section1ofFA2010ReportonTaxExpenditures.pdf> accessed 25 February 2019.

Department of Finance, *Islamic Finance in Ireland; An Information Note* (Department of Finance, Dublin, March 2010).

Department of Finance, *IFS2020: A Strategy for Ireland's International Financial Services sector 2015–2020* (The Stationery Office 2015).

Direction Générale des Finances, Bulletin Officiel Des Impôts, No 78 of 24 August 2010, 'Régime Applicable aux Sukuk d'investissement' (Direction Générale des Finances Publiques 4 FE/S2/10, 2010).

Eglington, K., remarks made at the 'The Future of Islamic Finance in Britain Panel', *Islamic Finance: The Way Forward Conference*, The London School of Economics and Political Science (27 February 2016).

El-Gamal, M., *Islamic Finance; Law, Economics and Practice* (Cambridge University Press 2006).

Ercanbrack, J., 'The Regulation of Islamic Finance in the United Kingdom' (2011) 13 Ecclesiastical Law Journal 69.

Ercanbrack, J., 'Regulating Islamic financial institutions in the UK' in Valentino Cattelan (ed) *Islamic Finance in Europe, Towards a Plural Financial System* (Edward Elgar 2013) 157.

Ercanbrack, J., *The Transformation of Islamic Law in Global Financial Markets* (Cambridge University Press 2015).

Financial Services Authority (now the Financial Conduct Authority) *Regulation of Home Reversion and Home Purchase Plans* (London 2006).

Foot, M., 'The Future of Islamic Banking in Europe', Speech given at the *Second International Islamic Finance Conference*, Dubai, United Arab Emirates (22 September 2003) <http://www.fsa.gov.uk/Pages/Library/Communication/Speeches/2003/sp150.shtml> accessed 25 February 2019.

Grais, W. and Pellegrini, M., 'Corporate Governance and Shariah Compliance in Institutions Offering Islamic Financial Services' *World Bank Policy Research Working Paper 4054* (World Bank 2006).

Gray, K. and Gray, S.F., *Land Law* (Oxford University Press 2007).

Hainsworth, A., 'Governance rules for Islamic financial institutions: the new frontier?' (2007) 9 Journal of International Banking and Financial Law 515.

Hasan, Z., 'Regulatory Framework of *Sharī'ah* Governance System in Malaysia, GCC Countries and the UK' (March 2010) 3–2 Kyoto Bulletin of Islamic Area Studies 82.

Hasan, Z., *Shari'ah Governance in Islamic Banks* (Edinburgh University Press 2012).

Hegazy, W.S., 'Contemporary Islamic Finance: From Socioeconomic Idealism to Pure Legalism' (2007) 7(2) Chicago Journal of International Law 581.

HM Land Registry, 'Practice guide 69: Islamic financing' (updated 16 March 2018) <https://www.gov.uk/government/publications/islamic-financing/practice-guide-69-islamic-financing> accessed 25 February 2019.

HM Treasury, *The Development of Islamic Finance in the UK: The Government's Perspective* (HM Treasury 2008).

Hussain, M., 'A general introduction to Islamic Finance' in Rahail Ali (ed) *Islamic Finance: A Practical Guide* (Globe Business Publishing Ltd 2008) 7.

Irish Funds Industry Association, *Ireland: Opportunities for Middle Eastern Fund Managers* (IFIA 2010).

Irish Revenue Commissioners, 'Islamic Finance, Tax Briefing Issue 78' (Irish Revenue Commissioners, October 2009) <http://www.revenue.ie/en/tax-professionals/historic-material/tax-briefing/2009/tax-briefing-78-2009.pdf> accessed 25 February 2019.

Irish Revenue Commissioners, *Guidance Notes on the Tax Treatment of Islamic Financial Transactions* (Irish Revenue Commissioners 2010).

Irish Revenue Commissioners, 'Tax Treatment of Islamic Financial Transactions', *Tax and Duty Manual* (Part 08A-01-01) (Irish Revenue Commissioners 2018).

Islamic Financial Services Board, *Guiding Principles on Sharī'ah Governance Systems for Institutions offering Islamic Financial Services* (IFSB 2009).

Islamic Financial Services Board, *Revised Guidance on Key Elements in the Supervisory Review Process of Institutions offering Islamic Financial Services (excluding Islamic Insurance (Takāful) Institutions and Islamic Collective Investment Schemes)* (IFSB 2014).

Islamic Financial Services Board, *Guiding Principles on Corporate Governance for Institutions offering only Islamic Financial Services (Excluding Islamic Insurance (Takaful) Institutions and Islamic Mutual Funds)* (IFSB 2015).

Islamic Financial Services Board, *Stability Report 2018*(IFSB 2018).

Jabbar, H.S.F.A., 'The Shari'a supervisory board of Islamic financial institutions: a case for governance' (2009) 30(8) Company Lawyer 243.

Klarmann, R.L., *Islamic Project Finance; a Legal Study with Particular Reference to the Laws of Switzerland and the United Arab Emirates* (Schulthess 2003).

Luxembourg for Finance, 'Islamic finance', January 2017 <www.alfi.lu/sites/alfi.lu/files/LFF_brochure_islamic_finance.pdf> accessed 25 February 2019.

Lenihan, B., *Dáil Eireann Debate*, Vol. 704 No. 4; 'Finance Act 2010: Report Stage (Resumed) and Final Stage' (10 March 2010).

Matheson, *News and Insights*, 'Matheson Advises on the First Irish Issuance of a Sukuk Bond Under Irish Tax Law' (5 April 2018), <https://www.matheson.com/news-and-insights/article/matheson-advises-on-the-first-irish-issuance-of-a-sukuk-bond-under-irish-ta> accessed 25 February 2019.

McAughtry, L., 'A safe haven in stormy seas: Shariah banks show strength amid global turmoil' 13(2) (2016) Islamic Finance News 1.

McCarthy, C., 'Regulation and Islamic Finance', Speech given at the *Muslim Council of Britain Islamic Finance and Trade Conference* (13 June 2006) <http://www.fsa.gov.uk/pages/Library/Communication/Speeches/2006/0613_cm.shtml> accessed 25 February 2019.

Menski, W., 'Accommodating religious needs in relation to marriage: Flying kites and navigating state law and other forms of law', paper presented for *Diritto & Religione, Prima giornata di studio 'Edoardo Dieni', Il riconoscimento civile dei matrimoni religiosi: conflitto di leggi o di culture?*, Università degli Studi dell'Insubria, Facoltà di Giurisprudenza, Como, Italy (28–29 November 2008).

Mokal, R., 'Liquidation Expenses and Floating Charges – the Separate Funds Fallacy' [2004] Lloyd's Maritime and Commercial Law Quarterly 387.

Oireachtas, 'Finance Bill 2010, Explanatory Memorandum' <https://data.oireachtas.ie/ie/oireachtas/bill/2010/9/eng/memo/b0910d-memo.pdf> accessed 25 February 2019.

Parker, M., remarks made at the 'The Future of Islamic Finance in Britain' Panel, *Islamic Finance: The Way Forward Conference*, The London School of Economics and Political Science (27 February 2016).

Philip, Lee, 'Ireland's First Islamic Financing Product: The First Of Many' (2018), <https://www.philiplee.ie/irelands-first-islamic-financing-product-the-first-of-many/> accessed 25 February 2019.

Ready, R.K., 'The Egyptian Municipal Saving Bank Project' (1967) 9(2) International Development Review 2.

Saleh, N.A., *Unlawful Gain and Legitimate Profit in Islamic Law* (2 nd edn, Graham & Trotman 1992).

Scully, G., 'Sector set for continued growth' Finance-Magazine (2007) <http://www.finance-magazine.com/supplements/abs2007/display_article.php?i=7477> accessed 25 February 2019.

Shafique, M., 'Food for thought: role of Shari'ah scholars' (April-June 2010) New Horizon 24.

Standard & Poor's, 'Islamic Finance Outlook 2018 Edition' (S&P Global Inc 2017), <img.en25.com/Web/StandardPoorsRatings/Islamic%20Finance%202018%20Digital.pdf> accessed 25 February 2019.

The Rte Hon Sir Edward George, Speech given at the Islamic Home Finance Seminar, London (27 March 2003) in Bank of England Quarterly Bulletin 0A42/12 (May 2003) 240.

Toan, R., 'Cross-Border *Ijarah*; A Case study in the US Taxation of Islamic Finance', in *Third Harvard Islamic Proceedings* (Harvard Islamic Finance Program 2000) 191.

Uz-Zaman, F., *Shariah-Compliant Financial Services: A Guide to Products, Markets and Trends* (VRL KnowledgeBank Ltd 2006).

Van Greuning, H. and Iqbal, Z., *Risk analysis for Islamic banks* (World Bank Publications 2008).

Vogel, F.E. and Hayes, S.L., *Islamic Law and Finance, Religion, Risk and Return.* (Kluwer Law International 1998).

Waters, D., 'Home reversions and Islamic mortgages get new consumer protections' (FSA/PN041/2006) (27 April 2006) <http://www.fsa.gov.uk/pages/Library/Communication/PR/2006/041.shtml> accessed 25 February 2019.

Weiss, B., 'Interpretation in Islamic Law: The Theory of Ijtihād' (1977–78) 26 American Journal of Comparative Law 199.

Wilson, R., 'Islamic Finance in Europe' RSCAS Policy Papers No 2007/02 (European University Institute for MUSMINE 2007).

PART 3

International Perspectives on Sharia Councils: Regulation and Governance

CHAPTER 9

The Legal Framework for Regulating Shariah Councils in the UK

A Potential Model for Ireland?

Amin Al-Astewani

Introduction

In December of 2017, the *Irish Times* revealed in a number of articles that a significant multitude of women are still travelling from Ireland to the UK for abortion services, with over 3,000 such voyages documented by the UK Department of Health in 2016.[1] This revelation bore a subtle yet striking resemblance with a similar revelation made by the *Irish Times* almost a decade before this, which few of its readers will now recall. In February of 2008, a reporter for the *Irish Times* revealed in a seminal article that several Irish Muslim women were applying to the Islamic Shariah Council in London for decrees of religious divorce, with the lack of any such councils in Ireland forcing them to access such services overseas.[2] The reporter in question correctly noted that the vast majority of cases processed by UK Shariah Councils relate to decrees of religious divorce, which are particularly desired by Muslim women on grounds of religious conscience despite having obtained a civil divorce.[3] The proliferation of such cases in Ireland have led voices within the Irish Muslim community to call for the establishment of Shariah councils in Ireland, to free Muslim women within the community from the need to access services provided by such councils abroad.[4]

1 See for example Ciarán D'Arcy, 'What is the situation with abortion in Ireland?' *The Irish Times* (Dublin, 15 December 2017) and Shane Hickey, 'More than 3,000 British abortions for women from Republic' *The Irish times* (Dublin, 18 December 2017).

2 Mary FitzGerald, 'Would sharia law work in Ireland?' *The Irish Times* (Dublin, 16 February 2008).

3 John Bowen, 'How could English Courts recognise Shariah?' (2011) 7(3) University of STLJ 411, 419–421.

4 Ibid. At the time of writing, there is still no evidence to suggest that a Shariah council has been formed in Ireland.

 | DOI:10.1163/9789004398252_010

Bearing in mind the significant increase in the size of the Irish Muslim population over the last three decades, the likelihood of Irish Shariah Councils emerging in the near future is particularly strong.[5] The emergence of such councils will without doubt raise a number of contentious socio-legal issues, the most prominent of which will arguably be how the Irish legal system should respond. This chapter addresses this particular issue. It will seek to examine the regulatory model currently used by the English legal system for governing UK Shariah councils in order to assess whether this could be adopted by the Irish legal system. The chapter will begin by comparing the general legal framework with regards to the accommodation of religious tribunals in both the Irish and English legal systems. It will then closely examine the particular framework adopted by the English legal system for the regulation of Shariah councils. The chapter will then conclude by evaluating the potential for this framework to be adopted within the Irish legal system, should Shariah councils emerge within its jurisdiction.

The chapter thus arranged would be a novel and ground-breaking contribution to the literature of religious tribunals within Western legal systems from more than one angle. Since its inception in the 1990s, the specific body of literature on UK Shariah councils has predominantly focused on the incompatibility of Islamic law with Western liberal ideals and the consequent impact this may have on members of the Muslim community who use Shariah councils.[6] Very little research has been done on the legal status of these councils from a traditional 'black-letter' perspective, and the way in which they are regulated by the English legal system. The examination in this chapter of the legal framework which regulates UK Shariah councils will thus attempt to fill this gap in the literature. Incorporating the Irish question within this examination further enhances its novelty. The literature on the resolution of marital disputes

5 For the dramatic changes in the demographics of the Irish Muslim community over the last three decades see Oliver Scharbrodt, 'Muslim Immigration to the Republic of Ireland: Trajectories and Dynamics since World War II' (2012) 47 EI 221, 230 and O Scharbrodt and T Sakaranaho, 'Islam and Muslims in the Republic of Ireland' 31(1) JMMA 469, 470.

6 See for example Michael King (ed) *God's Law Versus State Law* (Grey Seal Books 1995) 77; Jessie Brechin, 'A Study of the Use of Sharia Law in Religious Arbitration in the United Kingdom and the Concerns That This Raises for Human Rights' (2013) 15(3) ELJ 297; Dominick McGoldrick, 'Accommodating Muslims in Europe: From Adopting Sharia Law to Religiously Based Opt Outs from Generally Applicable Laws' (2009) 9(4) HRLR 605; Maria Reiss, 'The Materialization of Legal Pluralism in Britain: Why Shari'a Council Decisions Should be Non-Binding' (2009) 26(3) AJICL 743–756; Denis MacEoin, *Sharia Law or 'One Law for All'* (Civitas Institute for the Study of Civil Society 2009) 18–25 and Rowan Williams, 'Civil and Religious Law in England: A Religious Perspective' (2008) 10(3) ELJ 264–265.

within the Irish Muslim community is noticeably sparse, particularly with regards to the potential role of Shariah councils within the Irish legal system.[7]

1 English and Irish Legal Approaches towards the Accommodation of Religious Tribunals

Since the Toleration Act was passed in 1689, the UK has witnessed a steady increase in religious toleration which has continued into the twenty first century.[8] This predictably began as a negative freedom to practice religion in a way which had been previously forbidden for religious groups other than the Church of England. This included the right for such groups to establish their own places of worship and carry out religious activities which did not contravene the law in any of their aspects. In the twentieth century toleration of religion went further to confer positive rights to those who adhered to a religion or belief, as well as offer them exemptions from generally applicable rules.[9] The end of the twentieth century saw the passing of the Human Rights Act 1998, which marked the beginning of a movement to cement a positive right of religious freedom. This movement culminated with the passing of the Equality Act 2010 which treats religion and belief as a protected characteristic.[10]

Within this historical context of gradual toleration, several religious minorities in Britain established tribunals to serve the religious needs of their members, with prominent examples being the Catholic and Jewish communities.[11] These tribunals, in contrast to those belonging to the Church of England, all

7 In a seminal article which tentatively attempted to gauge how an Irish approach to Muslim divorce practice could be conceived, Enright noted that 'There is no centralised religious authority which makes policy or law for all Irish Muslims ... No significant research has been published on the role of these communities or their imams in assisting husbands and wives to resolve marital disputes and, further, only a few cases in the higher courts have been the subject of reported judgments. None of these cases, however, are concerned directly with domestic family law'. See Mairead Enright, 'Preferring the Stranger: Toward an Irish Approach to Muslim Divorce Practice' 49 IJ 65, 66.

8 Mark Hill, Russel Sandberg and Norman Doe, *Religion and Law in the United Kingdom* (Kluwer Law International 2011) 23–26; Lord Philips, 'Equality before the Law' (2008) 2(3) AQ 18–20.

9 Mark Hill, 'Religion and the State: Recognition, Regulation and Facilitation' in Russel Sandberg (ed), *Religion and Legal Pluralism* (Ashgate 2015) 25–34.

10 Equality Act 2010, s 2.

11 Professor Maleiha Malik has produced an excellent report under the auspices of the British Academy on the phenomenon of minority legal orders, focusing in particular on Christian, Jewish and Muslim legal orders in the UK, see Maleiha Malik, *Minority Legal Orders in the UK: Minorities, Pluralism and the Law* (The British Academy 2012).

function on a non-statutory basis and are not considered part of the civil court system. This includes Roman Catholic Church tribunals, whose decisions are not recognised at civil law.[12] They are nevertheless permitted to function on a voluntary jurisdiction and rely on the consent of both parties to submit to a particular decision when resolving disputes. In the words of Helen Grant, speaking as Parliamentary Under-Secretary of State:

> The use of religious councils or other extra-legal bodies to deal with civil disputes is well established and non-contentious. Communities have the option to use religious authorities to adjudicate disputes and to agree to abide by their decisions on a voluntary basis, but such decisions are subject to national law and are not legally enforceable.[13]

With regards to their particular status within the law, they are usually treated as unincorporated associations. These associations exist where two or more people become voluntarily bound together for common purposes and undertake mutual duties and obligations.[14]

A similar legal framework exists in Ireland for the accommodation of religious tribunals. Irish religious tribunals likewise function on a non-statutory basis and rely solely on a voluntary jurisdiction, with any decisions they make non-binding from a legal perspective.[15] Although the history of non-statutory religious tribunals in Ireland is less lively than that in the UK, there does exist a prominent tradition of marriage tribunals functioning under the auspices of the Roman Catholic Church.[16] These tribunals played a particularly significant

12 D'Auria states in her study of such tribunals, 'The decisions of Roman Catholic courts, called tribunals, are not recognised at civil law in England and, therefore, have no civil effect. A civil decree of nullity or a civil divorce decree absolutely satisfies the civil authorities of a person's freedom to remarry. However, the Catholic Church teaches that to marry is a right of natural law, and marriage is indissoluble; therefore, when a marriage fails, one's freedom to enter into a new marriage requires determination by an ecclesiastical tribunal' see Eithne D'Auria, 'The Use of Experts in the Roman Catholic Canon Law of Marriage' in Russel Sandberg (ed), *Religion and Legal Pluralism* (Ashgate 2015) 94.

13 See HC Deb April 2013 c291WH.

14 See Hill (n 9) 31–31 and Russel Sandberg, 'Islam and English law' (2010) 164 LJCLR 29–30.

15 *O'Keeffe v Cardinal Cullen* [1873] 7 I.L.T.R. 100, *The King v Conor Maguire* [1923] 57 I.L.T.R. 57 and *McGrath and O'Ruairc v The Trustees ofMaynooth College* [1979] I.L.R.M. 166 are prominent precedents in this regard.

16 For a detailed history see David Fitzpatrick, 'Divorce and Separation in Modern Irish History' (1987) 114(1) PP. 172, Norman Doe, *The Legal Framework of the Church of England: A Critical Study in Comparative Context* (Oxford University Press 1996) and John McAreavey, *The Canon Law of Marriage and the Family* (Four Courts Press 1997).

role in the 20th century by offering marriage annulment services during the period in which no civil divorce jurisdiction existed for Irish citizens.[17]

2 The English Legal Framework for Regulating Shariah Councils

When the first ever Shariah councils emerged in the UK in the 1980s, they were treated no differently by the English legal system from other long-established tribunals like the Jewish Beth Din tribunals and the Catholic marriage tribunals. The authority of Shariah councils to rule on religious matters such as religious divorce was thus derived entirely from the Muslim community, and did not derive from the state. Their decisions in principle had no legal status or authority. Clients who approached them for a religious divorce did so completely voluntarily and could not be summoned to do so. If a Muslim wife for example did not want to resolve her divorce according to Islamic law as per the wish of her husband, she was completely free to file a claim in the English courts where English divorce law would trump Islamic divorce law regardless of the husband's desires, as occurred in the unreported case of *Al-Saffar v Al-Saffar*.[18] In this respect the jurisdiction of Shariah tribunals relied completely on the members of the community themselves, who voluntarily decided to accept the religious jurisdiction of such institutions by virtue of the services they were able to provide.

The UK government has explicitly affirmed that British Muslims are free to govern their lives according to Islamic law, as long as any activity which they consequently engage in does not contravene the law of the land. This affirmation was made by the government in response to an e-petition submitted during the 2010–2015 Conservative–Liberal Democrat coalition government. The e-petition was titled 'Ban all sharia law in the UK' and stated:

---

17 See Maebh Harding, 'Religion and family law in Ireland: From a Catholic protection of marriage to a "catholic" approach to nullity' in J Mair and E Orucu (ed), *The Place of Religion in Family Law* (Intersentia 2011) 161. For parallels between the Irish and English legal systems in the areas of finance and contract, see Edana Richardson, 'Islamic Finance Disputes in Ireland: A comparative study of dispute resolution in Islamic finance contracts' (2017) 57 IJ 35.

18 *Al-Saffar v Al-Saffar* [2012] EWCA Civ. In this case the Muslim husband, Dr Al-Saffar, was refusing to pay his wife maintenance payments on the basis that they were 'illegitimate and illegal' according to Islamic law. Ward LJ declared such a belief as no defence to orders made by the English divorce courts, see <http://www.telegraph.co.uk/women/sex/divorce/9426373/Islamic-tradition-is-no-defence-against-divorce-ruling.html> accessed 06 November 2018.

> This is to stop all 85 sharia courts that are open and to stop anymore from opening. People residing in this country should obey by British law. No other law should ever be used in this country not now and not ever. I want to see all sharia law banned and any one found performing these acts should be prosecuted by British law.

If an e-petition gets 10,000 signatures, the government will respond to the petition, and if it gets 100,000 signatures, the petition will be considered for debate in parliament.[19] By the deadline date of April 2014 the e-petition had received 21,452 signatures, and so qualified for a government response. The government responded by stating:

> Sharia 'law' has no jurisdiction in England and Wales and the Government has no intention to change this position. Sharia principles are the code of personal religious law governing the conduct of Muslims. They can extend into all aspects of people's lives, but provided an activity prescribed by Sharia principles does not contravene the law of England and Wales, there is nothing that prevents people living by Sharia principles. Britain has a proud tradition of religious tolerance, within the law. We expect individuals and groups to exercise their religious beliefs in a courteous and considerate manner and to respect the rights of others. Freedom of expression is the hallmark of a healthy society; however, mutual concern and respect for our fellow citizens is essential if we want our neighbourhoods to be places where everyone can play their part and feel that they belong. There are a number of Sharia councils in England and Wales which help Muslim communities resolve civil and family disputes, by making recommendations, which they hope the parties will abide by. They are not part of the court system in this country and have no means of enforcing their decisions. If any of the decisions or recommendations they make are contrary to national law (including the Equality Act 2010) then national law prevails. This is no different to any other council or tribunal – whether or not based on Sharia principles. There can never be reliance on the fact that an act that is permitted under Sharia principles is a justification for committing what is, under the law of this country, a criminal act or indeed a breach of civil law such as the Equality Act 2010. Muslim women, for example, can find legal recourse in the legislation that has already been enacted, for example forced marriage issues, regardless of what is stated within Sharia principles. This Government will

19 See <https://petition.parliament.uk/> accessed 06 November 2018.

> challenge behaviours and views which run counter to our shared values. Promoting fairness in society is one of the Coalition Government's core commitments. This is everyone's responsibility; it is only together we are able to develop a stronger and more cohesive society. There can be no question of there being a parallel system of law in this country.[20]

The government's affirmation that Muslims can live 'by Sharia principles' is based on the traditional legal position in respect of religious individuals that they have the right to do whatever they like as long as this do not contravene an explicit provision of the law.[21] The government confirmation at the same time that Sharia councils in England and Wales are not part of the English judicial system and that their decisions have no legal force affirms the effectiveness of the legal framework that was applied to Shariah councils since their emergence.

It is primarily due to the existence of this legal framework that the government rejected Baroness Cox's attempt to limit the jurisdiction of Shariah councils with a private member's bill, which she initially introduced in the House of Lords in 2011.[22] Part 5 of the bill sought to create a new legal offence of 'falsely claiming legal jurisdiction' by amending the Courts and Legal Services Act 1990, with the aim of preventing Shariah councils from claiming legal jurisdiction in disputes outside the remit of Arbitration such as family and criminal disputes.[23] The government responded by stating that the criminal offence suggested in Part 5 was unnecessary because 'Sharia councils and other religious councils have no jurisdiction in this country, therefore any decision they make can never be legally binding' and 'relevant and specific protections are already in place in common law and in existing legislation'.[24]

For their initial period of existence, Shariah councils in the UK were thus regulated by the general legal framework developed for religious tribunals

20 <https://petition.parliament.uk/archived/petitions/48352> accessed 06 November 2018. In 2013 a debate also took place in Westminster Hall on the issue of Sharia councils, in which Helen Grant, Parliamentary Under-Secretary of State for Justice at the time, gave a similar but more elaborate response on the government's position in relation to Sharia tribunals, see HC Deb April 2013 c289-293WH.

21 *Donaldson MR, AG v Guardian Newspapers Ltd* (No 2) (1990] 1 AC 109; Lord Philips 'Equality before the Law' (2008) 2(3) AQ 18.

22 See Amin Al-Astewani, 'Reflections on the rise and fall of the Arbitration and Mediation Services (Equality) Bill' (2017) 4 PL 544, 549–550.

23 Arbitration and Mediation Services (Equality) Bill Pt 5 cl. 6(2); Caroline Cox, *A Parallel World: Confronting the abuse of many Muslim women in Britain today* (London: Bow Group, 2015) 39.

24 Hansard, HL, col.1712 (October 2012); Hansard, HL, col.903 (October 2015).

which had existed prior to their formation in the 1980s. Over time however, the English legal system developed a more nuanced model for regulating Shariah councils which was specifically tailored towards their nature, function and practices. It did so by providing three exceptional avenues for the decisions of Shariah councils to accrue legal status, and thus become enforceable by the civil courts. Thus although the default status of Shariah council decisions is that they are not legally binding, they may accrue legal status if they fulfil conditions and qualifications stipulated within these three legal avenues, which will now be examined. The first avenue was established via Contract law, the second via the Arbitration Act 1996 and the third via the Divorce (Religious Marriages) Act 2002.

2.1 *The First Exceptional Avenue for Shariah Council Decisions to Accrue Legal Status: Contract Law*

If a decision of a Shariah council relates to financial matters, then such a decision will be given legal effect for the purposes of contract law. This rule stems from the 1965 case of *Shahnaz v Rizwan*.[25] The main qualification is that both parties must have consented to have their original dispute resolved by the Shariah council. This qualification was established by Justice Rix in *Al-Midani* v *Al-Midani*, the first ever reported case to consider the legal status of a decision issued by a UK Shariah council.[26] The Islamic Shariah Council in London had in this case issued a decision on the division and distribution of assets in an inheritance dispute between Muslim litigants. Justice Rix decided that the decision had no legal effect because one of the parties had not consented to having the dispute adjudicated by the Shariah Council. The case includes an important account of the nature and function of the Islamic Shariah Council by an English judge:

The Shari'a Council was, as explained in its own brochure, established in 1982 by scholars representing a number of mosques in the UK...Some 1,500 cases, most of them divorce cases, had been referred to it by 1995...It acknowledges that it 'is not yet legally recognized by the authorities in the UK', but represents itself as gaining recognition and confidence among the Islamic community and at large. It would seem that Islamic divorce and matrimonial

25 *Shahnaz v Rizwan* [1965] 1 Q.B. 390. In this case the judge recognised the financial gift stipulated by Islamic law in marital contracts (known as the *mahr*) as valid for the purposes of contract law, finding that the Muslim wife in question was owed the *mahr* since the couple had divorced, thus establishing the principle that a provision of Islamic law or (by analogy) decision made according to Islamic law will be deemed valid for the purposes of contract law.

26 *Al-Midani and another v Al-Midani and others* [1999] CLC 904.

questions in general are the focus of its advisory and judicial work...It can grant Islamic divorce, but it emphasizes that such divorce nullifies only the Islamic marriage and has nothing to do with the civil contract...The bench of the Shari'a Council would seem to provide a welcome facility to the Muslim community of the UK to render decisions on Islamic law, particularly in the matrimonial and family sphere. Its authority appears to rest largely on consent, in as much as it responds to the needs of the community it serves, but it may be that under Shari'a law it has autonomous power, as a religious court, to promulgate decisions in favour of a claimant even against the will of a respondent... I am unable, however, to see how its judgment can be binding on the heirs or any of them without their consent. Certainly Myrna and Omar never gave their consent to the Shari'a Council's jurisdiction, unless the arbitration agreement bound them to do so.[27]

Justice Rix affirms in this statement the voluntary and religious nature of the Islamic Sharia Council, and recognises that the council provides a beneficial service to the Muslim community in rendering decisions on Islamic law. Two more significant cases have appeared since *Al-Midani* which clarify the position of the law in such cases, namely *Choudhury* v *Choudhury* and *Uddin* v *Choudhury*.[28]

2.2 *The Ramifications of Chowdhury v Chowdhury and Uddin v Chowdhury*

In *Choudhury* v *Choudhury* a decision was also issued by an Islamic scholar on the division of assets in an inheritance dispute between Muslim litigants. The agreement which was drafted as a result of this decision was deemed to have legal effect by the judge.[29] The crucial factor in this case which distinguishes it from *Al-Midani* was that the parties to the dispute had consented to having their dispute resolved by an Islamic judge.[30] The more recent case of *Uddin* v *Choudhury* involved a financial dispute between two spouses who had their

27 *Ibid*, 911, 912, 913.

28 *Choudhury v Choudhury* [2006] EWHC 1837 (Ch), *Uddin v Choudhury* [2009] EWCA Civ 1205.

29 *Choudhury v Choudhury* [2006] EWHC 1837 (Ch) 203.

30 The decision in this dispute was issued by the scholar of Bury Park Mosque in a meeting held at the family home of the litigants, and not by a formal Shariah tribunal. Nevertheless the scholar was for all intents and purposes acting as an Islamic judge in considering the case before him, just like an Islamic scholar employed by a formal Shariah council. His decision can thus be treated by analogy like a decision issued by a formal Shariah tribunal for the purposes of our discussion. The unreported case of *Al-Saffar v Al-Saffar* [2012] EWCA Civ also affirms the requirement of consent from both Muslim spouses in a divorce if they wish to resolve their divorce according to Islamic law.

marriage dissolved by the Islamic Shariah Council in Leyton at the request of the wife in 2004. The facts of the case are noteworthy as they depict the typical kind of case that Sharia tribunals receive throughout the year. The marriage had been arranged by the parents of both spouses, who had immigrated to England from Bangladesh. As per the usual practice in South Asian culture, the families exchanged gifts as part of the marriage ceremony, including substantial amounts of gold jewellery. These were completely unrelated to the dower (known in Islamic law as the *mahr*), which was stipulated in the marriage contract as £15,000. This remained unpaid upon completion of the Islamic marriage ceremony.

The couple conducted the Islamic marriage ceremony in 2003 with the intention of conducting a civil ceremony later on, but this never occurred. The marriage did not work out, and so the bride approached the Sharia council a year later to dissolve the marriage. The husband agreed to the procedure as long as the wife agreed to return the jewellery he had given her as well as the portion of *mahr* he had paid her. The wife denied she had been paid any *mahr*. The council subsequently dissolved the marriage in December 2004, with its records showing that the decision contained no stipulations concerning Jewellery or *mahr*.[31] The husband's father, Mr Uddin, decided to pursue the case in the civil courts, and claimed that the bride was obliged to return the gifts and jewellery worth over £25,000. The wife filed a counter-claim in court that she was owed the £15,000 of dower stipulated in the marriage contract.

The court[32] decided to appoint Sheikh Siddiqui, founder and chief judge of the recently formed Muslim Arbitration Tribunal, as the expert witness on Islamic law. Sheikh Siddiqui advised the judge that the gifts were not owed back to the groom's family according to Islamic law as they were not part of the dower. Moreover he advised that the bride was due the *mahr* in full because the marriage had not been consummated and this was not due to the refusal of the wife. The judge acted on Siddique's testimony, finding that the gifts need not be returned, and that the *mahr* was owed to the wife. On appeal, Lord Justice Mummery affirmed the ruling decided at first instance, stating that the marriage was 'validly dissolved by decree of the Islamic Shariah Council' and thus activated the obligation of the husband to pay his wife the financial gifts which had been stipulated in the Islamic marriage contract:

> On this point it seems to me that, on the basis of the evidence given by Mr Saddiqui and the findings of fact by the judge, it was a valid marriage

31 Bowen (n 3) 423.

32 In this instance the Central London County Court.

> under Sharia law and that it was then validly dissolved by decree of the Islamic Sharia council. This was not a matter of English law. There was no ceremony which was recognised by English law, but it was a valid ceremony so far as the parties were agreed and it was valid for the purposes of giving legal effect to the agreement which had been made about gifts and dower… Looking to the evidence of Mr Saddiqui as summarised by the judge in his judgment, it is not correct to say, as Mr Uddin does, that those gifts should be deducted from the dower or that there is no legal right to enforce the dower in the circumstances in which this marriage was dissolved. As a matter of contract, arising out of the agreement which the parties had made, I think that the judge was entitled in law to say that this was an enforceable agreement, and therefore he was right to grant judgment on the counterclaim.[33]

Lord Justice Mummery's reasoning closely follows that of Justice Winn in *Shahnaz,* who decided to treat the Islamic dower as a proprietary right for the purposes of contract law, stating that 'under Mohammedan law such right to dower, once it had accrued as payable, was enforceable by civil action and was regarded as an assignable proprietary right'.[34] *Uddin v Choudhury* is a landmark case in relation to the decisions of UK Shariah councils. It confirms that English judges are willing to recognize an Islamic decree of divorce issued by a Shariah tribunal as having legal effect for the purposes of contract law. This is an extremely significant judgement as it opens the doors for Muslim women who use Sharia tribunals to have their financial disputes resolved by the English courts despite not legally registering their marriages. Indeed in *Uddin* the court was ruling between two litigants who were not married in the eyes of English law, but were simply partners to a financial contract.

2.3 *The Second Exceptional Avenue for Shariah Council Decisions to Accrue Legal Status: The Arbitration Act 1996*

The second avenue for the decisions of Shariah tribunals to accrue legal status is provided by the Arbitration Act 1996. As Sandberg notes, the Arbitration Act is a facilitative piece of legislation which focuses on people rather than on dispute-resolution bodies.[35] It allows citizens to refer their disputes to private

33 *Uddin v Choudhury* [2009] EWCA Civ, 11, 13.

34 *Shahnaz v Rizwan* [1965] 1 Q.B. 390.

35 Sandberg (n 14) 33.

arbitrators rather than refer them to the civil courts.[36] More crucially it allows the parties themselves to decide what law the arbitrators will use to resolve the dispute, including religious law such as Jewish or Islamic law.[37] Once the parties choose to be bound by an arbitration agreement, then the decision of the arbitrator will become legally binding and will be enforced by the civil courts. Recent cases such as *Kohn v Wagschal & Ors*[38] affirm that the civil courts will enforce arbitration decisions made according to religious law. Limitations do however exist on arbitration. Criminal proceedings are completely beyond its jurisdiction.[39] English law retains a complete monopoly over criminal law.[40] Thus if a Shariah tribunal sought to enforce a punishment they would be liable under English criminal law for assault or false imprisonment. Arbitration decisions which do not comply with minimal standards of fairness or which fall foul of public policy can also be quashed by the courts via Section 68 of the Arbitration Act or via the Human Rights Act 1998.[41]

---

36 Arbitration Act 1996, s 1. This includes the ability to specify the religion of the arbitrator in arbitration clause which is part of a commercial contract, see *Jivraj v Hashwani* [2011] UKSC 40.

37 Arbitration Act 1996, s 46; Robert Blacklett, 'The Status of Religious "Courts" in English law' (2009) DIAN 11–14. This crucial element of the Act was emphasised by the government in its rejection of Cox's bill discussed earlier, which also sought to limit Shariah Councils' use of arbitration under the 1996 Act. The government stated in this regard: 'Couples, communities and other groups have the option to use arbitration and to apply religious considerations. For example, the Jewish Beth Din has long been recognised as able to conduct arbitrations applying Jewish law considerations. The Muslim Arbitration Tribunal, established in 2007, provides an alternative route to resolve civil law disputes in accordance with Sharia principles. In both cases this is because the Arbitration Act 1996 allows parties to an arbitration to agree any system of law or rules, other than national laws, to be applied by the arbitral tribunal' see Hansard, HL, col.1711 (October 2012).

38 *Kohn v Wagschal & Ors* [2007] EWCA Civ 1022.

39 Samantha Knights, *Freedom of Religion, Minorities and the Law* (Oxford University Press, Oxford 2007) 76.

40 In a Westminster Hall debate concerning the phenomenon of Shariah councils, the Parliamentary Under-Secretary of State for Justice stated in this regard 'Under criminal law, any person who commits a criminal offence is liable to be prosecuted for that offence, provided it is in the public interest to do so. In England and Wales, criminal proceedings are always heard in a criminal court. We do not recognise any criminal law decision made by an alternative court in this country. The Government have no intention of changing that position' see HC Deb April 2013 c292WH.

41 Sandberg (n 14) 33–38. The Parliamentary Under-Secretary of State for Justice has confirmed this principle, stating, 'There are a number of sharia councils in England and Wales that help Muslim communities resolve civil and family disputes by making recommendations by which they hope that the parties will abide, but I make it absolutely clear that they are not part of the court system in this country and have no means of enforcing their decisions. If any of their decisions or recommendations are illegal or contrary to

The English courts also retain ultimate jurisdiction over issues arising out of divorce, regardless of any private arbitration agreement the couple might have agreed upon.[42] Since the establishment of judicial divorce in the 19th century, English law has asserted an exclusive interest in the welfare of the child whose parents become divorced, as well as the financial consequences of the divorce.[43] This does not preclude private arbitration tribunals like religious tribunals judging on matters relating to divorce such as financial settlement and the welfare of the children involved. It simply means such judgements will have no legal effect unless they are approved by the courts via an order known as a consent order.[44] This fact was confirmed by Lord Bach when asked in the House of Lords how the English courts ensure that an agreement reached by parties in a Shariah tribunal complies with English legal tenets:

> There is no visible evidence available to a court that an application for a consent order has been made following negotiations and agreement made by the parties at a Sharia council. Therefore these applications are treated in the same way as any other application within family proceedings. There are many forms of alternative dispute resolution available to assist parties to reach an agreement in family cases, but whichever method is used by the parties, the principles applied by the court are the same. The court cannot simply 'rubber-stamp' an agreement in a family case, whatever the process by which the agreement has been reached, and courts can and do ask for further information where there is any doubt about the propriety of a proposed order. Any order made by consent and submitted to the court, whether the product of an agreement by a Sharia council or not, might be made by coercion and it is the function of the court to question any order which appears unfair. An order which on its face involved an undue advantage to one party or set out arrangements for contact which excluded care or contact with one parent would be the sort of order which alerts a court to potential coercion and the need to ask for further information and, if appropriate, to refuse to make the order requested. The statutory basis for any enforcement in the courts of any agreement facilitated by a Sharia council is the Arbitration Act 1996,

public policy – including equality policies such as the Equality Act 2010 – or national law, national law will prevail all the time, every time. That is no different from any other council or tribunal, whether or not based on sharia law' see HC Deb April 2013 c291WH.

42 *Hyman v Hyman* [1929] AC 601.

43 Gillian Douglas, 'Who Regulates Marriage? The Case of Religious Marriage and Divorce' in Russel Sandberg (ed), *Religion and Legal Pluralism* (Ashgate 2015) 57.

44 *Xydhias v Xydhias* [1999] 1 FLR 683.

> established by the previous Government. There are no plans to change this.[45]

This principle was also recently affirmed by Baker J in the recent High Court case of *AI v MT*, which involved a dispute between a Jewish couple over the custody of their children.[46]

2.4 *The Significance of AI v MT*

Although the decision did not by any stretch of the imagination 'open the way to Sharia divorces' as many media reports claimed,[47] it was nevertheless a very significant case for the jurisdiction of religious tribunals under arbitration law. The Jewish couple involved in the case asked Baker J during proceedings if they could have their dispute arbitrated by a Jewish Beth Din and agree to be bound by any arbitration award made by the Beth Din. Baker J declined to make such an order because it 'flouted the principle that the court's jurisdiction to determine issues arising out of the marriage, or concerning the welfare and upbringing of the children, cannot be ousted by agreement'.[48] He did however endorse the couple's decision to refer the dispute to a Beth Din on the basis that the outcome would not be binding unless it received a consent order from the court. The couple's dispute was then successfully resolved by the Beth Din

45 HL Deb Nov 2008 WA81. Bridget Prentice has also stated in this regard: 'In Muslim family disputes, the parties may choose to have their financial affairs and decisions about their children decided by a Sharia Council. If the parties wish to have that decision recognised by English authorities, they are at liberty to draft a consent order embodying the terms of the agreement and submit it to an English or Welsh court. This allows it to be scrutinised by an English or Welsh judge to ensure that it complies with English legal tenets. If the decision is made into a court order the English and Welsh courts can enforce it' HC Deb April 2008 c509W.

46 *AI v MT* [2013] EWHC 100 (Fam).

47 See for example <http://www.thetimes.co.uk/tto/law/article3674837.ece> accessed 06 November 2018; <http://www.telegraph.co.uk/news/uknews/9841370/Sharia-divorces-could-be-allowed-after-legal-ruling.html> accessed 06 November 2018; <http://www.standard.co.uk/news/uk/sharia-divorces-could-become-legal-8476904.html> accessed 06 November 2018. The case in fact had nothing to do with marital status either in civil or religious law. As has been established an English court can only issue a civil divorce, which is why Muslim and Jewish women need religious tribunals to get a religious divorce.

48 *AI v MT* [2013] EWHC 100, para [12]. Baker J also stated at para [27] 'insofar as the court has jurisdiction to determine issues arising out of the marriage, or concerning the welfare and upbringing of the children, that jurisdiction cannot be ousted by agreement. The parties cannot lawfully make an agreement either not to invoke the jurisdiction or to control the powers of the court where jurisdiction in invoked: see Lord Hailsham in *Hyman v Hyman* [1929] AC 601'.

and subsequently affirmed by Baker J via a consent order. Baker J highlighted the success of the case in satisfying both the religious beliefs of the couple as well as the principles of English law, stating 'The parties' devout beliefs had been respected. The outcome was in keeping with English law whilst achieved by a process rooted in the Jewish culture to which the families belong'.[49]

The case is thus significant in establishing the first ever precedent of an English court referring a divorce dispute for arbitration to a religious tribunal, with the option of granting the decision legal status via a consent order.[50] The case affirms at the same time that the civil courts retain ultimate jurisdiction over issues arousing out of divorce. A Sharia council or Beth Din tribunal may rule upon a divorce dispute using arbitration, but its ruling will not contain any legal force. The decision can only be made legally binding by a civil court via a consent order, which itself will only happen if the court is satisfied that the ruling is in line with English law. Baker J was particularly emphatic on this point, stating:

> In this case, having been reassured as to the principles which would be applied by the rabbinical authorities, which so far as the children were concerned were akin to the paramountcy principle on which English children's law is based, the court was content to accept and respect the parents' deeply-held wishes, subject to the proviso that the outcome could not be binding without the court's endorsement. It does not, however, necessarily follow that a court would be content in other cases to endorse a proposal that a dispute concerning children should be referred for determination by another religious authority. Each case will turn on its own facts.[51]

The case of *AI v MT* also highlights the increasing importance of arbitration in English family law, which has important repercussions for the legal status of religious tribunals such as Sharia councils. It is a well-established principle in English family law that it is in the best interests of couples to privately settle

49 *Ibid*, para [37]. Baker J also stated at para [35] '...this case illustrates the principle propounded by Archbishop Rowan Williams in his 2008 lecture "Civil and Religious Law in England: a Religious Perspective" (cited by Mr. Setright QC and Mr. Devereux) that "citizenship in a secular society should not necessitate the abandoning of religious discipline, any more than religious discipline should deprive one of access to liberties secured by the law of the land, to the common benefits of secular citizenship"'.

50 See *Ibid*, para [31] in which Baker J affirms that there is no precedent before the date of his order for referring a matrimonial dispute to arbitration.

51 *Ibid*, para [33].

their matrimonial disputes rather than become entangled in adversarial litigation.[52] This principle has become more firmly enshrined by the English legal system in recent years, with the Family Procedure Rules 2010 obligating courts to encourage parties to use an alternative dispute resolution procedure if the court considers this appropriate.[53] Baker J affirmed this principle in *AI v MT* by stating that the resolution of the dispute by non-binding arbitration via a religious tribunal was 'largely in accordance with the overriding objective of the Family Procedure Rules 2010' and that 'it is always in the interests of parties to try to resolve disputes by agreement wherever possible, including disputes concerning the future of children and ancillary relief of the breakdown of a marriage'.[54] He also highlighted the attractions of arbitration for divorced couples which include 'speed, confidentiality and cost…the parties are able to select the arbitrator as opposed to litigation where the parties are obliged to accept the judge allocated to hear the case'.[55] This increased prominence of private arbitration in English family law will give Shariah councils more opportunities to settle disputes between Muslim couples, as well as potentially receiving consent orders from the civil courts granting legal status to their decisions following the precedent of *AI v MT*.[56] At the same time the English courts will benefit from such a development, as their own workload will be reduced.

2.5 *The Third Exceptional Avenue for Shariah Tribunal Decisions to Accrue Legal Status: The Divorce (Religious Marriages) Act 2002*

The plight of Jewish women bound in limping marriages was specifically addressed by the Divorce (Religious Marriages) Act 2002, which inserted a new

52 Gillian Douglas, 'Who Regulates Marriage? The Case of Religious Marriage and Divorce' in Russel Sandberg (ed), *Religion and Legal Pluralism* (Ashgate 2015) 61.

53 The Family Procedure Rules 2010, s 3(2). The Children and Families Act 2014 now also obligates couples to attend a family mediation session before applying to court. Muslim counsellors working at Sharia tribunals could therefore qualify as mediators and thus be eligible to mediate between Muslim couples.

54 *AI v MT* [2013] EWHC 100, para [37], [30].

55 *Ibid*, para [32].

56 Thomson states in this regard: 'In principle, this judgement has set a precedent that can be applied in the future not only to Jewish couples but also to Muslim couples who have celebrated both a civil marriage and a *nikah* marriage; who wish to end both contracts by way of divorce; and who need the assistance of both a British Shari'a Council and an English civil court in deciding matters concerning the education, residence and contact with their children and associated ancillary financial relief' see Hajj Ahmad Thomson, *An Insight into the work of Islamic Shari'a Councils* (Wynne Chambers 2013) available at <http://www.wynnechambers.co.uk/pdf/An_Insight_into_Sharia_Councils_29OCT13.pdf> accessed 06 November 2018.

Section (10A) into the Matrimonial Causes Act 1973 for this purpose.[57] Section 10A allows a court to order that a decree nisi cannot become absolute until both parties dissolve the marriage according to 'the usages of the Jews' or 'any other prescribed religious usages'.[58] The London Beth Din has stated that Section 10A has reduced the number of Jewish women in limping marriages, by pressurising Jewish husbands to approach the Beth Din and agree to give their wives a divorce before the decree absolute is issued.[59] Other religious groups may also benefit from Section 10A under the term 'other prescribed religious usages', however they must first apply to the government for such an extension to be officially granted.

The government has explicitly stated that the section will be extended to the Muslim community if their representatives apply for such an extension to be made. No such application has of yet been made by the Muslim community.[60] The most likely reason that Shariah tribunals have not sought to have the section extended thus far is that Islamic law allows a Muslim women to apply for judicial divorce regardless of the wishes of the husband. In this sense there is no need for Muslim husbands to be pressurised by a civil court to grant their wives a religious divorce, as is the case with Jewish husbands. Shariah tribunals could however still benefit from Section 10(A). Many Muslim women petitioning for a civil divorce may also require an Islamic judicial divorce without realising that Shariah tribunals exist to grant such a divorce. They may on the other hand only realise or consider the need for an Islamic judicial divorce after civil proceedings. Section 10(A) would ensure that the civil courts send the Muslim couple to a Shariah tribunal before a decree absolute is declared. For this reason, it is highly likely that Shariah tribunals will seek to have the section extended to the Muslim community in the foreseeable future. This would open up another avenue for the decisions of Shariah tribunals to accrue legal status. It would also ensure that the process of Islamic divorce becomes more formalised and efficient.

The Divorce (Religious Marriages) Act 2002 is based on two important presumptions which are particularly pertinent for UK Shariah councils. The first of these presumptions is that an individual can be married according to both a civil and a religious marital bond. The second is that an English judge can only release such an individual from the civil marital bond, and has no power

57 Ralph Grillo, *Muslim Families, Politics and the Law: A Legal Industry in Multicultural Britain* (Ashgate 2015) 104.

58 See Matrimonial Causes Act 1973 s 10A.

59 Gillian Douglas et al, *Social Cohesion and Civil Law: Marriage, Divorce and Religious Courts* (Report of a Research Study funded by the AHRC, Cardiff Law School 2011) 48.

60 Grillo (n 57) 105.

to do so from the religious marital bond. This is why the Act makes provisions for English judges to send litigants to religious judges who are qualified to issue a religious decree of divorce before an absolute decree by civil law is subsequently issued.

The reason these two presumptions are particularly pertinent for UK Shariah councils is that Carroll had previously advanced the argument that a civil decree of divorce satisfies the requirements for divorce in Islamic law and thus renders the services of Shariah councils ineffective.[61] Carroll also suggested within this argument that a British Muslim cannot legally purport to get married 'twice', once according to Islamic law and once according to English law.[62] Shariah council judges were thus vindicated with the passing of the 2002 Act and have cited it as a support to justify the need for the services which their tribunals provide. Sheikh Al-Haddad of the Islamic Shariah Council has stated in this regard:

> One important thing to note here is marriages and divorce. We have the Islamic marriage, and the civil marriage. They are totally separate systems. Therefore I had a in depth conversation with the deputy minister for social affairs of Denmark. She actually visited us here back when she did her PhD, at that time when she came I remembered her. So when I met her last year, I told her the Islamic marriage is different from the civil marriage. She initially tried to argue that a civil judge can solve the problem, he can annul an Islamic divorce, so I had to explain to her that this is not allowed, even by the law of the land, the European laws themselves. In fact, I told the channel 4 news presenter who came to interview me last week, to go and explain to Lady Cox that the British system does not regulate *nikaah*, Islamic marriage, does not approve it, does not recognise, it does not mean anything for the civil law. So who will annul an Islamic marriage? Who will help those Muslim women in the UK who are Islamically married and want to remarry? A major misunderstanding amongst many even within our own Islamic community is that an English judge who issues a divorce under English law will also be giving an Islamic divorce. This is a big problem! Many Muslims believe they can

61 See Lucy Carroll, 'Muslim Women and the "Islamic Divorce" in England' (1997) 17(1) JMMA 105–110.

62 *Ibid*, 106. Carroll erroneously proposes in this regard that an Islamic marriage ceremony conducted before a civil ceremony would constitute a criminal offence, a proposition which has been refuted by the decision of *R v Bham* [1966] 1 QB 159 in which precisely such a conviction was quashed because the union was not intended by the parties to be a marriage recognised by English law.

> remarry after they get a civil divorce, when Islamically this is not allowed, it is a big problem. Hence in Holland they don't want Shariah councils, as they actually think that a civil divorce will count as an Islamic divorce, hence they say we are in no need for Shariah councils. In fact the English legal system itself does not recognise Islamic marriage, hence why the 2002 act which was confirmed in 2005 allows for an English judge to give provision to two Jewish parties to go and get a get before the absolute decree is given.[63]

Sheikh Al-Haddad makes two important points in this statement. The first is that a civil judge cannot annul an Islamic divorce according to Islamic law, contrary to the claim of Carroll. The second is that a civil judge cannot annul an Islamic divorce even according to the English legal system. He correctly states that English law does not recognise Islamic marriage, thus making it impossible for a civil decree of divorce to be considered as an annulment of the Islamic bond of marriage from the perspective of English law.[64] It is here that Haythem cites the 2002 Act to support this argument, because the Act is based on the presumption that an English judge cannot annul an Islamic divorce. The founder of the Muslim Arbitration Tribunal, Sheikh Siddique, has also emphasised this important distinction between the role and jurisdiction of English judges and that of Shariah tribunal judges:

> I think Muslim judges should sit in English courts, but what they are doing is not substituting the work of the Muslim Arbitration Tribunal, what the Muslim Arbitration Tribunal is doing is applying Islamic law, Muslim judges sitting in English courts are applying English law, which is entirely different, and both are very welcome, they don't contradict each other, they don't substitute or replace each other, because Muslim judges sitting in English courts are not applying Islamic law, they are applying English Law. No doubt they will have some discretion in which they can try to give as ethical a decision as possible, but that ethical decision should be

63 Recorded by the author in an interview with Sheikh Haytham Al-Haddad at the Islamic Shariah Council in London 09/10/2014. The interview transcript remains unpublished.

64 The fact that the Islamic marriage ceremony is not recognised by English law has been affirmed in *R v Bham* [1966] 1 QB 159 and was also confirmed by Bridget Prentice in the House of Commons, stating in response to a question asked about marriages registered by Shariah courts that 'Marriages conducted under sharia law are not legally recognised in England and Wales unless they also comply with the provisions of the Marriage Act 1949. The English and Welsh courts do not legally recognise divorces granted by any faith groups' see HC Deb Jan 2010 c24W.

> with all judges not just Muslim judges. So, I think that doesn't replace the idea that a Muslim court, or a Muslim tribunal, is giving its decision according to Islamic law. So I think both are absolutely fine.[65]

Sheikh Siddique emphasises here that the function of English civil judges is to apply English law and not Islamic law. For this reason he says that their work does not contradict the work of Shariah tribunal judges, who are applying Islamic law. He therefore concludes that the work of Shariah tribunals is in fact needed, as they serve a function which English judges do not and cannot serve within their judicial capacity.

3 Would the English Model Work in Ireland?

The preceding examination shows that the English regulatory model is marked as a whole by its refusal to directly intervene in the governance of Shariah councils. Instead it has opted to delegate a limited and qualified set of self-governing powers to such councils whilst reserving for itself the power to step in and police their activities should they transgress the boundaries of their prescribed jurisdiction. It has also developed indirect mechanisms of accommodating some of their practices in particular situations. The result is that Shariah councils are given ample space to freely offer their services to the Muslim community as long as they do not contravene any provisions of the law or challenge the jurisdiction of the state's secular courts. In three particular instances, their decisions can also accrue legal status if they fulfil the conditions prescribed by the law.

Is this model one which could work in Ireland? It is certainly not the only model available. Shariah councils enjoy no legal jurisdiction in France, despite the fact that France contains the largest population of Muslims in Western Europe.[66] On the other hand, the direct incorporation of Islamic Mufti tribunals in the Greek province of Western Thrace within the Greek judicial system is a rare European example of directly accommodating Shariah councils within

65 Recorded by the author in an interview with Sheikh Faizul Aqtab Siddiqui at the Muslim Arbitration Tribunal in Nuneaton 02/10/2014. The interview transcript remains unpublished.

66 John Bowen 'Islamic Adaptations to Western Europe and North America: The Importance of Contrastive Analyses' (2011) 20(10) ABS 7–9; Jonathan Laurence and Justin Vaisse, *Integrating Islam: Political and Religious Challenges in Contemporary France* (Brookings Institution Press 2006) 1.

the state judicial system.[67] The English model, also adopted to varying extents in a number of other European countries, is a compromise between these two models.[68] There are strong reasons to suggest that the English model would indeed work well in Ireland, and would be more suitable than the French and Greek models. For a start, the pre-existing parallels between the English and Irish legal systems in their general approach towards religious tribunals forms an apt foundation for the adoption of the English model. Both systems have historically been lenient in allowing religious tribunals to function on a non-statutory basis as long as they do not clash with the state's secular court system or violate any provisions within the law. For this reasons Catholic marriage tribunals have enjoyed a flourishing existence in both systems, positively complimenting the work of the state's secular courts. Indeed Irish Muslims can closely relate to the attempts historically undertaken by Irish Catholics to navigate between canon law and the Church's marriage tribunals on the one hand, and the secular state legal system on the other.[69]

There is however a more pertinent and particular reason to suggest the English model would work well in Ireland, and this relates to Ireland's constitution.[70] The Irish constitution represents an interesting fusion between two ideological traditions which strongly influenced Irish politics during the

67 This exceptional situation is explained by Greece's historical proximity to the Ottoman empire; the official recognition of Islamic tribunals is based on treaties conducted in the 20th century between Greece and Turkey which sought to protect the rights of the Muslim minority in Thrace to an Islamic alternative dispute-resolution system. See İlker Tsavousoglou, 'The Legal Treatment of Muslim Minority Women under the Rule of Islamic Law in Greek Thrace' (2015) 3 OLR 241, 242–243. For a more detailed analysis of the Greek accommodation of Islamic law, see Konstantinos Tsitselikis (ed), *Annotated Legal Documents on Islam in Europe: Greece* (Brill 2016). A note should be made that as a result of the 2018 European Court of Human Right's case *Molla Sali* v *Greece* (No. 20452/14), the Greek Parliament voted to limit the powers of Islamic tribunals operating in Thrace by giving the secular courts priority in all cases and thereby ensuring Greek Muslim women have full access to the civil courts should they wish to use them.

68 For the indirect accommodation of Shariah councils in Holland see Machteld Zee, 'The State and the Operation of Sharia Councils in the United Kingdom: A Response to Shona Lester' (2015) 17 JRS 4. For a more detailed discussion of regulatory models for Shariah councils in Europe, see Machteld Zee, 'Five Options for the Relationship between the State and Sharia Councils: Untangling the Debate on Sharia Councils and Women's Rights in the United Kingdom' (2014) 16 JRS 1–15 and Shona Lester, 'The State and the Operation of Sharia Councils in the United Kingdom: A Critical Response to Machteld Zee' (2015) 17 JRS 1–6 and Malik (n 11) 33–49.

69 Mairead Enright, 'Preferring the Stranger: Toward an Irish Approach to Muslim Divorce Practice' 49 IJ 65, 97.

70 Despite the historical connections and parallels between English and Irish Law, the existence of a written constitution is something which distinguishes Irish Law from its

drafting process in the 1930s, namely the 'inherited liberal democratic tradition of the Free State, and…the social teaching of the Catholic Church'.[71] The constitution's provisions on religion thus reflect these two traditions. Article 44 of the constitution, entitled 'Religion', contains two key provisions for the purposes of religious tribunals. The first is found in Article 44.1 which establishes a duty on the state to 'respect and honour religion'. The second and more pertinent provision is found in Article 44.2.5 which guarantees the right for every religious denomination to 'manage its own affairs, own, acquire and administer property, movable and immovable, and maintain institutions for religious or charitable purposes'. The High Court affirmed in the case of *McNally v Ireland* that these two provisions when read together gave religious groups the right to manage their own affairs and maintain religious institutions, creating what the court termed a 'constitutional domain of recognition'.[72] This constitutional setting therefore clearly aligns itself most closely to the English model of indirectly accommodating the practices of Shariah councils without directly intervening in their affairs. For this reason, along with the other reasons suggested above, it is posited that the English model is certainly a model which Ireland could successfully adopt should Shariah councils emerge in Ireland in the near future.

Bibliography

Books

Cox, C., *A Parallel World: Confronting the abuse of many Muslim women in Britain today* (London: Bow Group, 2015).

Doe, N., *The Legal Framework of the Church of England: A Critical Study in Comparative Context* (Oxford University Press 1996).

Grillo, R., *Muslim Families, Politics and the Law: A Legal Industry in Multicultural Britain* (Ashgate 2015).

English common-law counterpart, which from a Public Law perspective still maintains the unusual position of functioning without a codified constitution.

71 Gerard Whyte, 'Religion and the Irish Constitution', (1997) 30 JMLR 725,728. See also Brian Girvin, 'Church, state and the Irish Constitution: the secularisation of Irish politics?' (1996) 49(4) PA 599.

72 *McNally v Ireland* [2009] IEHC 573. In the case of *McGrath and Ruairc v The Trustees of Maynooth College* [1979] ILRM.166 the internal disciplinary rules of Maynooth College were held by the supreme court to fall within this constitutional domain, see Enright (69) 74.

Hill, M., Sandberg, R. and Doe, N., *Religion and Law in the United Kingdom* (Kluwer Law International 2011).

King, M., (ed) *God's Law Versus State Law* (Grey Seal Books 1995).

Knights, S., *Freedom of Religion, Minorities and the Law* (Oxford University Press, Oxford 2007).

Laurence, J. and Vaisse, J., *Integrating Islam: Political and Religious Challenges in Contemporary France* (Brookings Institution Press 2006).

McAreavey, J., *The Canon Law of Marriage and the Family* (Four Courts Press 1997).

Journal Articles and Academic Reports

Al-Astewani, A., 'Reflections on the rise and fall of the Arbitration and Mediation Services (Equality) Bill' (2017) 4 PL 544.

Blacklett, R., 'The Status of Religious "Courts" in English law' (2009) DIAN 11–14.

Bowen, J., 'How could English Courts recognise Shariah?' (2011) 7(3) USTLJ 411.

Bowen, J., 'Islamic Adaptations to Western Europe and North America: The Importance of Contrastive Analyses' (2011) 20(10) ABS 7.

Brechin, J., 'A Study of the Use of Sharia Law in Religious Arbitration in the United Kingdom and the Concerns That This Raises for Human Rights' (2013) 15(3) ELJ 297.

D'Auria, E., 'The Use of Experts in the Roman Catholic Canon Law of Marriage' in Russel Sandberg (ed), Religion and Legal Pluralism (Ashgate 2015) 94.

Douglas, G., et al., *Social Cohesion and Civil Law: Marriage, Divorce and Religious Courts* (Report of a Research Study funded by the AHRC, Cardiff Law School 2011).

Douglas, G., 'Who Regulates Marriage? The Case of Religious Marriage and Divorce' in Russel Sandberg (ed), Religion and Legal Pluralism (Ashgate 2015) 57.

Enright, M., 'Preferring the Stranger: Toward an Irish Approach to Muslim Divorce Practice' 49 IJ 65.

Fitzpatrick, D., 'Divorce and Separation in Modern Irish History' (1987) 114(1) PP. 172.

Girvin, B., 'Church, state and the Irish Constitution: the secularisation of Irish politics?' (1996) 49(4) PA 599.

Harding, M., 'Religion and family law in Ireland: From a Catholic protection of marriage to a "catholic" approach to nullity' in J Mair and E Orucu (ed), The Place of Religion in Family Law (Intersentia 2011).

Hill, M., 'Religion and the State: Recognition, Regulation and Facilitation' in Russel Sandberg (ed), Religion and Legal Pluralism (Ashgate 2015) 25.

Lester, S., 'The State and the Operation of Sharia Councils in the United Kingdom: A Critical Response to Machteld Zee' (2015) 17 JRS 1–6.

MacEoin, D., Sharia Law or 'One Law for All' (Civitas Institute for the Study of Civil Society 2009) 1.

Malik, M., *Minority Legal Orders in the UK: Minorities, Pluralism and the Law* (The British Academy 2012).

McGoldrick, D., 'Accommodating Muslims in Europe: From Adopting Sharia Law to Religiously Based Opt Outs from Generally Applicable Laws' (2009) 9(4) HRL 605.

Philips, L., 'Equality before the Law' (2008) 2(3) AQ 18.

Reiss, M., 'The Materialization of Legal Pluralism in Britain: Why Shari'a Council Decisions Should be Non-Binding' (2009) 26(3) AJICL 743.

Richardson, E., 'Islamic Finance Disputes in Ireland: A comparative study of dispute resolution in Islamic finance contracts' (2017) 57 IJ 35.

Sandberg, R., 'Islam and English law' (2010) 164 LJCLR 29.

Scharbrodt, O. and Sakaranaho, T., 'Islam and Muslims in the Republic of Ireland' 31(1) JMMA 469.

Scharbrodt, O., 'Muslim Immigration to the Republic of Ireland: Trajectories and Dynamics since World War II' (2012) 47 EI 221.

Thomson, H.A., *An Insight into the work of Islamic Shari'a Councils* (Wynne Chambers 2013).

Tsavousoglou, I., 'The Legal Treatment of Muslim Minority Women under the Rule of Islamic Law in Greek Thrace' (2015) 3 OLR 241.

Whyte, G., 'Religion and the Irish Constitution', (1997) 30 JMLR 725.

Williams, R., 'Civil and Religious Law in England: A Religious Perspective' (2008) 10(3) ELJ 264.

Zee, M., 'Five Options for the Relationship between the State and Sharia Councils: Untangling the Debate on Sharia Councils and Women's Rights in the United Kingdom' (2014) 16 JRS 1.

Zee, M., 'The State and the Operation of Sharia Councils in the United Kingdom: A Response to Shona Lester' (2015) 17 JRS 4.

CHAPTER 10

The Usefulness of the 'Parity Governance Model' in Muslim Family Law Debates

Samia Bano

Introduction

Drawing upon feminist scholarship this chapter evaluates the possible value and or potential limitations of the 'parity governance' model (broadly conceived as gender parity) to be constitutively applied as a framework of 'democratic governance' to Muslim legal pluralist models of dispute resolution (identified as sharia councils and the Muslim Arbitration Tribunal).

Debates on multiculturalism and its normative concern for justice, equality and fairness have of course long been debated, theorized, critiqued and challenged. The twin goals of the 'accommodation' of cultural and religious differences and practices and the limits of such 'recognition' has led to the emergence of a renewed liberal political discourse and public policy development(s) dealing with the specific conflicts of 'minority rights', individual rights versus group rights and the tensions created by different sets of obligations owed to self, family, community and state law. Political and social theorists have, for example, long traced the European liberal legal tradition of 'minority rights' with a focus on problems generated by conflicting of norms and normativity (social and legal/state law norms) and the extent to which individuals are able to choose between two or more sets of conflicting norms in the face of group loyalty versus state law obligations.

In this chapter I draw upon the 'parity governance' model in a multicultural context to interrogate issues of power and unequal power relations in relation to promoting personal and community autonomy, and to consider its plausibility for positive law obligations for religious group autonomy. To what extent, for example, can the 'parity governance model' promote and enhance personal autonomy, challenge unequal religious practice and gender inequality but also protect religious autonomy and religious freedom in community private governance mechanisms? Can this model contribute to protecting and providing remedies to women when conflicting demands arise from state law and from religious and cultural practices?

 | DOI:10.1163/9789004398252_011

In doing so the chapter also raises another set of related questions. Firstly a closer analysis on the institutional design of private community governance in Britain identified as sharia councils and the Muslim Arbitration Tribunal: what is it about these bodies that signifies 'Islam' 'Muslim practice' and 'Muslimness'? How are these bodies conceptualized in relation to ideas of liberal justice, human rights and equality? What are the contours of the debates and the resolution of family law disputes within the processes of what we understand as dispute resolution? Can we capture an assertion of Muslim subjectivity and Muslim autonomy in these spaces? And does this assertion of Muslim subjectivity undermine state law legal processes?

The diverse, contested and varied experiences of South Asian Muslim women utilizing unofficial dispute resolution mechanisms such as sharia councils and more formalized religious bodies such as the Muslim Arbitration Tribunal is increasingly being documented and demonstrating the ways in which debates on belonging, identity and rights cannot be understood as fixed and unchanging.[1] Debates across UK and Europe have focused on policies of multiculturalism and the extent to which minority religious practices are tolerated and or endorsed by national domestic courts. Further afield debates in Canada, US and increasingly Australia highlight issues of conflict, equity and discrimination. Muslim women remain at the centre of these debates while feminists from across the political spectrum seek to defend or resist calls for greater accommodation of religious norms and values and practices in western democratic societies. This has led to enormous conflicts, crossing political spectrums and the extent to which state law should recognize alternative systems of family law dispute resolution. As Marie Ashe and Anissa Helie explain,

> 'Civil governmental recognitions of jurisdiction in specifically-religious courts may be the most extraordinary of the accommodations currently being provided to religious organisations. The toleration of judicial autonomy in such bodies in itself manifests a striking sharing of sovereignty. And the ceding to religious bodies of a central feature of governmental sovereignty – the judicial power – becomes particularly problematic when that power is utilized in order to enforce religious law that conflicts with fundamental principles of the civil law'.[2]

1 See Samia Bano, *Muslim Women and Shari'ah Councils: Transcending the Boundaries of Community and Law*, (Palgrave MacMillan 2012); John Bowen, *On British Islam. Religion, Law and Everyday Practice in Sharia Councils* (Princeton University Press 2016).

2 See Marie Ashe and Anne Helie, 'Realities of Religico-Legalism: Religious Courts and Women's Rights in Canada, the United Kingdom and the United States' (2014) 20 U.Cal.-Davis J International Law & Policy 139, 142.

Debates have therefore focused on the extent to which religious legal practices comply with liberal legalism and gender equality raising a further set of questions: Do such bodies discriminate against Muslim women? Are women's rights, liberty and equality under threat? Is justice being administered in the shadow of the law? The controversy of Sharia, it seems, will not only not disappear but is increasing in its intensity and vigour both by its opponents and its supporters. This raises the important question raised again by Ashe and Helies as to whether such bodies should be tolerated at all? Can the 'problem' in fact be resolved? 'The non-settled status of sharia-related questions' they argue 'invites broader more historically-informed, and more comparative inquiry concerning the policies that should shape liberal-governmental interaction with religious courts in general'.[3] Why, for example, under a liberal multiculturalist framework is the demand for religious and communal group autonomy considered both inevitable and necessary rather than questioning the basis upon which demands are made and met?

In Britain, new methods of dispute resolution in English family law have also led to an unprecedented rise in the number of scholarly and policy critiques questioning their effectiveness and the challenge to liberal legal principles of 'equality before the law', 'justice' and 'common citizenship'.[4] Debates have focused on the wider discussions of promoting 'access to justice' for all citizens and better understanding of the relationship between cultural and social norms that may underpin new forms of dispute resolution. Indeed the contemporary landscape of civil and family justice in England and Wales is part of a renewed recognition by the state to build upon mechanisms of Alternate Dispute Resolution (ADR) that are evidenced by the increasing use of arbitration, mediation, conciliation and initiatives developed by practitioners such as collaborative law. As part of these contemporary developments, issues of cultural and religious diversity are addressed including demands for the accommodation of religious dispute mechanisms as part of new dispute resolution initiatives. We have seen, for example, a rise in cross-cultural mediation mechanisms in determining both the use and delivery of services and the desire to accommodate the needs of all users, irrespective of cultural and religious differences. In essence, what we see then is not only the emergence of new forms of legal cultures but also the ways in which new forms of informal and formal adjudication in all their complexity emerge and develop within groups, communities and networks.

---

3 Ibid 143.

4 See John Eekelaar and Maclean M. (eds) *Lawyers and Mediators. The Brave New World of Services for Separated Families* (Hart Publishing 2016).

1 Multiculturalism and Managing Migrant Communities

Debates on the nature and settlement of postcolonial migrations are often discussed in relation to discussions on identity, ethnicity, religion, migration and the impact of transnational populations upon settled communities. Within a wide body of scholarship and sociological research we are better able to understand how notions of diaspora, hybridity and globalism intersect with social and class divisions, gender, ethnicity and class. Today, therefore, there is a growing literature which seeks to understand identities as multiple, fluid, dynamic and partial and which can only be understood in interaction with other identities, ethnicities and social structures. This understanding of identity as fluid and changing has led many commentators to conclude that, at specific times, a particular aspect of the group identity emerges. In Britain, for example, we have seen the emergence of a 'renewed' Muslim religious identity as part of South Asian Muslim communities[5] and demands for the accommodation of religious systems of law to be made under this understanding of identity.

The term multiculturalism in Britain today is debated, discussed, contested, challenged and more recently dismissed. Indeed some of the problems attributed to multiculturalism including the perceived lack of integration of minority ethnic communities into British society, the emergence of parallel and segregated minority ethnic communities and the failure to foster a national British identity only illustrates the shifts and contradictions in its meaning and what it was originally perceived to stand for. Current public commentary therefore pays much more attention to its perceived principle failure rather than any real success. Whether the term itself has any epistemological value is itself open to question as are questions on measurable outcomes. At its best, multiculturalism promotes tolerance, equality and respect for cultural and religious difference, promoting positive relations between minority and majority communities but at its worst it promotes segregated, polarised and parallel communities who have little care or understanding how the 'other' may live. For many, it is this politics of difference and the threshold of tolerance that remains problematic. For example, at which point does a cultural practice become intolerant and oppressive and to whom? For many liberal multiculturalists the threshold is to protect vulnerable members within communities and in Muslim communities this has often meant Muslim women being protected against what is often deemed oppressive, archaic and traditional religious practices. In other words, the principles of freedom and choice are seen

5 See Tariq Modood, 'Part 1 Accommodating religions: Multiculturalism's new fault line' (2013) 34(1) *Critical Social Policy* 121.

as easily compromised in Muslim communities where the protection of Muslim women becomes the benchmark upon which we must fight for women's rights and liberal values of freedom, justice and equality. In her work Lila Abu-Lughod warns of the dangers this can bring, explaining that

> '....generalizing about cultures prevents us from appreciating or even accounting for people's experiences and the contingencies with which we all live. The idea of culture increasingly has become a core component of international politics and common sense. Pundits tell us that there is a clash of civilizations or cultures in our world. They tell us there is an unbridgeable chasm between the West and the 'Rest'. Muslims are presented as a special and threatening culture – the most homogenized and the most troubling of the Rest. Muslim women in this new common sense, symbolize just how alien this culture is'.[6]

Today, in an age where the practice and discourse of multiculturalism and policies of diversity and managing diversity is coming under increasing attack from all sides of the political spectrum questions of culture (whose culture?) and rights (whose rights?) become ever more urgent in the context of the settlement and management of minority ethnic and religious groups in western democratic societies.

The twin policies of social cohesion and integration has led to what Patel (2008) identifies as a move away from multiculturalism and towards what she describes as 'multi-faithism' with government policies specifically promoting and nurturing 'faith communities'. For Patel the encroaching of secular spaces that are increasingly being taken up by religious groups means that women from minority backgrounds are left with even less choice. She explains,

> 'Ironically, the current promotion of faith based projects in all areas of civil society will compromise the gender equality agenda for black and minority women in particular. It will divert women away from the legal justice system into the hands of religious conservative and fundamentalist leaders. The cry of religious discrimination can and will be used to claim access to and control over resources, whilst at the same time it will serve to perpetuate discrimination against women and other sub groups and to deter state intervention in family matters'.[7]

6 Lila Abu-Lughod, *Do Muslim Women Need Saving?* (Harvard University Press 2013) 6.

7 Pragna Patel, 'Faith in the State? Asian Women's Struggles for Human Rights in the UK' (2008) 16(1) Feminist Legal Studies 9, 25.

Not only does this lead to a denial of rights for women from minority ethnic backgrounds but this critique also flags up central questions of power, voice and representation and the use of male interlocutors in forging majority/ minority relations between communities and the state. Further critique points to an outcome for minority ethnic communities who maybe feel disempowered from processes of power but the focus on cultural and religious difference that has in fact led to a form of limited autonomy over internal 'community' affairs, such as religious observance, dress and food. In other words, the emphasis upon communities to focus on their culture and religion has in effect led to a shift away from public decision-making spaces. More worrying however it has also led to the emergence of community leaders who often have the undemocratic mandate to represent their communities. For example male leaders, who over time have become the primary interlocutors and who are afforded the right to speak on behalf of the whole community are seen as both legitimate and with authority. Women are in effect then side-lined and given less voice and capacity to engage with community and state practices.

2 Islam and the 'Muslim Question'

The 'Muslim Question' (generated by a series of questions over integration/ loyalty to the state/ citizenship and claims for religious communal autonomy in family law matters, to name but a few) has in recent times, come to be understood (by scholars and policy makers alike) as one of *the* defining questions in the twenty first century when framing, challenging and debating issues ranging from the limits of liberal free speech, minority rights, questions of modernity, immigration, liberalism, multiculturalism and most importantly of course issues of gender equality, injustice and personal autonomy for potentially vulnerable Muslim women living within Muslim families and communities. This literature is accompanied by an expansive body of scholarship tracing the social and lived realities of Muslim communities in the UK,[8] rights of minorities communities and multiculturalism[9] to charting the rise of anti-Muslim discrimination and 'Islamaphobia'[10] and tracing the rise of religious

8 See Russell Sandberg, Gillian Douglas, Norman Doe, Sophie Gilliat-Ray and Asma Khan, 'Britain's Religious Tribunals: "Joint Governance" in Practice' (2012) 33(2) Oxford Journal of Legal Studies 263; Farah Ahmed, 'Personal Autonomy and the Option of Religious Law' (2010) 24(2) *International Journal of Law, Policy and the Family* 222.

9 See Modood (n 5).

10 There is a wide body of scholarship that examines the nature and practice of Islamaphobia. Problems on definition exist. See Salman Sayyid and AbdoolKarim Vakil (eds), *Thinking Through Islamaphobia: Global* Perspectives (Hurst Press 2009).

intolerance and the emergence of a politics of fear and the limits of anti-discrimination legislation. Furthermore it seems that the 'Muslim Problem' is inextricably linked to the 'Secularism Problem' with the juxtaposition of religion and secularism and the public and private spheres deemed, imaginary, problematic and illusory. For example the work of Saba Mahmood[11] (2011), Talal Asad[12] (2011), Oliver Roy[13] (2010) and Salman Sayyid[14] (2014) demonstrate *how* debates on secularism are closely linked to the ways in which Muslim mobilisations in the West are managed, controlled and designated in western European societies often through security and racist governmentalities. In Britain, for example, the government's Prevent strategy has been critiqued for not only the loss of civil liberties but its focus on Muslim communities and the potential consequences that this kind of exceptionalism promotes. This body of literature raises important questions regarding the separation of religious and political spaces in liberal politics and the junctures upon which religious personal practices can be located and accommodated as part of the liberal human rights framework. As Sayyid points out, 'secularism is one of the categories often deployed in discussions about the difficulties of exercising Muslim agency'.[15] Therefore, what are the dialogic processes and challenges between community and state law relations if Muslim communities seek not to operate from a liberal legal and ethical framework ? What are the other possibilities for communicative or intercultural dialogue(s)? Are minority Muslim communities in Europe simply in need of secularization?

Critiques on liberal legal models aim therefore to de-center the 'West' and challenge the 'Western imaginary' as *the* dominant loci of politics, governance and identity. Indeed the contemporary binary oppositions of Islam and the West are not only widely acknowledged as a reflection of the hegemony of western legal liberalism but the framing and naming of Islam and Muslim legal pluralism has led to disjunctures between 'official laws' and 'law as a lived social reality'. Questions of 'norms' 'truth' and claims-making have focused on the uneasy tensions produced by communities with liberal and democratic principles of liberal legal conceptions of justice, equality before the law, human

11 See Saba Mahmood, 'Secularism, Hermeneutics, Empire: The Politics of Islamic Reformation' (2006) 18(2) *Public Culture* 323.

12 See Talal Asad, *Foundations of the secular: Christianity, Islam, Modernity* (Stanford University 2003).

13 Oliver Roy, *Holy Ignorance: When Religion and Culture Part Ways* (Columbia University Press 2010).

14 See Salman Sayyid, *Recalling the Caliphate: Decolonisation and the World Order* (Hurst Press 2014).

15 Ibid 32.

rights and citizenship. The focus on Islam and Muslims remains important for both communities and state-law relations because 'the act of naming is also the act of becoming'.[16] In other words, the ways in which Muslims name themselves as Muslims and construct *ways* of belonging (for example belonging to the Muslim community or the Muslim Ummah) coupled with the ways in which communities are understood (or imagined) in non-Muslim societies contributes to policy initiatives and community-state relations. Furthermore the ways in which Muslim communities 'imagine' the Muslim Ummah can help our conceptualisations of community and Muslim autonomy. Therefore the rubric upon which we frame debates can also help to reframe debates on cultural and religious autonomy and finding legal remedies to protect vulnerable members of communities subject to religious personal systems of law, most often Muslim women.

Indeed this act of becoming has taken shape and form in a myriad of ways as epitomized by the emergence of local grassroots Muslim community groups (including private community governance) and the different levels of state funding and state support. Over the past three decades, for example, we have seen the emergence of local Muslim women's groups, refuges and counselling services to the setting up of national organisations such as the Muslim Council of Britain[17]and the Muslim Women's Network[18] and numerous sharia councils and the Muslim Arbitration Tribunal.[19] The 2011 Census identified Islam as the second largest religion in the UK with a population of 2,786,635 and 4.4% of the total population. This act of becoming has therefore taken shape, for example, under the rubric of multiculturalism, policies of integration, socio-economic factors vis-a-vis community, state and cultural interlocutors. So what are the cultural impacts of these new formations in our understandings of Islam and Muslims living in non-Muslim majority societies? What does the description of a 'Muslim community' mean for Muslims and non-Muslims alike? What are the processes of governance and governmentality that *signify* Muslim communities? And how can we conceptualise, identify and address issues of cultural inter and intra community conflicts addressing issues of unequal gender relations without relying on reified notions of culture, religion, belonging, identity and law?

16 Ibid 4.

17 See Muslim Council of Britain at www.mcb.org.uk.

18 See Muslim Women's network at www.mwnuk.co.uk.

19 See Muslim Arbitration Tribunal at www.mat.org.uk.

3 Muslims and Problem with Democracy?

In their article Ruiz and Rubio-Marin (2009)[20] point out that democratic parity 'must define what democracy is fundamentally about'. Similarly in her work Ann Philips[21] concludes that, 'Democratic parity matters because without it we do not yet have democracy'. Whilst we also learn that this model 'has its own distinctive logic' such observations clearly point to an implicit relationship between the two leading to some kind of normative conception of democracy. Of course all claims about meaning and value of concepts such as democracy merit scrutiny and both scholars successfully draw upon a political theory of democracy that promotes gender equality in ways that aims to avoid the pitfalls of essentialism and normative truth/ claims-making-as theorizing choice, capability and capacity from a feminist perspective. Feminist political theorists and philosophers have also (over the past two decades) developed new models to challenge discrimination and oppression occurring within particular cultural and religious settings (for example Shachar[22] and her model of transformative accommodation).

In this part of the chapter, I pose a series of questions to consider the ways in which the idea and meaning of democracy as a common *signifier* of democracy may serve to ascribe meanings and value (within minority Muslim communities) in fixed and problematic ways. For example the assumptions and goals of democracy; the way in which it engages and inter-sects with non-state norms and minority communities, while raising a critical reading on the relationship between Democracy, the West and Islam.

Our efforts to complicate the concepts and practice of democracy are important if democracy also exhibits an ensemble of practices and democratic institutions that seek to regulate the exercise of communal and private governance based upon orientalist tropes of Muslims simply lacking the credentials of freedom and democracy. The meaning, relevance and perils of democracy therefore raise important questions and challenges. For example, in his work on governmentality Foucault[23] poses a series of questions relating to the problems of government and the role of individuals. How should 'we govern oneself, how to be governed, by whom should be accept to be governed and how to be the best possible governor'? This series of lectures reveals important

20 Blanca Rodriguez-Ruiz and Ruth Rubio-Marin, 'Constitutional Justification of Parity Democracy' (2009) 60 (5) Alabama Law Review 1171.

21 Anne Phillips, *Multiculturalism without Culture* (Princeton University Press 2007).

22 Ayelet Shachar, 'Privatizing Diversity: A Cautionary Tale from Religious Arbitration in Family Law' (2008) 9(2) Theoretical Inquiries in Law 573.

23 Michel Foucault, *Discipline and Punish The Birth of the Prison* (London Penguin 1979) 35.

insights into the intricate and complex relationships between governance and the process of governing and the ways in which governance is both 'thought' and practiced' by the liberal political processes. Governmentality he argues is in evidence across multiple sites (such as population) where technologies operate to regulate conduct and behaviours in ever complex ways displaying the myriad and multiple forms of political power in action. The multiple dynamics of power seek to define/ address/ manage and control with implications for all in minority and majority communities. Social and legal norms operate within and across communities in relation 'to the division of labour, authority between family members and intimate behaviour'. We have, of course a long and expansive body of postcolonial scholarship that produces important insights into relations of power, legality and identity.

Yet even this (brief) overview of governmentality, power and state law relations raises important questions in relation to relations of power, dialogue, inter cultural dialogue, positionality and rights and contributes to our understanding of the myriad and complex lived social realities of law and legalities that take shape in many different forms both in state law relations and as private governance within minority communities. The rise of racist governmentalities, for example, also raises an important set of questions as the logic of democracy that can also rest upon a logic of West and non West and those who are democratic versus non democratic. One could, for example, question upon what basis the *idea* of democracy is predicated in its application to minority Muslim communities living in western societies? Western exceptionality and a fixed description democracy (and democratic discourse) reveals a tenuous relationship between ideas of belonging, identity and a convergence of being democratic and being western. Postcolonial critiques, for example, point to the western hegemony and a fixed western identity as the primary signifiers of democracy, today. So how can we better understand the category of democracy as it applies to Muslim communities? These critiques remain important for the dislocation within Muslim communities from ideas of citizenship, democracy and belonging are in evidence and raise a series of questions, what are the primary features of democracy and how can do we understand questions of autonomous individuals, decision-making and capacity in relation to Muslim women and religious models of dispute resolution? What is the capacity of Muslim dispute resolution bodies to transform to accommodate 'difference within difference'? How do these organisations envisage democratic arrangements and governance? Are we able to produce alternative accounts both as insiders and outsiders of communities and groups? It is imperative, of course that we unpack this *idea* of a Muslim community as the Muslim Ummah. As Sayyid points out, 'The Muslim question encompasses the difficulties associated with the emergence of a distinct political identity that appears to be transgressive of the norms, conventions and structures that underpin the contemporary world.'[24] Yet suprising perhaps in a world of difference, complexity and challenge the emergence of fixed notions of identity and religious have only in recent times gained increasing urgency. Furthermore, as a political signifier, democracy, with its particular cultural formations in the 'west', provides the essence of human identity transcending cultural and religious divides and acting as a designator of freedom, capacity but also government practices and hybrid western identities. We therefore understand democracy as closely aligned to a western identity and to be to be anti-western is to be anti-democratic.

4 Institutional Design of Muslim Dispute Resolution Mechanisms

An analysis of the institutional design and power relations embedded within sharia councils is of fundamental importance in order to consider the ways in which these bodies, today are not only increasingly understood as the primary expression of 'Muslim legal pluralism' but also in order to consider the possible ways in which the 'parity governance' model may be useful in the process of the internal reform. All such bodies are of course plural, that is they are constructed around multiple and often conflicting schools of thought and the boundaries upon which they operate are constructed and depend upon a vast number of social and religious rules and norms. More importantly such rules, principles, procedures and sources are structured by a whole host of factors including, religious, ethnic, gender and class differences. The rule-making capacity of such bodies may be relational and specific to local contingencies but is also dependent upon certain shared cultural and religious attributes that attribute identity and the boundaries of such alternative dispute resolution mechanisms to the authority of the religious scholar(s). In the case of sharia councils, important questions remain in relation to what kinds of structures are created and what types of communication take place between the sources of authority, religious scholars and primary users most often Muslim women. Furthermore, in what ways do principles of justice, rights and gender equality differ from liberal values and how do such bodies operate as decision-making processes? What is the institutional design and the constitutive elements in the operation of justice? And does this system of dispute resolution recognize

24 See Sayyid (n14) 3.

its own contingencies? In other words, is it even possible to have gender parity in sharia councils and religious tribunals?

Democracy and equality remain the two foundational principles of the parity governance model with gender representation at its core. Conversely, the model of dispute resolution dominant in contemporary British sharia councils remains grounded in normative Islamic principles that render gender differentiated rights and duties and are marked by contested concepts of Islamic jurisprudential schools of thought. Therefore there is an obvious challenge to the application of a parity design model upon these bodies but if these challenges can be overcome what are the options for parity design as a process of reform within these bodies? In this part of the paper, I discuss the normative desirability or change in the institutional design or formal structure of these bodies but also focus upon the ambiguous and contested concepts of religion that underpin these bodies. Parity claims, first and foremost, provide female members with exercising their rights within a liberal and egalitarian public culture. It strongly maintains that the equal representation of women is central to ensuring that liberal societies properly invoke the principles of democracy and equality. Women members from minority groups often pay a high cost if they are denied exercising their rights that are bestowed upon all citizens.

The history of sharia councils has been widely documented in Britain and can be traced to a diverse set of social, political and religious developments in civil society and as part of emergence of a Muslim identity both forged and as part of multicultural practices. The question of how such bodies should be classified and understood, for example as groups, associations, institutions or alternative disputes resolution mechanisms, often rests upon the way they may operate and the nature of their relationship to multicultural practices and internal rules of process, institution, whether they rely on a hierarchal relationship and the structures and processes of decision-making and methods of enforcement. Moreover, over the past three decades, a growing number of scholars have explored the changing and contested nature of this relationship, revealing a new discursive space of engagement, contestation and negotiation between minority religious communities and the state. This would include for example the emergence of sharia councils as part of mosques and religious community centres more specifically in Britain charting from the past four decades. While these bodies can be identified as being autonomous and constructed by the institutional autonomy and frameworks of local religious loyalties and Islamic schools of thought, many may actively seek to avoid any interaction with each other and any possible conflict with a secular state and civil law. In other words, such bodies exist also to distinguish themselves from other religious groups and religious practices to emerge as offering a very specific type of expertise.

Therefore to understand the emergence of sharia councils in Britain we need to begin, not with an overview of how they may function, but the ways in which they have emerged as part of multicultural Britain and the recognition of cultural and religious practices as part of British Muslim lives. They are part of British Muslim communities that have established very specific ways in which family law disputes are resolved, yet there is on-going debate within British Muslim communities regarding their role, identity and future. There are complex variations and permutations of shariah councils as they are neither unified nor represent a single school of thought but instead are made up of various different bodies representing the different schools of thought in Islam and ethnic religious groups.

Debate on the emergence of sharia councils has largely been discussed and scrutinised in relation to debates on liberal multiculturalism and its limits on minority-group rights. There is no single and authoritative definition of the term 'sharia council' and therefore no obvious consensus on the role of these bodies within British Muslim communities. In essence, a sharia council has three key functions, namely issuing Muslim divorce certificates, reconciling and mediating between parties and producing expert opinion reports on matters of Muslim family law and custom to the Muslim community, solicitors and the courts. Existing scholarship for example provides little insight into the nature of rules within these bodies as institutionalised systems of dispute resolution. Concern in particular has focused on the rights and autonomy of minority group members and the potential conflicts generated by minority community norms and values in conflict with majority group norms and culture. Hegemonic relations of state law are understood as oppressive and over-bearing while undermining individual members' sense of belonging and autonomy as part of their faith communities. Protection of the individual vis-à-vis the group therefore has become imperative to the liberal project. However as Karayanni[25] points out, 'as this theory of group rights crystallised, a major problem arose: how should liberal multiculturalism relate to religious minority groups that adhere to practices viewed as illiberal, for which they seek accommodation – in the form of jurisdictional autonomy over their members in matters of family law, recognition of their dress codes, absolution from criminal

25 See Michael Karayanni, 'The Acute Multicultural Entrapment of the Palestinian-Arab Religious Minorities in Israel and the Feeble Measures Required to Relieve It' in Robert Provost (ed), *Mapping the Legal Boundaries of Belonging, Religion and Multiculturalism from Israel to Canada* (Oxford University Press 2014).

liability when they perform certain religiously motivated activities or other judicial leniencies?'

This body of work challenges both the essentialism and uniformity assumed in state law relations and celebrates cultural and religious difference as demonstrative of the emerging parallel systems of law operating in British society. More specifically, it contributes to our understanding of how contemporary societies are 'increasingly confronted within minority groups demanding recognition of their ethnicity and accommodation of their cultural and religious differences'. However this literature also adopts a somewhat legal prescriptive analysis to understanding the emergence of sharia councils and their relationship with and in opposition to state law. In short, there is little substantive and empirical analysis on the internal dynamics of power within these mechanisms of dispute resolution. Conceptualizing unofficial dispute resolution in this way is premised on the idea of homogeneity within 'Muslim communities' with little explanation on how these bodies are constituted within local communities. Furthermore, the primacy of a Muslim identity means that little is learnt about cultural and religious practices that may affect the autonomy of women using these bodies and how such processes are contested, redefined and used strategically to serve particular ends. Existing literature does not, for example, give due salience to the interconnection between the sharia councils, forms of power and gender inequality.

At present the nature and scope of sharia council activity in England and Wales remains largely unknown and undocumented. However a report by the Ministry of Justice entitled *An exploratory study of Shari'ah councils in England with respect to family law* identified 30 councils that worked on issues of Muslim family law and issued Muslim divorce certificates. Although this project did not look at smaller Shari'ah councils it suggests a relatively small number of key councils operating in England. The project found much diversity in the size of the councils, the number of religious scholars providing advice and assistance, and in the composition of council members. Most councils were embedded within Muslim communities, forming part of mosques and community centres and appear to have evolved according to the needs of the communities in which they are located.

Another example of Muslim legal pluralism is the Muslim Arbitration Tribunal (MAT) that was set up in June 2007 and aims to settle disputes in accordance with religious Sharia law. The authority of this tribunal rests with the Arbitration Act 1996 which permits civil matters to be resolved in accordance with Muslim law and within the ambit of state law. For many, this process of resolving disputes may provide the ideal forum that allows the arbitrating parties to resolve disputes according to English law while fulfilling any obligations under Islamic law. The advantages of arbitration, it is argued, allow the parties to achieve some level of autonomy in the decision-making process. This, coupled with the informal setting, lower costs, flexibility and time efficiency means that for some it may prove a more attractive alternative to the adversarial courts system in England and Wales. However there remain real concerns over whether this process can restrict women's equality and over issues of fairness and justice in family law. At present, there are five tribunals operating as part of the MAT across Britain. Apart from addressing religious divorce and other Muslim family law matters (including marriage contracts, wills and inheritance disputes), these tribunals also arbitrate on matters relating to forced marriage and domestic violence. The MAT states that all agreements are settled in accordance with:

1. Qur'anic Injunctions and Prophetic Practice as determined by the recognised Schools of Islamic Sacred Law;
2. as fairly, quickly and efficiently as possible; and
3. where appropriate, that members of the Tribunal have responsibility for ensuring this in the interests of the parties to the proceedings and in the wider public interest.

It is held that Islamic decisions can be reached quickly and cheaply, and can be used as evidence before the civil court when seeking other remedies. It does not deal with criminal offences but states that 'where there are criminal charges such as assault within the context of domestic violence, the parties will be able ask MAT to assist in reaching reconciliation which is observed and approved by MAT as an independent organisation. The terms of such reconciliation can then be passed by MAT on to the Crown Prosecution Service (CPS) though the local Police Domestic Violence Liaison Officers with a view to reconsidering the criminal charges. Note that the final decision to prosecute always remains with the CPS'. Concern remains however that Muslim women participating in these processes continue to be risk of domestic violence and encouraged to reconcile with dangerous partners. Bowen (2016) has conducted in depth empirical research with this body and points to the fact that unlike Sharia councils it is run by the Hijaz community based the Muslim sufi faith.[26] As Bowen explains, 'If the London ISC scholars seek to base their legitimacy on correct following of jurisprudence and adherence to explicit procedural rules, MAT is based on Sufi sanctity'.[27]

26 See John Bowen, *On British Islam: Religion, Law and Everyday Practice in Sharia Councils* (Princeton University Press 2016).

27 Ibid 143.

In 2008, MAT produced a report entitled, *Liberation from Forced Marriages*, which stated that MAT was the most appropriate forum for the Muslim community to resolve problems such as forced marriage.[28] It put forward the following proposals to combat the practice of forced marriage as a community driven initiative with emphasis placed upon protecting British citizens marrying abroad who are victims of forced marriage. This includes requesting the foreign spouse to submit voluntarily 'an oral deposition to the Judges of MAT, satisfying them that the marriage he/she entered into was neither forced nor coerced'.[29] As a voluntary deposition by the British citizen rather than a legal requirement the Judges of MAT would then produce a written declaration that they were satisfied that the marriage entered into was without any force or coercion. The proposal further states that

> 'the British citizen can then use this declaration to support the application of the foreign spouse to settle in the UK. If however, the foreign spouse fails to produce such a declaration from MAT or any other appropriate evidence, then it would be open for the ECO at the entry clearance point, to draw such inferences deemed appropriate as to the status of the marriage'.[30]

The decisions of MAT judges are recorded on tape and hearings recorded on camera. Evidence may include speaking to family members 'to highlight the wider consequences of participating or being complicit in a coerced or forced marriage'. The use of community elders as a source of social scrutiny to embarrass perpetrators is also proposed as a source of action. So the proposal envisages a scenario where the MAT hopes to work closely with both perpetrators and victims of forced marriage. Indeed, since its establishment, the MAT has generated much hostility in the press which has focused on the assumed threat it poses to English law and the due process of law. So what is the remit of religious courts under the Arbitration Act 1996? The establishment of the MAT has been controversial for a number of reasons. Firstly, it has been claimed that Sharia courts have been allowed through the back door; secondly, that they directly challenge the superiority of the English legal system; and finally that they undermine the principles upon which English family law are based. As Blackett says,

28 A copy of this report can be found at www.matribunal.com (last accessed 8 Dec 2018).

29 Ibid 12.

30 Ibid 13.

> 'it is important to point out that the Muslim Arbitration Tribunal does not resemble or operate as a court but is an arbitration tribunal that must have the consent of the parties to rule on an issue. MAT has no power of enforcement but decisions can be enforced by the English county or high courts. This process therefore means that the decisions made by these arbitration bodies have to be in line with principles of English law or judges will not enforce them under sovereign rule'.[31]

5 Democratizing Muslim Legal Pluralism? Parity and Muslim Dispute Resolution

In an earlier paper of this chapter I explored the problems of 'democracy' and what has been described as a emergence of forms of Muslim exceptionalism whereby liberal governance specifically targets Muslim communities. In this part of the paper I question whether the Parity Democracy Model offer insights into the ways in which these processes of dispute resolution can promote gender parity in family law disputes? Empirical research on sharia councils suggests that the boundaries of community groups are often closed with a form of 'operative closure' that operate selectively and exclusively to reproduce norms that promote the closing of boundaries. We also know that this can lead to intra cultural gender inequalities as this process can allow dispute resolution to evolve from a system of personal decision-making to one of oppressive norms and the application of sanctions including the loss of personal decision-making and the normative values upon which the process is based upon. Whilst the rationale for applying a parity governance model upon community dispute resolution processes maybe questioned, nevertheless, it raises important questions on the ability of such a model to provide a framework to the administration and functioning of these types of councils. As Ziegert points out 'The impossibility of communication *between* systems but the apparent historically varied correlations between the legal system and various other social systems require a more accurate observation as to how such relationships become possible and what form they take'.[32] There is now an important body of work which explores the liberal basis upon which religious and

31 See Roger Blackett, 'The Status of "Religious Courts" in English Law Decisions' (2009) Decisions, Decisions: Dispute Resolution and International Arbitration Newsletter 11.

32 See Klaus A Ziegert, 'Systems Theory and Qualitative Socio-Legal Research' in Reza Banakar and Max Travers (eds) *Theory and Method in Socio-Legal Research* (Hart Publishing 2005).

cultural autonomy may be recognized and accommodated in English law. Attempting to create new forms accommodation, however, also raises questions of power and the extent to which minority groups rely on the political system to supply a normative framework for the political system's operations.

In his work, Eekelaar puts forward a model he describes as 'cultural voluntarism' which would allow individuals to continue following group norms as long as they comply with civil law norms.[33] He explains:

> 'family courts could make orders based on agreements reached under religious law but only if the agreement was genuine and followed independent advice, and was consistent with overriding policy goals (for example the best interests of the child). State law would be available at all times to anyone who chose to invoke it and access to it should be safeguarded and encouraged'.[34]

Drawing upon this work, Malik[35] describes the emergence of 'minority legal order (s)' in Britain, defined around two key aspects: 'first, by its distinct cultural or religious norms; second, by some 'systemic' features that allow us to say that there is a distinct institutional system for the identification, interpretation and enforcement of these norms'. This can be identified as Sharia councils and other forms of Muslim dispute resolution processes. Malik puts forward a number of democratic participatory models that would allow both systems to operate with in-built democratic processes to deal with potential conflicts and tensions but also concludes that although there are good reasons to encourage cooperation between the state and minority legal orders, this cannot be implemented until further research is conducted to deal with how issues of justice and access to justice are addressed.[36] Again the concern is how to ensure the vulnerable members within groups are given adequate protection and safeguards.

Yet the question over the norms that act as the foundational bases upon which Muslim legal pluralism rests and the extent to which these forms can be tested, challenged and transformed is left largely unaddressed by both Eeklaar and Malik. While recognizing the problem of power and power relations in relation to norm-making whereby norms may be imposed by persons or elites

33 See John Eekelaar, 'Law and Community Practices' in John Eekelaar and Mavis Maclean (eds) *Managing Family Justice in Diverse Societies* (Hart Publishing 2013).

34 Ibid, 16.

35 See Maleiha Malik, *Minority legal Systems in the UK: Multiculturalism, Minorities and the Law* (British Academy Policy Papers 2012) 12.

36 Ibid 65.

within communities in order to advance their own interests or ideologies under the guise of the interests of the community they do not offer an adequate response to how this problem can be overcome. Whilst scholarship therefore considers the effects of religious accommodation in terms of the nature and extent to which this is practiced within Muslim communities, we also need to think through carefully the consequences for all members of communities including minorities within minority groups before a model of Muslim dispute resolution based upon the foundational principles of democracy and rights is adopted. What exactly is the basis upon which these processes operate that can lead to a potential re-allocation of family law disputes. Critics such as Shah (2014) argue that such models are, in the end, disempowering communities as they are simply constrained by liberal values, values that are 'apparently non-contestable' and do 'not problematize the potentially violent, oppressive, or absurd consequences of applying such a framework to non-liberal communities that is, communities that do not operate from within a liberal ethical framework'.[37] Not only is the western legal system inherently 'euro-centric' he argues but he challenges critiques of homogeneity…'for seldom is homogeneity regarded as a precondition to the recognition of various types of jurisdiction, while heterogeneity does not prevent recognition in different ways'.[38] Liberal Law in this reading is therefore a problem because it is based on a dominant cultural framework. This analysis should also not be taken as a claim that it is impossible for community dispute resolution mechanisms to develop alternatives to civil law mechanisms. Sharia councils, for example, themselves are products of the western Muslim diaspora, and not a result of a moral critique imposed from 'outside'. Observing the temporal conditions of sharia councils raises many issues concerning the relationship between religious identity, norms, power and politics. It is important to consider whether a parity model of gender equality could potentially allow Muslim women to be part of process of reshaping and reconceptualising community norms within community dispute resolution mechanisms – so how would this potentially take place and what would be the possible outcomes?

As discussed earlier, notions of choice, agency, autonomy, welfare and responsibility underpin feminist critiques of religious personal systems of law in the UK and its potential to promote equality, justice and human rights for women living within minority religious communities. This literature has been accompanied by a rise in Muslim feminist scholarship with critiques on

37 Prakash Shah, *Family, Religion and Law. Cultural Encounters in Europe* (Routledge 2014) 49.

38 Ibid 52.

rethinking and reinterpreting the meaning and practice of Muslim marriage, divorce and matrimonial rights upon breakdown of the relationship as part of a rethinking and reformulating of Islamic texts and intellectual thought and practice in order to 'accommodate' the needs of Muslims living in Muslim minority contexts. With a focus on issues of sexual rights, financial obligations, honour, authority, consent and choice, this scholarship also provides important insights into the conceptual frameworks upon which issues of Muslim marriage and divorce in Islam are discussed in Muslim communities living in the 'west'. The emergence of Muslim family law in the UK must be understood as part of specific historical, social and political conditions under which post-colonial migrations emerge. Within this context feminist methodologies, ethnographic research and critiques of the 'Muslim female subject' have led to new understandings and critical approaches in the practice of Muslim family law in the UK. What is the potential of this scholarship to critically engage with Islamic feminist critiques on textual interpretations and new methodologies in re-reading sacred texts and their application to Muslim dispute resolution mechanisms?

Muslim feminist interrogation with issues of power, authority and the dynamics of power within the institutions of marriage, family, community in British Muslim communities reveals important insights into the ways in which the initiatives such as the new marriage contract and Muslim dispute resolution have been shaped, accepted, contested, resisted and challenged as part of new Muslim feminist scholarship.[39] This research also opens up important conceptual questions regarding issues of authority and power within Muslim diasporic communities and produces important insights into ways in which democratic models such as the 'Parity Democracy model'[40] may potentially remain limited in developing ways to challenge unequal intra community norms and values that may discriminate against its most vulnerable members, Muslim women. Furthermore the multicultural context upon which Muslim communities operate must also include critiques of democracy, dialogue and power if we are to consider the plausibility of developing positive law obligations for religious group autonomy whilst respecting the rights of individuals.

---

39 See Ziba Mir-Hosseini, Kari Vogt, Lena Larsen and Christian Moe (eds) *Gender and Equality in Muslim Family Law: Justice and Ethics in the Islamic Legal Tradition* (I.B.Tauris 2015).

40 See Ruth Rubio-Marin, 'A New European Parity-Democracy Sex Equality Model and why it won't Fly in the United States' (2012) 60(1) The American Journal of Comparative Law 99.

6 Parity and Sharia Councils: The Question of Gender Equality

The 'Parity Democracy Model' is an important strategic intervention in promoting equality. While recognising the limitations of the formal substantive sex equality framework it seeks to enable women to participate equally in all domains of citizenship. Its rationale therefore includes a transformation and redefinition of the liberal autonomy paradigm from one of independence to interdependence. In this way it resonates closely to the work of Black feminist activists and scholars, who, for example, have long recognized this paradigm shift of separated public and private spheres as individual and state law relations to intersectional analyses whilst recognising the specific forms of subordination found in the family, home and community. Feminist scholarship has long addressed the fact that 'woman' is not a unitary category and instead it acts as a site of multiple contradictions with 'effects that may reinforce or undermine social divisions'.[41] We see in evidence that 'the lives of different categories of women are differentially shaped by articulating relations of power; and how under a given set of circumstances we ourselves are 'situated' in these power relations vis-à-vis other categories of women and men'.[42] The challenge of universalism is addressed by creating spaces of 'strategic essentialism'[43] framed from the vantage point of a dominated subject position. Models, which therefore aspire to 'parity', are important in relation to debates on rights, democracy and law. As Rubio-Marin states,

> 'it seems unlikely that one could press for a gender parity democracy model in the United States without integrating some conception of racial parity democracy. This makes the project more daunting and less viable both theoretically and politically because the forces of racism and patriarchy would presumably join in opposing it'.[44]

Intersectional analyses however raise important challenges while interrogating power relations and the defining of racial and sexual categories as oppositional and in conflict.

The question of choice, consent, agency, capabilities and autonomy has long remained both an important and a vexed question for feminist scholars from

41 See Avtar Brah, *Cartographies of Diaspora: Contesting Identities* (Routledge 1993) 89.

42 Ibid 93.

43 See Gayatri Spivak, 'Can the subaltern speak?' in Cary Nelson and Lawrence Grossberg (eds.) *Marxism and the Interpretation of Culture* (Macmillan 1988).

44 See Rubio-Marin (n 40) 105.

multiple traditions including western and postcolonial feminist paradigms. The debates are underpinned by important questions of moral self and viable choices all taking place relationally under various the contexts of identity and belonging Feminist scholarship informs us that agency cannot be exercised without choice and the relationship between choice and agency is a complex one. This relationship between agency and choice becomes even more complicated within wider debates of identity, belonging and citizenship for women living within minority Muslim communities. For many feminists' autonomy and choice remain difficult and elusive concepts to define each overlapping but also pointing to points of departure and how individual meanings and interpretations challenge the very foundations upon which they maybe understood. Furthermore, the acquiesce of choice is an important aspect of understanding how choice may operate.[45]

For many scholars, the question of personal autonomy and choice underpins debates on the recognition of religious councils and tribunals in Britain. The debates fall largely within two spectrums of scholarly work. The first can be described broadly as orientalist discourses which accord Muslim women little if any agency and personal choice as members of Muslim families and communities and the second points to the fact that all debates on equality and free choice are circumscribed by 'difference' along multiple and complex factors including, context, place and time with notions of belonging, identity and being. The extent to which free choice is therefore expressed can simply be one based on personal and strategic decision-making in the face of conflicting and competing demands.

Thus the language of choice, commitment and faith as described by the religious scholars fits in neatly with the discourse of belonging to a wider Muslim community (*Umma*) and the importance attached to the development and formation of a local Muslim community-identity. In this way the community space (inhabited by Shariah councils) is deemed the obvious site upon which the long established practice of Muslim dispute resolution takes place. And in this respect it seems clear that the religious scholars seek to establish authority with respect to family law matters and require all participants to take the proceedings seriously. While the process of disputing itself reveals striking similarities to the development of family mediation in English family law, most religious scholars describe this process as distinct from the English family law approach to settling family disputes and the process is in fact framed as in opposition to state law mediation practices. It is also conceptualized in terms

45 See Rosemary Hunter and Sharon Cowan (eds) *Choice and Consent: Feminist Engagements with law and subjectivity* (Routledge 2007).

of a *duty* upon all Muslims to abide by the requirements of the Shariah and the stipulations of the Shariah councils. This shared understanding stems from the belief that the secular space inhabited by English family law principles cannot bring about in itself genuine resolution of matrimonial disputes for Muslims living in Britain.

In my earlier research, with the exception of one interviewee, all the women had contacted a Shariah council voluntarily, notwithstanding guidance they may have received from family, friends and/or the local Imam. In most cases, initial contact had been made via the telephone, and this was followed up with an application form citing the reasons for seeking a religious dissolution of marriage. The most obvious questions concern the autonomy and independence of the women during this process of dispute resolution and their experience of mediation and reconciliation. Although not all women are marginalized and denied equal bargaining power during official mediation processes, there exists evidence to suggest that there is deep anxiety amongst many women at the prospect of initiating both official and unofficial mediation, an anxiety that persists throughout the process. Feminist scholars have warned of the dangers of trying to resolve marital disputes outside the protection of formal law. This may include situations where cultural norms deny women decision-making authority or where the mediator is not neutral and yet still provides the normative framework for discussion a situation which can transform the nature of the discussion and curtail the autonomy of the disputant. Roberts (2008) raises concerns that negotiations might well occur in private 'without the presence of partisan lawyers and without access to appeal'.[46] Some studies point to the fact that official mediation places women in a weak bargaining position, and encourages them to accept a settlement considerably inferior to one that they might have obtained had they gone through the adversarial process. Mediation can therefore promote a particular familial ideology that is based upon social control and patriarchal norms and values, and operates through subliminal, covert forms of power and coercion. In contrast, formal law provides protection against abuse in the private sphere, and so in response to the move towards private legal ordering, critics argue that mediation fails to deliver on the key issue of 'justice'. This can be described as a development of social and legal norms as one which

> 'exists within society a network of social norms which is formally independent of the legal system, but which is in constant interaction with it. Formal law sometimes seeks to strengthen the social norms. Sometimes

46 See Marian Roberts, *Mediation in Family Disputes: Principles of Practice* (Ashgate 2008).

> it allows them to serve its purposes without the necessity of direct intervention; sometimes it tries to weaken or destroy them and sometimes it withdraws from enforcement, not in an attempt to subvert them, but because countervailing values make conflicts better resolved outside the legal arena'.[47]

Feminists have extensively critiqued this tenuous relationship between family and state intervention across a wide spectrum of disciplines. Yet it is precisely the fact that women have such divergent experiences of family mediation that renders problematic any proposals to develop family mediation as a more formalized process to suit the specific needs of minority ethnic communities. There seems to be an inherent conflict between recognizing identities as multiple and fluid and formulating social policy initiatives that are based upon specific cultural practices, precisely because cultural and religious practices are open to change, contestation and interpretation. At the very least, we must ensure that mechanisms are in place so that those who choose not to participate in such processes are not compelled to do so. It is in this context that concerns have been raised about how such proposals will lead to delegating rights to communities to regulate matters of family law, which is effectively a move towards some form of cultural autonomy. Maclean rightly asks: 'What are the implications for family justice of this move towards private ordering? Is this form of 'privatization' safe?'[48] Undoubtedly, in this context formal law provides protection against abuse in the 'private' sphere – the sphere in which this legal ordering operates. Maclean goes on to ask: 'is it dangerous to remove disputes from the legal system with the advantage of due process, plus protection of those at the wrong end of the far from level playing field, and visible negotiation and settlement which takes place of not in court than in the shadow of the law?'[49]

The debates in Ontario, Canada have also formed the backdrop to understanding this relationship between civil and religious law. In Ontario, the extent to which family disputes should be allowed to take part under the Ontario Arbitration Act was brought into sharp relief when the Canadian Society of Muslims sought to establish as Sharia Tribunal and use the Ontario Arbitration Act to resolve family law type disputes.

47 See Eekelaar (n 33) 45.

48 See Mavis Maclean, *Making Law For Families* (Hart Publishing 2000) 67.

49 Ibid.

The demand for recognition of religious arbitration was made under the context of multiculturalism and underpinned by s15 of Charter of Rights and Freedoms, a charter which guarantees fundamental freedoms including religious equality. This commitment to cultural and religious pluralism is enshrined in the Multiculturalism Act 1985 and it is this context upon which debates on the limits of law, legality and rights are regularly debated and addressed. It is useful to evaluate the developments in Canada often referred to as the 'Ontario controversy' to consider not only the commonalities and differences between the two contexts but also questions of reform and positive law obligations.

The Arbitration Act 1991 was adopted in the Province of Ontario specifying the procedures that consenting parties could apply if they chose to resolve their disputes outside the adversarial civil law system. Of particular concern was its use among wider religious communities as traditionally the Act had been used by the Jewish Orthodox communities only to form tribunals to deal with commercial disputes and agreements (including performing religious divorces). Was this option available to all religious communities seeking to resolve matrimonial disputes? Whatever the answer to this question it became apparent that its use by Muslims communities in Canada was not only perceived as controversial but it was also unforeseen. The call itself was made by a former Muslim leader and President of the Canadian Society of Muslims, Syed Mumtaz Ali who argued that Muslims should be granted greater autonomy in matters of family law as existing provisions and constitutional arrangements failed to support the practice of their religious lives. The significance of ethnic, class and kinship differences within in Muslim communities was erased to promote the view that all Muslims were religiously obligated to use Sharia to resolve family law matters. Ashe and Helie refer to this as a form of 'religio-legal pluralism' whereby religious communities are given greater autonomy in family law matters but this is only enforceable via the power of state law and civil consent orders.[50] The fact that this form of religious pluralism would not only be endorsed but be supported by the state raised alarm bells for many, notwithstanding Muslim women's organisations. And what exactly would be the role of the courts in this process? How would this type of religious governance take place? The most important and defining factor in this form of religious pluralism was the continued use of and primacy of state law. As Baines explained, 'Ali did not propose to sever the relationship between arbitration tribunals and

50 Ashe and Helie (n 2) 151.

courts. Instead he sought to restrict the role of courts to purely procedural matters: judges should not be called upon to interpret sharia law'.[51]

Under this process the courts delegated to religious authorities in matters of family law. The fact that judges were unable to intervene in potential oppressive contexts based upon orthodox religious principles was of huge concern to many Muslim women and feminists. For example, one prominent Muslim woman activist Shahnaz Khan explained,

> 'It is unlikely that all "consenting" adults particularly women, would willingly and gladly consent to arrange their lives according to laws which give them unequal status before the law. Although we may characterize some women as "choosing" no doubt they would experience a certain amount of pressure to conform. However should they decline to be governed by Muslim Personal Status Laws and find themselves ostracized by their families and their community, they would have to confront the discrimination of the larger Canadian population…'[52]

Of particular concern was the unproblematised use of Sharia law and the failure of Syed Ali and others to the potential of intra community inequalities and injustice experienced by vulnerable women. The argument that all Muslims are obligated to use Sharia principles to resolve matrimonial disputes is also flawed and open to dispute. Opposition, therefore came from various Muslim women's and feminist organisations including the Canadian Council of Muslim Women (CCMW) and the National Association of Women and Law (NAWL). The primary argument made was that the establishment of such tribunals led to a violation of freedoms offered to all women under existing legislation.

The Boyd Report was then commissioned in response to calls for the establishment of a civil law system to incorporate Muslim family law matters and found that religious arbitration in family law matters should be allowed to continue as long as procedural safeguards to protect vulnerable parties who may be compelled to use these services were put in place. However this was opposed by the largest Muslim women's organisation in Canada (The Canadian Council of Muslim Women) arguing that this undermined the Canadian constitution which promotes 'equality before the law' for all its citizens. The resulting Boyd Report and critiques of Muslim women's choice in face of

---

51 See Beverley Baines, 'Must Feminists Identify as Secular Citizens? Lessons from Ontario' in Linda. C. McClain and Joanna L. Grossman (eds) *Gender Equality, Dimensions of Women's Equal Citizenship* (Cambridge University Press 2009).

52 Ashe and Helie (n 2) 152.

moves towards religious autonomy led to the introduction of Bill 27 by Ontarian Premier McGuinty intending to ban all religion based arbitration of family matters marking what Ashe and Helie describe as 'Ontario's commitment to religious pluralism and its rejection of legal – and specifically religio-legal-pluralism'.[53]

Canadian Muslim women's organisations challenged this proposal and the findings of the Boyd Report which called for the recognition of religious tribunals as long as some safeguards were in place. The furore led to the government rejecting that position. As Eekelaar (2013) points out:

> 'The result was that, while religious bodies may still carry out arbitration in family latters under the Arbitration Act they must do so according to the law of Ontario or of another Canadian jurisdiction. Furthermore, regulations require family law arbitrators to undergo training in the law of Canada, that cases are screened for 'power imbalances and domestic violence, by someone other than the arbitrator' and that a written record be kept of the proceedings'.[54]

Ayelet Shachar (2008) points out succinctly that 'The vision of privatized diversity in its fully-fledged 'unregulated islands of jurisdiction' variant poses a challenge to the superiority of secular family law by its old adversary: religion'.[55] This vision of privatized diversity can be applied to the new MAT if we understand privatized diversity as a model in which to achieve and possibly separate the secular from the religious in the public space, in effect encouraging individuals to contract out of state involvement and into a traditional non-state forum when resolving family disputes. This would include religious tribunals arbitrating according to a different set of principles than those enshrined in English law.

For Shachar there are real concerns of individuals being expected to live 'as undifferentiated citizens in the public sphere, but remain free to express our distinct cultural or religious identities in the private domain of family and communal life'.[56] For her and many other liberal scholars, the issue surrounds the contentious question of where private identity and life ends and public identity begins. She quite rightly points out that, if we are expected to express personal identities in the private, at which point in the public sphere do they

53 Ashe and Helie (n 2) 156.
54 Eekelaar (n 33).
55 See Shacher (n 22) 573.
56 Ibid 580.

cease to be so? Shachar also discusses the fact that the vision of privatized diversity will evoke different feelings for different people. For those who want to establish a pluralistic system of law that recognizes claims of culture and religion, this would not be so terrifying, but those who are 'blind' to these needs will see it as challenging the superiority of universal laws that apply to all:

> 'for others who endorse a strict separationist approach, or "blindness" towards religious or cultural affiliation, the idea that we might find unregulated "religious islands of binding jurisdiction" mushrooming on the terrain of state law is seen as evidence of the dangers of accommodating diversity, potentially chipping away, however slightly as the foundational, modernist citizenship formula of "one law for all"'.[57]

In 2011 a private members bill, the Arbitration and Mediation Services (Equality) Bill was introduced by Baroness Cox in the House of Lords. This Bill was reintroduced in October 2015 and 2016–17 and has generated considerable media attention as it aims to make clear the limits of arbitration and make amendments to the Arbitration Act to ensure its compliance with the Equality Act 2010 while seeking to outlaw discrimination on the grounds of sex. Clause 7 of the Bill proposes an amendment to the section of the Courts and Legal Services Act 1990 and criminalizes 'falsely claiming legal jurisdiction' to prevent the ousting of jurisdiction in matters of family and criminal law. Although the Bill does not specifically mention Islamic law it was widely believed to target Muslim communities and to attempt to limit the powers of organisations such as MAT and Shariah councils. But for many scholars it raised the question of the extent to which state law should intervene in religious councils and tribunals. It has been criticized for promoting the idea that the practice of Muslim family law is not only based upon unfair and unequal principles but specifically targets and discriminates against Muslim women as primary users of Muslim dispute resolution bodies. Furthermore the formalist top-down state interventionist approach as epitomized by the Bill in seeking to limit the powers of religious bodies as also been criticized as being predicated on fixed and homogenous notions of Islam and Islamic legal practice which fails to recognize the dynamism and pluralism within the communities themselves. As Eekelaar (2013) argues:

> 'It is a mistake to think of Shari'a as a monolithic system, impervious to change. In fact the bodies apply it in different ways, and it is subject to

57 Ibid.

> internal arguments and contestation. Might it be better to allow it to develop within its communities and responding to its internal critiques and influenced by the culture around it? Alongside this, its adherents could be encouraged to make more use of the civil law, including a greater readiness to enter legally recognized marriages without thereby severing their relationship with their religious norms'.[58]

But what are the experiences of Muslim women using religious mechanisms of dispute resolution in family law matters? Do religious tribunals promote patriarchy and gender inequality? At present, we have three significant pieces of research which provide important insights into how Sharia councils in Britain govern as alternative dispute resolution mechanisms in the field of family law. In my work, *Shariah Councils and Muslim Women: Transcending the Boundaries of Community and Law* I draw three key conclusions from undertaking extensive empirical research with 5 shariah councils and interviews with 25 British Muslim women. Firstly, the claim that seeing culture and forms of religious practice as a mode of legitimizing claims to power and authority dramatically shifts the way we understand the debate on liberalism and universalism versus relativism. In other words, that view that Muslims increasingly seek the freedom to live under sharia is not only extremely problematic but fails to capture the complexity of British Muslim identity as fragmented, porous and hybrid. Second, anthropological scholarship points to the importance of locating gender and gender relations as key sites to the debate; thus, the ways in which Muslim women engage with sharia councils in Britain illustrates how processes and concepts of sharia law are mobilized, adopted and transformed. Underlying this process are power relations that define the nature of the interaction, define meaning of sharia within sharia councils and construct possibilities of change and action. Finally, an essentialised understanding of Muslim religious practice does not reflect the experience of British Muslim women. A more dynamic understanding of British Muslim identity is required, which does not label the needs of Muslims to accommodate sharia as fixed but understands this process as temporal, with shifts from cultural to religious practice and vice versa. Elham Manea argues that limited recognition of legal pluralism and multiculturalism has led to the recognition of culture and religion as homogeneous that ignores individual voices and arguments and the expense of collective arguments.[59] In particular her empirical research with sharia councils

58 Eekelaar (n 33) 32.

59 See Elham Manea, *Women and Shari'a Law: The Impact of Legal Pluralism in the UK* (I.B. Tauris 2016).

and Muslim women users of these bodies found examples of practices such as forced marriage, under age marriage, condoning domestic violence, criminal sanctions and inequities in inheritance.

7 Conclusion

For many liberal scholars the practice of religious personal systems of law raises the paradox of what Shachar refers to as 'multicultural vulnerability', namely the dilemma of protecting individual choice and personal autonomy with group and community rights. The arena of family law succinctly illustrates this conflict, as Shachar explains:

> 'Clearly, when the state awards jurisdictional powers to the group in the family law arena, it enhances the group's autonomy. At the same time, this re-allocation of legal authority from the state to the group may also expose certain individuals within the group to systemic and sanctioned in-group rights violations'.[60]

Such concerns also mirror current debates over the establishment of 'Sharia courts' in Britain and the accommodation of plural systems of family law.

Some form of accommodation will include a shift of dispute resolution from the public to the private sphere and this raises serious concerns on how power is then effectively reconfigured from the state to the family and community. From such a perspective, the differential treatment of women in the process of marriage and divorce can lead to a conflict between equality and autonomy and the conflicting interests of the protection of family, culture and religion as enshrined by the norms and values of Sharia councils and the MAT.

As to the question of gender parity as a model of governance and reform it provides an important starting point for Muslim women to explore ways in which their use is based upon choice, gender equality and justice. As Anitha and Gill (2009, 168) point out:

> 'Women exercise their agency in complex and often contradictory ways, as they assess the options that are open to them, weigh the costs and benefits of their actions, and seek to balance their often competing needs with the expectations and desires. While there remains a need to recognise gendered power imbalances at the same time there also remains a

60 Shachar (n 22) 98.

> need to respect women's exercise of agency…We need to give more support to those women who wish to express their subjectivity within the framework of the communities of which they perceive themselves to be such a fundamental part'.[61]

Furthermore, the process of 'reform' within communities is often a long and fractured one, contextual and dependent upon multiple variables including state support and subsidy. Narratives from Muslim women using religious mechanisms of dispute resolution reveal both the strategic and the complex use of these bodies. In the case of Muslim legal pluralism, we can then see in evidence different forms of mobilizations with underlying cultural and religious meanings which interact, conflict and re-order themselves according to the different communities in which they are located and state law, and vice versa. We see also that the decision-making processes produce an internal legal structure – a process of mixing-up, overlapping and often in conflict. The application of gender parity can also mean a conflict of meanings of equality and community recognition or legitimacy of various legal and social domains that mix up notions of law and decision-making.

Bibliography

Abbas, T., *Muslim Britain: Communities under pressure* (Zed books, 2005).

Abu-Lughod, L., *Do Muslim Women Need Saving?* (Harvard University Press 2013).

Ahmed, F., 'Personal Autonomy and the Option of Religious Law' (2010) International Journal of Law, Policy and the Family 24.

Ali, S., *Modern Challenges to Islamic Law* (Cambridge University Press 2016).

Anitha, S. and Gill, A., 'Coercion, Consent and the Forced Marriage Debate' (2009) in Feminist Legal Studies 165.

Arjana, S., *Muslims in the Western Imagination*, (Oxford University Press 2015).

Asad, T., *Foundations of the secular. Christianity, Islam, modernity*. Stanford: (Stanford University 2003).

Asad, T., Thinking about the secular body, pain and Liberal Politics, (2011) Cultural Anthropology, Vol 26, Issue 4.

Ashe, M. and Helie, A., Realities of Religico-Legalism: Religious Courts and Women's Rights in Canada, the United Kingdom and the United States, (2014) University of California, Davis vol 20.2.

61 See Sundari Anitha and Aisha Gill, 'Coercion, Consent and the Forced Marriage Debate' (2009) 17(2) Feminist Legal Studies 165.

Baines, B., Must Feminists Identify as Secular Citizens? Lessons from Ontario, in *Gender Equality, Dimensions of Women's Equal Citizenship* eds. Linda. C. McClain and Joanna L. Grossman (Cambridge University Press 2009).

Bano, S., *An exploratory study of Shariah councils in England with respect to family law*, Ministry of Justice (2012).

Bano, S., *Muslim Women and Shari'ah Councils: Transcending the Boundaries of Community and Law*, (Palgrave MacMillan 2012).

Booth, P., 'Judging Sharia' (2008) 38 *Family Law* 935.

Bottomley, A. and Conaghan, J., *Feminist legal Theory and Legal Strategy*, (Oxford Blackwell. 1993).

Boyd, S., *Challenging the Public/Private Divide: Feminism, Law and Public Policy*, (Toronto University, Toronto press 1997).

Bowen, J., *On British Islam. Religion, Law and Everyday Practice in Sharia Councils* (Princeton University Press 2016).

Brah, A., *Cartographies of Diaspora and Contesting Identities*, Routledge (1993).

Crenshaw, K., 'Demarginalising the Intersection of Race and Sex: A Black Feminist Critique of Antidiscrimination Doctrine', *Feminist Theory and Antiracist Politics*, (1989) University of Chicago Forum, 139.

Douglas, G. Gilliat-Ray, S., Doe, N., Sandberg, R. and Khan, A., *Social Cohesion and Civil Law: Marriage, Divorce and Religious Courts*, Cardiff University (2011).

Eekelaar, J. and Maclean, M., (ed) *Managing Family Justice in Diverse Societies* (Hart 2013).

Foucault M, *Discipline and Punish The Birth of the Prison* (London Penguin 1979).

Gillat-Ray, S., Britain's Religious Tribunals: 'Joint Governance' in Practice (2012) Oxford Journal of Legal Studies.

Hall, S., 'The West and the rest: discourse and power' in Stuart Hall and Ben Gieben (eds), *Formations of Modernity*, (Cambridge: Polity Press 1992).

Hunter, R. and Cowan, S., Introduction in (eds), Rosemary Hunter and Sharon Cowan, *Choice and Consent: Feminist Engagements with law and subjectivity* (Routledge 2007).

Hussain, Y. and Bagguley, S., *Citizenship, Ethnicity and Identity: British Pakistanis after the 2001 riots.* (Sage 2005).

Karayanni, M., The Acute Multicultural Entrapment of the Palestinian-Arab Religious Minorities in Israel and the Feeble Measures Required to Relieve It in (eds) Robert Provost, *Mapping the Legal Boundaries of Belonging, Religion and Multiculturalism from Israel to Canada* (Oxford University Press 2014).

Khan, S., Canadian Muslim Women and Shar'ia Law: A Feminist Response to 'O Canada!' (1993) *Canadian Journal of Women & Law* 6.

Maclean, M. (ed.), *'Making Law for Families'*, Onati International Series in Law and Society, (Oxford-Portland 2000).

Maclean, M. and Eekelaar, J., *Lawyers and Mediators : the Brave New World of Services for Separating Families* (Hart Oxford 2016).

Mahmood, S., 'Secularism, Hermeneutics, Empire: The Politics of Islamic Reformation' (2006) 18 *Public Culture* 323–347.

Malik, M., *Minority legal Systems in the UK: Multiculturalism, Minorities and the Law* (2012) (British Academy Policy Papers.

Manea, E., *Women and Shari'a Law: The Impact of Legal Pluralism in the UK* (I.B. Tauris 2016).

Modood, T., 'Accommodating religions: Multiculturalism's new fault line', (2013) *Critical Social Policy* 31. 3

Muslim Arbitration Tribunal (2008) *Liberation from Forced Marriages*, London.

Nobles, R. and Schiff, D., *Observing Law Through Systems Theory*, (Hart Publishing 2014).

Patel, P., Faith in the State? Asian Women's Struggles for Human Rights in the UK, *Feminist Legal Studies* (2008) 16 (1).

Phillips, A., (2007) *Multiculturalism without Culture*, (Princeton University Press 2007.).

Redfern, A. and Hunter, M., *International Commercial Arbitration* (Cambridge University Press 2004).

Roy, O., *Holy Ignorance: When Religion and Culture Part Ways* (Columbia University Press 2010).

Rubio-Marin, R., A New European Parity-Democracy Sex Equality Model and why it won't Fly in the United States (2011) *The American Journal of Comparative Law*. Vol 1. 60 99.

Rodriguez Ruiz, B. and Rubio-Marin, R., Constitutional Justification of Parity Democracy (2009) Alabama Law Review Vol 6. 5 1170.

Sayyid, S., (2009) Contemporary Politics of secularism in (eds) Geoffrey B. Levey and Tariq Modood *Secularism, Religion and Multicultural Citizenship*, (Cambridge University Press 2009).

Sayyid, S., and Vakil, A.K., (eds), *Thinking Through Islamaphobia: Global* Perspectives (Hurst Press 2009).

Sayyid, S., *Recalling the Caliphate: Decolonisation and the World Order* (Hurst Press 2014).

Shachar, A., (2008) 'Privatizing Diversity: A Cautionary Tale from Religious Arbitration in Family Law' 9 *Theoretical Inquiries in Law* 573.

Shah, P. Family, *Religion and Law. Cultural Encounters in Europe* (Routledge 2014).

Shah-Kazemi, S., 'Untying the Knot: Muslim Women, Divorce and the Shariah', The Nuffield Foundation (2001)

Spivak, G.,'Can the subaltern speak?' in Nelson, N. and Grossberg, L. (eds) *Marxism and the Interpretation of Culture*, Chicago: Illinos UP (1988).

Sundari, A. and Gill, A., Coercion, Consent and the Forced Marriage Debate in the UK (2009) *Feminist Legal Studies* 12 165–184.

Index

www.ingramcontent.com/pod-product-compliance
Lightning Source LLC
LaVergne TN
LVHW010641300926
849161LV00005B/1014